MW01205364

CULT GIRLS

MANSON FAMILY WOMEN & GIRLS'
BIOS, PSYCHOLOGY & CRIMES

DR. PAUL DAWSON

VISTAR BOOKS

Published by Vistar Pictures Ltd.

CULT GIRLS

MANSON FAMILY WOMEN & GIRLS' BIOS, PSYCHOLOGY & CRIMES

Revised: November 7th, 2020

Copyright © 2020 by Dr. Paul Dawson

BOOKS BY DR. PAUL DAWSON:

ALL ABOUT KIP; ANGELINA JOLIE PSYCHOANALYZED; BIPOLAR ZOO; BIPOLAR JUNGLE; BORDERLINE PERSONALITY DISORDER; BPD RECOVERY; CAMPUS KILLER'S SECRET OBSESSION; CHARACTER INTELLIGENCE; CHARLES MANSON'S GIRLS; CULT GIRLS; DARKSIDE VAMPIRE HUNTERS; FACES OF TED BUNDY; FOUR SERIAL KILLERS; GRACE KELLY SESSIONS; HOW TO GET SOBER; JACKIE O TAPES; JACKIE O SESSIONS; JFK KILLERS EXPOSED; JFK JR. MURDERED; JODI ARIAS; JOHNNY DEPP DIAGNOSED; MAID GUY; MANSON INTERVIEWS RAW; MARILYN MONROE DIAGNOSED; MARILYN MURDEREED; MASKS OF A LADY KILLER; MASKS of PREDATORS; MASKS of SEX PREDATORS MASKS of TED BUNDY; MY PRINCESS DIANA THERAPY SESSIONS; MY TED BUNDY INTERVIEWS RAW! NARCOTERRORIST PSYCHOPATHS; PLEDGED; PRINCESS DIANA DIAGNOSED; PSYCHOLOGY OF HIDDEN INFLUENCE; PSYCHOLOGY of MEN WHO ABUSE WOMEN; PSYCHOPATHS; ROCK STARS DIAGNOSED ROYAL SESSIONS; ROYAL SESSIONS 2; ROYAL SESSIONS 3; ROYALS THERAPIST; ROYALS THERAPIST 2; RUNAWAY BOYS; RUSH PARTY MURDERS; SERIAL KILLERS; SERIAL KILLERS 2; SERIAL KILLERS 3; SEX CRIMES; SEX, LOVE & SMART DATING; SHAPE-SHIFTER BUNDY; SKULL SCRAPERS (SERIES OF 10 THRILLER NOVELS); SPIES & ASSASSINS; SPIRITUAL THERAPY; TED BUNDY'S DEATH ROW CONFESSIONS TERRORIST IMPERATIVE; THE MASKS OF KARLA HOMOLKA

CULT GIRLS: MANSON FAMILY WOMEN & GIRLS' BIOS, PSYCHOLOGY & CRIMES by Dr. Paul Dawson presents the shocking story of young women and girls who joined the pseudo-hippie Charles Manson Family cult in the late-1960s. CULT GIRLS presents the biographies of the Manson cult women and girls. The psychology behind the Manson Family from the viewpoint of women and girls is detailed. The Manson Family crimes are revealed. Dr. Dawson & Charles Manson's prison interviews are included.

Dr. Dawson brings a forensic-clinical psychologist's perspective on understanding the development of Manson's cult. CULT GIRLS reveals the deeper psychology behind the Manson Family. Dr. Paul Dawson explains the forming of the Manson Family, which was 5:1 girls-to-guys. A particular emphasis is on the development and life passages of the young women in the Manson Family.

Many of the girls Manson recruited for his hippie-murder cult seemed to be wild-and-crazy teenagers, hippie girls stoned on drugs, with parental issues, caught up in an identity-crisis turmoil which Manson exploited. Yet the Manson Family kids were often educated and from middle-class homes. This book follows their lives from the late-1960s until now. Some continued a criminal pattern, and others went straight in later life.

Dr. Dawson provides a rare, exciting, and fascinating investigation and assessment inside the dangerous, paradoxical Manson Family cult. CULT GIRLS presents the traumatizing, astonishing admissions and scandalous interview comments of the psychopathic-serial killer, Charles Manson, with a focus on revealing Charles Manson's girls and the deeper psychology of the Manson Family. Extensive photos.

He was the wild-eyed, scraggly-haired Dark Prince of the 1960s. Manson was the demon-hippie, psycho-serial-killer-by-proxy of the Woodstock era who sent his Manson Family of fanatical, cult-crazed robots out to commit multiple homicides in the mansions of Los Angeles. Charles Manson, an alarming, terrifying paradox, was one of the most dangerous serial killers in the American history of crime.

Dr. Dawson conducted a series of interviews with Charles Manson, the poster boy for killer-cult leaders, incarcerated in San Quentin State Prison, in September 1988. The focus of this book is on the psychology of the Manson Family, bios of the Manson Family women and girls, the Manson Family crimes, and Dr. Dawson & Charles Manson's prison interviews.

In CULT GIRLS, Dr. Dawson provides a unique, sensational, and spellbinding investigation and assessment inside the treacherous, enigmatic mind of this infamous icon of criminal evil. Manson's depraved aura, the repulsion of this homicidal-cult guru, the cult-kingpin murder rampage is investigated in depth.

Dr. Dawson reveals Manson's darkest secrets, elicits Manson Family confessions, confronts and provokes the murderer by probing his mind and challenging Manson's-spooky justifications. Manson, an enigma, is evaluated, and his cryptic crimes are explored. Psychological concepts illuminate persuasive, lucid light on Manson's and his cult's ghastly crimes of assault, torture, and mass murder.

Dr. Dawson earned a Ph.D. in clinical psychology from The New School for Social Research, Graduate Faculty in New York City. He has been a psychologist in clinics, schools, mental hospitals; he was a chief psychologist of a state prison system; he has been in private practice & consulting in New York. Dr. Dawson has written over 60 books.

CULT GIRLS:

MANSON FAMILY WOMEN & GIRLS' BIOS, PSYCHOLOGY & CRIMES

TABLE OF CONTENTS:

Chapter 6: Patricia Krenwinkel. Patricia
Dianne Krenwinkel, an American criminal, convicted of mass murder, was a Manson Family member.

Chapter 7: Crazy slogans. Manson's crazy
slogans and gibberish. Berne's Transactional Analysis and *Games People Play*. Heinlein's *Stranger in a Strange Land* was about free love and alienation. Dale Carnegie's *How to Win Friends and Influence People*.

Chapter 8: Lynette "Squeaky" Fromme.
Lynette Alice "Squeaky" Fromme, an American criminal, convicted of attempting to assassinate President Ford in 1975, was the leader of the Manson Family when Charlie went to prison - released from prison in 2009.

Chapter 9: Emotionally damaged. Manson
targeted emotionally damaged girls with family conflicts. He used pimp tricks to control girls. TA's games. Psychobabble jargon. New-Age-guru jargon. A 5-to-1 ratio of girls-to-guys in Manson's Family.

Chapter 10: Mary Brunner. Mary Theresa
Brunner, an American criminal, involved in Gary Hinman's murder, Hawthorne gun robbery & shootout, was a hardcore member of the Manson Family.

Chapter 11: Counterculture. Summer of Love.
Teen runaways. Haight and Ashbury scene exploited by Manson. Diggers. Free food, free sex, free crash pads, free medical clinic.

Chapter 12: Linda Kasabian. Linda Darlene
Kasabian, an American criminal, involved in the Tate/LaBianca murders, was a member of the Manson Family. She testified against the Manson Family killers.

Chapter 13: Guru. Manson, a fast-talking hustler, streetwise, was perfect to be a crazy guru. Moving from San Francisco to L.A. and the Spahn's Movie Ranch. Free sex, sex orgies, drugs, rock and roll, and a quasi-hippie commune or criminal cult.

Chapter 14: Dianne Lake. Dianne Lake, American, was a Manson Family member.

Chapter 15: Alienated. Manson got into various types of mind control, new-age-buzz words, and guru jargon, which could appeal to the alienated-young people of the 1960s counterculture.

Chapter 16: Ruth Ann Moorehouse. Ruth Ann "Ouisch" Moorehouse, an American criminal, was involved in attempted murder, was a hardcore Manson Family member. She fled and escaped a jail sentence.

Chapter 17: Psychopathy. This chapter presents a detailed outline of Manson's psychopathy symptoms.

Chapter 18: Barbara Hoyt. Barbara Hoyt, American, was a member of Manson's Family, Manson Family members attempted to murder her, so, she testified against Manson and Manson Family killers. She went to college and became a nurse. She died in 2017.

Chapter 19: Genetic factors. Charles Manson and possible genetic/neurological factors. Charles Manson's Interself Test Profile.

Chapter 20: Nancy Pitman. Nancy Laura Pitman, an American criminal, convicted of accessory to murder, and she did 18 months in prison. She was a hardcore member of the Manson Family.

Chapter 21: Cults. Charles Manson used techniques of mind control, which are used by cults to indoctrinate, brainwash, and break down a person's sense-of-self.

Chapter 22: Catherine Gillies. Catherine
Gillies, a devoted follower of Charles Manson and Manson Family member, died in 2018 at age 68.

Chapter 23: Charisma. This chapter reveals
Manson's horrifying charisma. Manson was a magnet for young people in conflict, criminals, and mentally deranged drifters who joined the Manson Family. Charlie's characteristics in common with destructive-cult leaders. Manson's power to hold the center-of-attention.

Chapter 24: Sandra Good. Sandra Good, a
devoted follower of Charles Manson and hardcore Manson Family member, a close friend of Lynette "Squeaky" Fromme. She did prison time, criminal record.

Chapter 25: Prison interviews. Dr. Dawson &
Charles Manson's prison interviews.

Chapter 26: Kathryn Lutesinger. Kathryn
Lutesinger joined the Manson Family after her boyfriend, Bobby Beausoleil, introduced her to the Manson Family. She was arrested in police raids with the Manson Family, criminal record.

Chapter 27: Prison interviews. Dr. Dawson &
Charles Manson's prison interviews.

Chapter 28: Susan Bartell. Susan Bartell, joined
the Manson Family after the Tate-LaBianca murders, was involved with the John "Zero" Haught "suicide," arrested in raids on the Manson Family, left the Manson Family in the mid-1970s.

Chapter 29: Prison interviews. Dr. Dawson &
Charles Manson's prison interviews.

Chapter 30: Catherine Share. Catherine Share,
an American criminal, Manson Family member, arrested and convicted and did five years in prison for Manson-related crimes. She's distanced herself from the Manson Family.

Chapter 31: Prison interviews. Dr. Dawson & Charles Manson's prison interviews.

Chapter 32: Review of other Manson Family members & associates.

Chapter 33: Prison interviews. Dr. Dawson & Charles Manson's prison interviews.

Chapter 34: Tate mass murders. Tate, Sebring, Folger, Frykowski, Parent murders. Murderers: Charles Manson, Tex Watson, Susan Atkins, Patricia Krenwinkel, Linda Kasabian (lookout).

Chapter 35: Prison interviews. Dr. Dawson & Charles Manson's prison interviews.

Chapter 36: LaBianca murders. Leno and Rosemary LaBianca murders. Murderers: Charles Manson, Tex Watson, Leslie Van Houten, Patricia Krenwinkel.

Chapter 37: Prison interviews. Dr. Dawson & Charles Manson's prison interviews.

Chapter 38: Gary Hinman's murder. Murderers: Bobby Beausoleil, Susan Atkins, Mary Brunner, Bruce Davis, Charles Manson.

Chapter 39: Prison interviews. Dr. Dawson & Charles Manson's prison interviews.

Chapter 40: Donald "Shorty" Shea murder. Murderers: Charles Manson, Bruce Davis, Steve Grogan; suspected murderer participants: Tex Watson, Bill Vance, Larry Bailey (aka Larry Giddings).

Chapter 41: Prison interviews. Dr. Dawson & Charles Manson's prison interviews.

Chapter 42: Bernard "Lotsapoppa" Crowe shooting. Shooter: Charles Manson over a drug deal that went wrong.

Chapter 43: Prison interviews. Dr. Dawson & Charles Manson's prison interviews.

Chapter 44: John "Zero" Haught. "Suicide-by- Russian-roulette" death. But suspected murder. He was possibly murdered by Bruce Davis on orders of Charles Manson, who suspected Zero of snitching to police.

Chapter 45: Prison interviews. Dr. Dawson & Charles Manson's prison interviews.

Chapter 46: Ronald Hughes. A lawyer who represented Charles Manson. Manson Family members suspected of murdering him.

Chapter 47: Prison interviews. Dr. Dawson & Charles Manson's prison interviews.

Chapter 48: Hawthorne Shootout. Weapons robbery to hijack a commercial jet. They arrested: Mary Brunner, Catherine Share, Charles Lovett, Lawrence Bailey, Kenneth Como, and Dennis Rice.

Chapter 49: Prison interviews. Dr. Dawson & Charles Manson's prison interviews.

Chapter 50: Review of the James and Lauren Willett murders. Murder suspects arrested and later convicted: Michael Monfort, James Craig, Nancy Pitman, Priscilla Cooper. Involved: Lynette "Squeaky" Fromme, jailed, released, and not charged.

Chapter 51: Prison interviews. Dr. Dawson & Charles Manson's prison interviews.

Chapter 52: The attempted murder of Barbara Hoyt. The murder charge reduced to trying to dissuade a witness from testifying. The plotters (Share, Fromme, Rice, and Grogan) served a 90-day jail sentence at the Los Angeles County Jail. Moorehouse charged initially with attempted murder, failed to show up at the sentencing hearing, fled, and never served her jail sentence.

Chapter 53: Prison interviews. Dr. Dawson & Charles Manson's prison interviews.

Chapter 54: Squeaky's attempted assassination. Lynette "Squeaky" Fromme, arrested for attempting to assassinate President Ford; she was convicted and served 34 years from 1975 until her release on parole in 2009.

Chapter 55: Prison interviews. Dr. Dawson & Charles Manson's prison interviews.

Chapter 56: Review of some of the other suspected Manson Family murders and various crimes.

Chapter 57: Prison interviews. Dr. Dawson & Charles Manson's prison interviews.

Chapter 58: Charles Manson. Charles Milles Manson was an American criminal, Manson Family cult leader, and aspiring musician. Convicted of mass murder and died in 2017 in prison.

Note to readers: Dr. Dawson's prison interviews with Charles Manson and other sources form the basis of CULT GIRLS. If you want the biographies of all the men in the Manson cult as well as the women, buy a copy of MANSON FAMILY MANUAL by Dr. Paul Dawson (Amazon books). If you want more prison interviews with Dr. Dawson & Charles Manson, buy a copy of CHARLES MANSON: My prison interviews with Charles Manson by Dr. Paul Dawson (Amazon books).

Warning: Graphic Content

CULT GIRLS:

MANSON FAMILY WOMEN & GIRLS' BIOS, PSYCHOLOGY & CRIMES

Prologue

My name is Leslie Van Houten. My mind wanders back to those magical nights during the Summer of Love in 1967. Dancing to those bands in San Francisco's Golden Gate Park. It was a hub of psychedelic exploration and creative energy, centering around the Haight-Ashbury district where bands like the Grateful Dead, Jefferson Airplane, and Janis Joplin entertained us. I'm very sentimental about those romantic days that seemed so innocent and full of life.

Smoking pot with Bobby Beausoleil and Catherine Share, I was part of the hippie counterculture, enjoying the vibes. Bobby and Catherine had connected in the music industry. Beausoleil's contacts at the Autumn label had helped Share to get a record deal. Her stage name was Charity Shayne on the folk-pop single Ain't It? Babe, released in 1965. And Bobby was playing in bands and composed the music soundtrack on Kenneth Anger's movie *Lucifer Rising*.

I had gotten to the Spahn's Movie Ranch through other people who had been there and were driving up and down the coast. I was in the hippie movement. I met these people who said they lived in a commune in L.A. And that they lived for the day and the moment. A lot of the Leary kind of philosophy of be here now. When I dropped out, I was separated from my family.

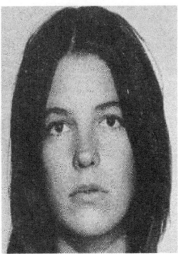

Left: Bobby Beausoleil. Right: Leslie Van Houten. Beausoleil and Van Houten were lovers in the late 1960s.

When I was caught after the murders, my family had anger and resentment. When my mother came to visit, I told her that she'd be better off just to leave me alone. She said she was not made of that kind of stuff. I wasn't physically enamored with Manson. I was caught and mesmerized by his mind. And the things he professed. I had come to the ranch by way of Robert Beausoleil, and Beausoleil was very important to Manson.

Because Beausoleil was my lover, Manson treated me in a way that I belonged to Bobby Beausoleil. I knew that something ominous and threatening was going to happen in the Tate murders. But not specifically in advance. Manson worked to shed ourselves of our egos and get rid of our own identity. To do what would make us one with one another. He insulted our families and our morals we'd been taught.

Left to right: Bobby Beausoleil, Leslie Van Houten, and Catherine "Gypsy" Share. Beausoleil, Van Houten, and Share started as creative young people enjoying the romance of the 1967 Summer of Love.

Because most of us were middle-class Anglos, he challenged us. Would you die for me? This was over some time. Not long before the murders, Manson said he would take the lead and show the blacks how it should be done. I found out he had some sort of bum drug deal and had shot someone.

I know now that Sharon Tate had something to do with Terry Melcher. But at the time, each of us knew very little about what was going on. Pat Krenwinkel told me about the Tate murders the next morning. I was sad that it had to occur. It was justified to make a statement following Charles Manson's orders. I didn't realize I was traveling on an evil path that would wreck my life and that I'd end up spending decades in prison.

Left: Leslie Van Houten, Monrovia High School homecoming queen.
Right: Van Houten, 1965, age 16.

I started dropping acid when I was 16. I was going to school. But the more I dropped acid, the harder it was to relate to different people other than the others who were dropping acid. All the hippies were migrating to the places where they felt comfortable with one another. I've had a lot of other women inside tell me they were glad they didn't run into Charlie. Because they too would have done murders. I think a lot of parents were concerned with the idea that it could have been their children.

I was taking LSD. I had been traveling around with a couple of other people I had met up in San Francisco. I had a break-up with my first boyfriend. And when you're young and very much in love, the break-up can be difficult. I was trying to make it on my own in San Francisco, and I couldn't. So a couple of people came along and said, "Well, come with us." It was a live-for-today situation.

Left: Spahn's Movie Ranch. Right: Manson Family cult members at Spahn's Movie Ranch.

So I went with them. Then I ended up going to Spahn's Movie Ranch. When you drop acid at first, it is a 9-hour experience. At first, you can go back to work on Monday after using it for a weekend. But the more you take, the less you can relate to others. And you're lost. The more I became isolated from people with different viewpoints, the more I became immersed in the acid reality. It's a fairy-tale world. I met Charles Manson, who was dominant.

I felt he knew what he was doing. We'd take acid in a group, and Manson would speak to us. If you didn't do what Manson wanted, you would not be in his good graces. I admired him, and I became dependent on him and his moods of the day. Charlie was always careful that nobody could put definite things on him. He always protected himself in different ways. At one point, I believed he was Jesus Christ. We went to bed together a couple of times. But I didn't consider him a lover. I feel like I was a pawn in whatever his scheme was.

Left: Charles Manson and his cult under arrest at Spahn's Movie Ranch.
Right: Leslie Van Houten police mugshot.

I was still under Manson's control then. Now I feel he's a very pitiful and pathetic human being. I'm sorry people give him attention. His only danger is in the attention he gets. If he were ignored and left alone, he would probably fade away. I believed that Manson was Jesus Christ, and the murders were something that had to be done. I did not feel good about it. It was like war. We were going through combat training at the ranch. Prepped like that.

Manson said the racial war was coming. About 18 years ago, I realized that was the wrong way to think. It's been very difficult for me to cope with this. It has not been until the last couple of years that I think I can be forgiven by God for what I've done. Part of my job at the ranch was to read to Manson from the bible.

It's been very difficult for me to find forgiveness spiritually. A.A. talks a lot about God as we understand him and turning my will over, removing defects of character. The more I study A.A., the more I realize I had to find some sort of peace. Not just with the crime but life after.

Manson cult women and girls:

All of the women who were enticed into Manson's circle were between the ages of 13 and 25 and were runaways, homeless, wannabe hippies, warped by father issues, distorted by an identity crisis, or feeling they didn't fit in their families or the American culture. Women wanted to support other women, in general, these women liked each other which bonded the Manson cult – it wasn't just Charlie harassing them with his philosophy, drug abuse, and sex orgies.

When they met Manson, they joined a group of other unrestricted women who traveled the country in a bus or ended up at the Spahn's Movie Ranch pseudo-hippie commune. In the 1960s counterculture, young people were experimenting with drugs and "free love" and protesting the Vietnam War and fighting for civil rights. The women took LSD trips with Manson who lectured them about the coming revolution, Helter Skelter, which was just Charlie's pretext to get revenge against Hollywood and the music industry that rejected him.

Chapter 1

The summer of 2019 marked the 50th anniversary of the Manson Family murders in the summer of 1969. In 12 chapters, I theorize the psychology behind Charles Manson's creepy ability to recruit, organize, and control his band of mostly criminal pseudo-hippies in the late 1960s.

Charles Manson (1934-2017) directed some of his cult followers to commit the Tate-LaBianca murders and also the killings of Gary Hinman and Shorty Shea. Besides the documented fatalities, the Manson Family committed other suspected slaughters and crimes.

Some key Manson Family killers included Charles Manson, Charles "Tex" Watson, Leslie Van Houten, Patricia Krenwinkel, Susan Atkins, Bruce Davis, Steven "Clem" Grogan, and Bobby "Cupid" Beausoleil.

Left to right: Charles Manson, ca 1970; Summer of Love poster; the hippie counterculture, ca the late 1960s.

On the night of August 9th, 1969, Manson ordered his murder crew of Charles "Tex" Watson, Susan Atkins, Patricia Krenwinkel, and Linda Kasabian to kill everybody at the home of Sharon Tate and Roman Polanski. Murdered that night were Sharon Tate and her guests Jay Sebring, Abigail Folger, and Wojciech Frykowski. Steven Parent, who was visiting the caretaker, was also killed.

The next night Charles Manson directed his Manson Family killers to murder Leno LaBianca and Rosemary LaBianca. Other Manson Family murder victims included Gary Hinman and Donald "Shorty" Shea.

In this book, I reveal the forming of the Manson Family, which was 5:1 girls-to-guys. I based the CULT GIRLS on prison interviews I conducted with Manson and other research. A particular emphasis was on the development and life passages of the young women in the Manson Family.

Pictured are Manson Family girls (ca 1969-1970).

Many of the girls Manson recruited for his hippie-murder cult were: 1) wild-and-crazy teenagers; 2) many were hippie girls stoned on drugs; 3) the girls had parental issues; 4) they had identity-crisis turmoil, which Manson exploited. However, the Manson Family kids were often educated and from middle-class homes. This book follows their lives from the late-1960s until now. Some continued a criminal pattern, and others went straight in later life.

I present some of the traumatizing, astonishing admissions and scandalous interview comments of the psychopathic-serial killer, Charles Manson, with a focus on revealing the Manson Family's psychology, Manson Family members, and their crimes. Charlie was the wild-eyed, scraggly-haired Dark Prince of the 1960s.

Charles Manson was the demon-hippie, psycho-serial-killer-by-proxy of the Woodstock era. Manson sent his Manson Family of fanatical, cult-crazed robots out to commit multiple homicides in the mansions of Los Angeles.

The Milgram Shock Experiment

In 1963, Stanley Milgram created an experiment to see if participants would follow orders even when the requested behavior went against their moral beliefs or good judgment.

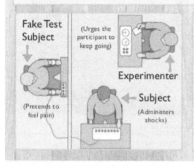

Fake Test Subject

(Urges the participant to keep going)

Experimenter

Subject (Administers shocks)

(Pretends to feel pain)

A researcher asks the participant to administer electric shocks to a test subject when he answers questions incorrectly. The test subject is an actor, who makes noises of pain when he receives the shocks. The participant is made to believe that each shock is stronger than the last one.

The Milgram experiments showed why people obey orders. The Manson Family members wanted rewards such as approval from Charles Manson. So some Manson cult members would murder if Manson ordered it.

Charles Manson, an alarming, terrifying paradox, was one of the most dangerous serial killers in the American history of crime. I focused my forensic-clinical psychologist's perspective in the Manson interviews, which I completed in 1988 and are now available for the first time after more than 30 years. Buy a copy of CHARLES MANSON: MY CHARLES MANSON PRISON INTERVIEWS by Dr. Paul Dawson for more on my interviews with Manson.

I interviewed Charles Manson in September 1988. Manson, the poster boy for killer-cult leaders, was incarcerated in San Quentin State Prison, San Quentin, California. My interviews resulted in a scarce, sensational, and spellbinding investigation and assessment inside the treacherous, enigmatic mind of this infamous icon of criminal evil. I investigated, in-depth, Manson's depraved aura, the repulsion of this homicidal-cult guru, and his murdering, cult-kingpin rampage.

The Stanford Prison Experiment (SPE). Guards became too cruel, and Prisoners suffered too much, and Zimbardo stopped the experiment in 6 days instead of 2 weeks. It was in the basement under the Stanford University psychology department. It showed the power of an authority figure playing a designated role. Manson, an authority figure who controlled his cult, got young women and men to kill for him.

I revealed Manson's darkest secrets, elicited Manson Family confessions, confronted and provoked the murderer by probing his mind, and challenging Manson's-spooky justifications. Manson, an enigma, finally answered questions about his cryptic crimes he had suppressed for many years. My psychological concepts illuminate persuasive, lucid light on Manson's ghastly crimes of assault, torture, and mass murder.

Charles Manson died November 19th, 2017, at age 83 of a heart attack. He was a dangerous cult leader who attracted and controlled mostly young women and girls who joined his Manson Family in the late 1960s. The Manson Family had about a 5:1 ratio of females to males. Why did girls follow Charles Manson? How did Manson manipulate and control mostly girls to murder and commit crimes for him?

Manson Family girls had a news conference during the Manson Family murder trial (1970). Nancy Pitman (right) was involved in the 1972 James and Lauren Willett murders. She was convicted of accessory to murder and did 18 months in prison.

CULT GIRLS reveals the Manson Family story based on my research, prison interviews, and psychological assessment of Charles Manson. In this book, CULT GIRLS, I aim to present a more systematic, organized guidebook and overview of the Manson Family with some updates on the status of the Manson-cult members. The focus is on the significant women and girls in Manson's cult.

Manson, charismatic, established himself as a cult leader and authority figure of a group of mostly teens and twenty-something girls. How could such a scruffy, bearded, little con artist like Charles Manson be such a magnet for many troubled young girls? And some disaffected, alienated, and isolated young-male drifters?

Charles Manson's followers outside the courthouse in L.A. while some Manson Family members were on trial for murder (1970). Manson's brainwashed girls were set off into a self-destructive direction for years and in some cases, decades of criminal behavior. Sandra Good (left) and Nancy Pitman (center) both did prison time for later crimes. Manson set his hardcore Manson Family members on a criminal path. Many of them continued a life of crime. Young women and some men continued on a path of self-destruction. The Manson Family crimes of the late-1960s didn't end after Charlie, and his killers went to prison.

Are you familiar with the 1963 Milgram obedience study? Stanley Milgram, a Yale University psychologist, did a series of social psychological experiments on obedience to authority figures. The investigation focused on the conflict between obedience to authority and personal conscience.

Experimenters ordered subjects in Milgram's experiments to keep giving electric shocks to people who pretended to yell in pain from another room. Would a person have to be an antisocial personality or be a hardcore psychopath to continue following orders to shock people?

Left to right: The happy 1960s hippie countercultural dream. The violent death of the Sixties' dream: chaos at Altamont; Manson Family murders.

However, 65% of the subjects never stopped giving shocks. The significance of Milgram's studies of obedience to authority figures is that they reveal the power of social pressure. Milgram's experiments provide a frame of reference on real-life extreme, destructive obedience as in the case of Charles Manson and his Manson Family of killer robots stalking and murdering people in the mansions of the Los Angeles area in the late 1960s.

The hypothesis that Stanley Milgram tested was the degree of pain an individual is willing to inflict upon another individual because an authority figure ordered it. The Milgram experiments showed why people obey orders. The Manson Family members wanted rewards such as approval from Charles Manson.

The Manson Family wanted to avoid the negative consequences of disobeying Manson. Manson was a legit-authority figure to the Manson Family. Manson created extreme-criminal situations. His cult members obeyed and murdered even when they were required to violate their moral values and conscience or sense of right and wrong.

A similar study was conducted in 1971 by Zimbardo, a Stanford University psychologist: The Stanford Prison Experiment (SPE). Young male students played the roles of Prisoner and Guard. Zimbardo's team constructed a prison-like setting in the basement of the Stanford psychology department.

Zimbardo planned the SPE experiment to take two weeks. The unexpected brutality of the Guards was intense. The Prisoners suffered to a high degree. So the study was stopped in six days.

Zimbardo's experiment illustrated the power of social situations to shape an individual's behavior. They performed their guard task like robots as a consequence of their role. Zimbardo was Prison Superintendent. The excess aggression and cruel behavior were surprising.

Left to right: Susan Atkins, Patricia Krenwinkel, and Leslie Van Houten in front of Charles Manson.

The Zimbardo and Milgram experiments showed the potential impact of a cult leader and authority figure like Charles Manson. The young, mixed-up girls and some young-male drifters and criminals obeyed Manson. The Manson cult followers ignored their conflicts and moral conscience objections.

The hardcore, drugged-out, brainwashed Manson Family females and guys were under Manson's spell and followed Charlie's orders. Eventually, police arrested most of the Manson Family. Some Manson Family members convicted of murder are still in prison nearly 50 years later.

Chapter 2

LESLIE VAN HOUTEN (1949-): Leslie Van
Houten (aka Lulu, Leslie Marie Sankston, Leslie Sue, Leslie Owens, Louella Maxwell Alexandria, Morning Flower) was a member of the Manson Family. Van Houten, convicted of murdering Leno and Rosemary LaBianca, was sentenced to life in prison when California banned the death penalty. Leslie is often recommended for parole. But California's governors have rejected her parole on the basis that she posed an unreasonable danger to society. She has admitted to stabbing Rosemary LaBianca about 16 times.

Leslie Van Houten, 71 in 2020, was born into a middle-class family in Altadena, California, on August 23rd, 1949. She was outgoing and athletic in her teens and was elected high school homecoming princess. Van Houten got off track by experimenting with drugs such as LSD, hashish, and marijuana. She continued to abuse mood-and mind-altering drugs.

Leslie Van Houten pictured at the time of her murder trials.

In the summer of 1968, she got involved with some horrible company. She met Bobby Beausoleil and Catherine "Gypsy" Share, who told her about Charles Manson in glowing terms. Share said Manson was Christlike and had all the answers to questions they had about life. In other words, Manson was a guru who would cure their teenage-identity crisis.

By the fall of 1968, Van Houten had joined the Manson Family cult at Spahn's Movie Ranch just outside of Los Angeles. At 19, Van Houten was one of the youngest Manson Family members. She, like the other Manson Family cult members, was brainwashed with sex orgies, Manson's psychobabble and pimp tricks, lots of continuous drug abuse, and threats of violence to keep her in line. Manson appointed her one of his sexiest "front-street" girls he used to pimp out to men he wanted to use and manipulate with sex favors.

As time went by in 1969, Manson began to realize he was not getting his big break as a rock star with a record deal, and Manson's jive talk turned from peace and love to the "Helter Skelter" revolution and murder. She said that, besides the sex and drugs, all the Manson Family did was listen to the Beatles' *White Album* and read the biblical book of *Revelations*. Manson was setting his hippie cult up for darker purposes, including violent revenge and murder.

Pictured are Leslie Van Houten with Susan Atkins and Patricia Krenwinkel during their murder trial. The girls often acted in an immature, arrogant, and obnoxious way, which shocked the public. They giggled, sang Manson's strange lyrics, and chanted. Manson was programming them.

Manson's twisted plan to stimulate Helter Skelter was to commit mass murder and get revenge against the Hollywood establishment by the Tate/LaBianca murders. Manson ordered Van Houten to join Tex Watson and Patricia Krenwinkel in murdering Leno and Rosemary LaBianca.

In late 1969, Van Houten and the other Manson Family killers were arrested and later convicted of murder. The victims' families strongly oppose releasing Manson Family killers on parole. Van Houten, while a model prisoner, as of February 2019, remains in prison in the California Institution for Women in Corona, California.

Leslie Van Houten represents the surprising twist Charles Manson was able to accomplish in brainwashing a beautiful, middle-class girl who was a two-time homecoming queen or princess in high school but had a weakness for abusing drugs. Because Manson ordered her to help murder the LaBiancas, she admitted she stabbed Rosemary LaBianca 16 times and was convicted of murder. Although Van Houten said, she stabbed her after she was dead because Watson ordered it. After all, Manson wanted them all to get their hands dirty doing the murders.

Leslie Van Houten during her murder trial.

But she was still under Manson's brainwashing spell during her murder trial. She turned off the public by giggling, laughing, singing, and chanting during her murder trial to show her rebellious attitude. Decades later, at parole hearings, she claimed to be under the influence of drugs like LSD or speed and in emotional conflict at the time of the murders.

Because she was a model prisoner, she's been approved for parole. Sharon Tate's sister got 140,000 citizens to sign a petition to keep Van Houten locked in prison. So, California's governor has denied her parole release.

Leslie Van Houten, on January 30, 2019, was recommended for release on parole again. But California's Governor Newsom disapproved of her release.

Leslie Louise Van Houten and her older brother grew up in a middle-class household. Her father Paul was an automotive auctioneer, and her mother Jane was a schoolteacher. After Leslie, there were two more additions. The Van Houtens adopted a young boy and girl that had been orphaned in Korea.

Leslie Van Houten during her murder trial.

In 1963 Leslie's parents divorced, Paul moved out, and the children stayed with Jane. Meanwhile, Leslie began attending Monrovia High School, where she was twice elected homecoming princess. She got into abusing hallucinogenic drugs, and her grade average went down. She dropped her extracurricular activities, got pregnant, and had an abortion. Sex and drugs were leading her off the track.

After graduating high school in 1967, Leslie moved in with her father, attended a business college, and studied to become a legal secretary. She got into New-Age spiritualism and wanted to live in a yoga-spiritual community.

In the summer of 1968, Leslie was visiting friends in San Francisco. At that time, she met Catherine Share, Bobby Beausoleil, and his wife, Gail. She began traveling with them. In September, they took her to meet Charles Manson at Spahn's Movie Ranch. She returned to the ranch three weeks later; this time, she didn't leave. Caught up in the hippie counterculture, Leslie wanted to join a commune.

Left: Leslie Van Houten, high school homecoming queen. Middle: Van Houten's police mugshot, 1969. Right: Van Houten, 2002 parole hearing. Van Houten transformed from a decent looking high school girl to a burned-out, drug-addicted murderer. She has since reformed herself in prison and has been recommended for parole.

Leslie became hypnotized by Charlie Manson. She admitted, "I was absolutely intrigued and mesmerized by Manson, and I believed that he was someone very special and extraordinary". She didn't realize he was just a con artist and hardcore street criminal.

Leslie followed Manson's orders. So the night of the LaBianca murders, she wanted to prove herself a real Manson Family robot. Van Houten identified with and followed Patricia Krenwinkel. Since Krenwinkel was committing homicide, she would also.

Van Houten, Patricia Krenwinkel, and Charles "Tex" Watson killed Rosemary and Leno LaBianca by stabbing them many times. It was reported Leslie wiped the house down for fingerprints, changed clothes, and eventually hitchhiked back to Spahn's Movie Ranch.

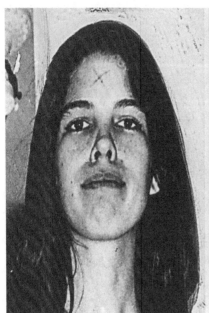

Left: Leslie Van Houten, 1970. Right: Van Houten in a recent photo, still in prison nearly 50 years later.

Leslie was arrested with the family in both the August 16, 1969, Spahn's Movie Ranch, and October 10, 1969, Barker Ranch raids. Police questioning revealed that Susan Atkins was involved with the Gary Hinman murder; that Linda Kasabian, Susan Atkins, and Patricia were at the Tate residence on the night of the killings. Linda Kasabian, the driver, and lookout, didn't kill anyone and later testified against the others.

Leslie's behavior at the Tate/LaBianca murder trial was suspicious, hostile, and somewhat silly. She and Atkins and Krenwinkel sang Manson's crazy songs on their way to court. She wasn't involved with the Tate murders. Van Houten's lawyers tried unsuccessfully to separate her from the other defendants. She was convicted of two counts of first-degree murder and one count of conspiracy to commit murder and sentenced to death.

Left: Leslie Van Houten and John Waters, director. Right: Recent photo of Van Houten.

Like the other Manson Family killers, in 1972, Leslie's death sentence was commuted to life imprisonment when California briefly outlawed the death penalty. Leslie began having problems with eating and developed severe anorexia related to the stress of prison. However, she overcame her eating disorder within a few years.

Van Houten's attorney Ronald Hughes, who may have been murdered by the Manson family, had disappeared in the middle of the first trial. So, Leslie was granted a second one. In January of 1977, her second trial began and ended with a deadlocked jury in September.

Van Houten had long since disassociated herself from Manson. She seemed to be quite a different person from the first trial. Between her second and third trials, she was out on bail for about six months, during which she lived with a friend and worked on her case. In March of 1978, Leslie's third trial started. She was convicted and sentenced to life imprisonment.

Left: Nancy Pitman, Manson Family member. Middle/right: Steve "Clem" Grogan, Manson Family member. Nancy Pitman only did 18 months in prison for accessory to murder in the Willett murder case. Grogan was convicted of murdering Donald "Shorty" Shea and was released from prison in 1985 – 34 years ago. Yet Leslie Van Houten is in prison nearly 50 years later.

Leslie had a jailhouse marriage with William Syvin, a former prisoner that she had corresponded with. However, the marriage ended because it was revealed that he was planning to break her out of prison.

Van Houten did some positive things in prison:

1) she received a B.A. in English Literature from Antioch University; 2) she has been active with both Alcoholics Anonymous and Narcotics Anonymous; 3) she edited a prison newspaper; 4) she has taught other inmates how to read.

Some predicted that out of all the Tate/LaBianca killers, Leslie has the best chance of getting paroled. The governor rejected parole for Van Houten in 2019. While she has been denied parole numerous times, the board of prison terms has recommended her for parole recently.

Left: Lynette "Squeaky" Fromme, Manson Family member. Right: Leslie Van Houten, 2015. Fromme, convicted of the attempted assassination of President Ford, was released on parole in 2009. In 2020, Van Houten is still in prison.

INTERVIEW COMMENTS – LESLIE VAN HOUTEN:

Barbara Walters (YouTube) interviewed Leslie Van Houten, at age 28, in 1977:

Van Houten: I started dropping acid when I was 16. I was going to school. But the more I dropped acid, the harder it was to relate to different people other than the others who were dropping acid. All the hippies were migrating to the places where they felt comfortable with one another. I've had a lot of other women inside tell me they were glad they didn't run into Charlie. Because they too would have done murders. I think a lot of parents were concerned with the idea that it could have been their children.

Left: Leslie Van Houten as a young girl. Right: Leslie Van Houten, circa 1970. Van Houten went from a nice, popular, middle-class girl, who was homecoming princess in high school, to a Charles-Manson-robot-killing machine in 1969.

Van Houten: I was taking LSD. I had been traveling around with a couple of other people I had met up in San Francisco. I had a break-up with my first boyfriend. And when you're young and very much in love, the break-up can be really difficult. I was trying to make it on my own in San Francisco, and I couldn't. So a couple of people came along and said, "Well, come with us." It was kind of a live-for-today situation. So I went with them. Then I ended up going to Spahn's Movie Ranch. ...When you drop acid at first, it is a 9-hour experience. At first, you can go back to work on Monday after using it for a weekend. But the more you take, the less you can relate to others. And you're lost. The more I became isolated from people with different viewpoints, the more I became immersed in the acid reality. It's a fairy-tale world. I met Charles Manson, who was dominant.

Leslie Van Houten, circa the 1970s, and Van Houten after nearly 50 years in prison. Should she be released from jail on parole?

Van Houten: I felt he knew what he was doing. We'd take acid in a group, and Manson would speak to us. ...If you didn't do what Manson wanted, you would not be in his good graces. I admired him, and I really became dependent on him and his moods of the day. ...Charlie was always careful that nobody could put definite things on him. He always protected himself in different ways. At one point, I believed he was Jesus Christ. ...We went to bed together a couple of times. But I didn't consider him a lover. I feel like I was a pawn in whatever his scheme was.

Van Houten explained how she was, like the other Manson Family members, brainwashed through drugs, sex, and Manson's New Age mumbo jumbo or psychobabble. Manson then sent her out to kill like the others.

<u>Van Houten (YouTube) spoke at her parole hearing in 1991 when she was 42-years-old:</u>

The parole hearing staff asked her to comment on defending Manson when she was first in prison.

Van Houten: I was still under Manson's control then. Now I feel he's a very pitiful and pathetic human being. I'm sorry people give him attention. His only danger is in the attention he's given. If he were ignored and left alone, he would probably just fade away. I believed that Manson was Jesus Christ, and the murders were something that had to be done. I did not feel good about it. It was like war. We were going through combat training at the ranch.

Prepped like that. Manson said the racial war was coming. About 18 years ago, I realized that was the wrong way to think. It's been very difficult for me to cope with this. It has not been until the last couple of years that I think I can be forgiven by God for what I've done. Part of my job at the ranch was to read to Manson from the bible.

It's been very difficult for me to find forgiveness spiritually. A.A. talks a lot about God as we understand him and turning my will over, removing defects of character. The more I study A.A., the more I realize I had to find some sort of peace. Not just with the crime but life after.

Larry King (YouTube) interviewed Leslie Van Houten in 1994, 25 years after the murders in 1969:

Van Houten: I had gotten to the Spahn's Movie Ranch through other people who had been there and were driving up and down the coast. I was in the hippie movement. I met these people who said they lived in a commune in L.A. And that they lived for the day and for the moment. A lot of the Leary kind of philosophy of be here now. When I dropped out, I was separated from my family.

When I was caught after the murders, my family had anger and resentment. When my mother came to visit, I told her that she'd be better off just to leave me alone. She said she was not made of that kind of stuff. I wasn't physically enamored with Manson. I was caught and mesmerized by his mind. And the things he professed. I had come to the ranch by way of Robert Beausoleil, and Beausoleil was very important to Manson.

Robert was my lover. Manson treated me in a way that I belonged to Bobby Beausoleil. I knew that something was going to happen in the Tate murders. But not specifically in advance. Manson worked to shed ourselves of our egos and get rid of our own identity. To do what would make us one with one another. He insulted our families and our morals we'd been taught.

Because most of us were middle-class Anglos, he challenged us. Would you die for me? This was over some time. Not long before the murders, Manson said he would take the lead and show the blacks how it should be done. I found out he had some sort of bum drug deal and had shot someone.

I know now that Sharon Tate had something to do with Terry Melcher. But at the time, each of us knew very little about what was going on. Pat Krenwinkel told me about the Tate murders the next morning. I was sad that it had to occur. It was justified to make a statement following Charles Manson's orders.

Dramatic film and stage play portrayals of Leslie Van Houten:

- In 2019, Van Houten was played by Victoria Pedretti (listed in the credits as "LuLu") in Quentin Tarantino's film *Once Upon a Time in Hollywood*.
- In 2018 she was portrayed by Gabrielle Klobucar in the made for TV documentary *Inside the Manson Cult: The Lost Tapes.*
- Later in 2016, Greer Grammer was cast as Van Houten in Leslie Libman's film *Manson's Lost Girls*, which starred MacKenzie Mauzy as Kasabian.
- Tania Raymonde portrayed Van Houten in Susanna Lo's 2016 film *Manson Girls.*

Left: Greer Grammer. Center: Grammer portrayed Leslie Van Houten (right) in Manson's Lost Girls, 2016. Right: Leslie Van Houten, 1969 police mugshot.

- In the 2015 NBC fictional series *Aquarius*, which centers on the Los Angeles Police Department and the Manson murders, Emma Dumont played a character named "Emma" who is loosely based on Van Houten.
- The 2009 film *Leslie, My Name is Evil* (released in some countries under the titles *Manson Girl* and *Manson, My Name Is Evil*) is partially based on Van Houten's early life and stars actress Kristen Hager as Van Houten.
- In *Helter Skelter* (2004 remake of the 1976 film), actress Catherine Wadkins portrayed Van Houten.
- In 2003, Amy Yates portrayed Leslie Van Houten in the film *The Manson Family*.
- San Francisco-based actress Connie Champagne played Van Houten in Dude Theater's long-running 1989 stage play *The Charlie Manson Story*, first at Climate Theater & then Theatre Artaud, a black comedy directed by Christopher Brophy. The production was the first to de-glamorize the Manson-myth and to question Manson's belief in the so-called Helter Skelter.
- Actress Cathey Paine portrayed Leslie Van Houten in the 1976 made-for-TV film *Helter Skelter*.

Left: Barbara Hoyt, Debra Tate (Sharon Tate's sister). Right: Pictured is Barbara Hoyt, circa 1969-1970s.

Barbara Hoyt, who lived with the Manson Family at Spahn's Movie Ranch for six months, can be understood to focus light on a fundamental issue concerning the Manson Family convicted killers who are still in prison. Were the Manson cult killers drug-crazed, zombie robots following Charlies Manson's orders?

Hoyt asserted that some Manson Family members, such as herself, refused to kill anybody. Others volunteered to Charlie willingly to go commit mass murder. I'm including Hoyt's letter here and also in the chapter on Barbara Hoyt.

She wrote this letter against Leslie Van Houten getting released on parole based on her experience living with Leslie Van Houten and other Manson Family groupies at Spahn's Movie Ranch. Hoyt did leave the Manson Family, testified against the Manson Family at the murder trials, got an education, worked as a nurse, and turned her life around as a law-abiding citizen.

Left: Barbara Hoyt and Brooks Poston. Right: Patricia Krenwinkel and Leslie Van Houten. Hoyt and Poston left the Manson Family as the violence and murder escalated. Krenwinkel and Van Houten participated in the Manson cult mass murders.

The hostile critic in the back row might dismiss Hoyt as self-righteous and hypocritical since Hoyt was a member of the Manson Family for at least six months.

Some might check out the Manson Family circus at Spahn's Movie Ranch, the drug abuse, the weird sex orgies, rumors of murders, and run like hell away from the Manson Family after one day – not hangout and live dangerously with Charlie Manson's cult for six months.

Although some former Manson followers rationalized that at first, the Manson Family was about the usual flower child or hippie commune values of doing drugs, dancing, and free love.

Left: Leslie Van Houten at her 2000 parole hearing. Right: Van Houten after decades in prison; Van Houten ca 1970.

Hoyt read a letter at Leslie Van Houten's 2007 parole hearing which was attended by Los Angeles Deputy District Attorney Patrick Sequeira:

"Dear Board of Prison Terms: My name is Barbara Hoyt. I testified in many Manson related trials against these defendants for seven years. I also testified before you on 10/20/06 against Bruce Davis. I lived with the Manson Family for six months when I was seventeen years old."

"One of the ways I have to judge whether or not a particular defendant has changed or is sorry is by how truthful they are in the present about their roles in the past. If they are lying or minimizing their actions, I know it because I was there."

"I was struck by Leslie's 2006 parole hearing because she made that task more difficult by refusing (like Sadie – Susan Atkins) to discuss the crime events at all. She not only murdered these poor people but she is now playing Mansonesque games, i.e., demanding that their memory cease to exist."

Left: Leno LaBianca, Rosemary LaBianca. Right: Patricia Krenwinkel, Leslie Van Houten, ca 1970.

"This is a major red flag for me. In none of Leslie's prior parole hearings that I have watched has she ever owned up to how aggressive she was, or how aggressive her participation was in these crimes. If there was something she wanted and you got in her way, she could be quite abusive."

"Her demeanor never changed after the murders. Her affect was never sad to me. According to Sadie (Susan Atkins), who I overheard talking about the murder to Ouisch (Ruth Ann Moorehouse), Leslie forced Mrs. LaBianca into her bedroom, put a pillowcase over her head, and wrapped a lamp cord around her neck, and shoved her onto the bed and held her down so Katie, Patricia Krenwinkel, could stab her, which she attempted, but her knife bent on the victim's collarbone."

"When Mrs. LaBianca overheard her husband being murdered, she jumped up from the bed with superhuman strength, screaming, 'What are you doing to my husband?' She managed to keep Leslie and Katie at bay by swinging the lamp at them with the cord still around her neck."

Left to right: Susan Atkins, Patricia Krenwinkel, and Leslie Van Houten during the Manson murder trial, ca 1970.

"So, Leslie got Tex. She knocked the lamp from Mrs. LaBianca's hands, and Tex, with a large knife, stabbed her, bringing her to the floor.   Several people lived with the Manson Family, who, despite believing that Charlie was Jesus Christ, that despite fearing the coming of the end of the world and Helter Skelter, despite the cult techniques of indoctrination, chose not to harm others, even if it meant not surviving Helter Skelter."

"There was also a group of Manson Family members who couldn't wait to kill. Leslie was in the latter group. I believe that even without Charlie, she would have harmed others in some capacity. I saw an interview with Leslie's father, and he stated that he has never asked her about the murders and she has never commented about it, that he has not lost any sleep over this entire – over this crime and that he doesn't think about the victims, and that he forgave Charles Manson a long time ago."

Left: Van Houten after many years in jail. Right: Van Houten, ca 1970. Leslie turned off the public because she was laughing, giggling, singing, and disruptive at the Manson murder trial.

"It must be nice. If my child had been involved in a murder, I would have asked a lot of questions, and I would have lost a lot of sleep. Leslie's ability to kill – or excuse me – Leslie's ability to feel no concern for others isn't a trait she learned from Charlie but from her father. Charlie just gave her a place to express herself."

"She chose to kill. She asked to kill. She wasn't a mindless, drug-crazed zombie soldier for Charlie, as she described herself in an earlier parole hearing. She had lots of fun. She played games, camped, sang songs, raced in dune buggies, had casual sex with favorite partners."

"She enjoyed herself. She was not an innocent who was plucked from her home. She came to the Manson Family with her group, including Bobby Beausoleil and "Gypsy" Share, who were both involved in another murder and attempted murder. Leslie also at the time, knew what she did was wrong."

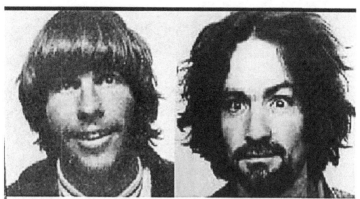

Charles "Tex" Watson and Charles Manson

"On the morning following the LaBianca murders, I entered the back house of the ranch to find Leslie on the bed, counting coins. A call came from the field phone that a man was on his way looking for Leslie. She told me the man had given her a ride last night from Griffith Park and for me to hide her, which I did. In 1977 Leslie was out of prison for a few months."

"I feel from her statements that the only person she feels is a victim is herself. I compare the Manson story with that of Hitler because there are so many similarities. Both groups consisted of antisocial people who, in their blood-thirsty quest for personal power, were willing to kill innocent people to get it."

"At least Hitler's cronies were held responsible for their murders despite pleas that they were only following orders, and so should the Manson followers who chose to kill. Both groups have left behind a legacy of evil that haunts us still today."

Left: Leslie Van Houten, ca the early 1970s. Right: Van Houten after nearly 50 years in jail. Van Houten had three murder trials.

"I believe that if Leslie were truly and deeply sorry, she would stop these parole hearings and let the victims' families have some peace and serve her time in silence and dignity. In closing, I would like to say to Leslie that there is a fact that you seem to be unaware of, and that is, that murder is something that you can never recover from or make right."

"The victims never get their lives back. The families never get to stop mourning. The witnesses never again get to live without fear, and the killers spend the rest of their lives in prison. You demanding to be able to leave prison would mean that you would be the only one to be able to walk away from the carnage you caused, and that would be a travesty of justice. Thank you. Barbara Hoyt."

Left to right: Leslie Van Houten as a child, teenager, high school homecoming queen, and in a police mugshot while a member of the Manson Family cult, ca 1969. Mood and mind-bending drugs and Manson cult brainwashing did have an impact on Van Houten.

Leslie Van Houten's summary: While Van Houten was recommended for parole on July 23, 2020, Governor Newsom will probably reject parole for her. Governor Newsom turned her down for parole on June 4, 2019. Van Houten, in 2020, is in the California Institution for Women in the Chino district of Corona, California.

Newsom commended Van Houten for her efforts at rehabilitation and conceded her youth at the time of the crimes, but he is concerned about her potential for future violence. I believe in tough sentences for murder. Deborah Tate, Sharon Tate's sister, has been against any Manson Family member's release from prison.

Governor Newsom turned down Van Houten for parole in 2019 and commented: "Ms. Van Houten and the Manson family committed some of the most notorious and brutal killings in California history. When considered as a whole, I find the evidence shows that she currently poses an unreasonable danger to society if released from prison at this time."

However, since several Manson Family members have been released who were convicted of murder or accessory to murder or attempted assassination of President Ford, in fairness, Van Houten could be released after serving about 50 years. Steve "Clem" Grogan, convicted of murdering Donald "Shorty" Shea, was released in 1985 – 35 years ago as of 2020.

Nancy Pitman only did 18 months in prison after being convicted as an accessory to murder in the Willett murder case. Lynette "Squeaky" Fromme was released in 2009 after serving 34 years for attempting to assassinate President Ford.

The strict position is that Leslie Van Houten, and the other remaining Manson Family convicted murderers, deserve to be left in prison for life because they took others' lives in 1969. Serving nearly 50 years in prison is not enough.

What do you think? Leslie Van Houten has changed in prison; she's recovered from Charles Manson's brainwashing and the impact of abusing drugs. She's been recommended for parole in recognition of her showing remorse, making some amends, and her positive efforts in prison. Perhaps the victims' families should consider forgiving Leslie Van Houten and support her release.

Chapter 3

Manson had combined a bag of tricks he picked up on the street and in prison to attract, hypnotize, and control his Manson Family. Although Charles Manson was a criminal psychopath, he was able to turn on some charm, play guitar, and sing bizarre songs he wrote to entertain his followers and recruit new Manson Family members.

Manson aspired to be a rock star without much talent or the discipline to work at it or the personality to network contacts. Manson came across as a messiah or authority and father figure to the middle-class and some college-educated kids who were often estranged or alienated from their parents and families.

Manson stroked the egos of young people who often were damaged by abusive parents. Or the kids had an identity crisis because their families neglected them or had kicked them out because of drugs and alcohol abuse.

Some Manson Family members. The ratio was about 5:1 females-to-males. The photo shows seven girls and two guys. The photo shows six of Charlie's hardcore Manson Family female members, including from the right-front clockwise: Lynette "Squeaky" Fromme, Ruth Ann "Ouisch" Moorehouse, Sandra Good, Catherine "Cappy" Gillies, Mary Brunner, and Catherine "Gypsy" Share. All six women have criminal records, and most did years in prison. Ouisch fled and avoided serving her jail sentence for attempted murder.

Manson gave them a vision of transforming their lives. Manson, a sinister- psychopathic killer, initially conned his Manson Family by promising his followers sexual paradise and druggie dreamland.

He told his pseudo-hippie gang they were superior to others because they'd pull off "Helter Skelter," a race war that would lead to Shangri-La run by the Manson Family with Charles Manson calling the shots. Then Charles Manson would rule the world. Grandiose and insane but swallowed whole by his ragtag, stoned followers who Manson kept loaded on drugs.

Aspiring rock musician Charles Manson and his Manson Family cult invaded The Beach Boys (left). Manson and his followers moved into Dennis Wilson's mansion in Pacific Palisades for a few months. Dennis Wilson and Charles Manson (right).

Manson glorified his criminal-counterculture lifestyle. He sent his cult followers out to steal items, including cars, and gather stale food out of garbage dumpsters. He used his Manson Family girls as prostitutes to trade sex for various things he wanted. For a time, his Manson Family moved in with Dennis Wilson, one of The Beach Boys.

In exchange for sex with Manson's girls, Wilson let the Manson Family hang out at his mansion in L.A. and drive his expensive cars. The Manson Family cost Dennis Wilson over $100,000 for the cost of food, medical, dental, damage to his cars, home, and items stolen from Wilson. The followers' self-esteem and identity were closely associated with Manson's aims. If one looked at Charles Manson objectively, he was just an ex-convict who was hustling on the dark side by using a group of young kids to do his bidding.

Left to right: Leslie Van Houten, high school beauty queen; 11th-grade high school yearbook photo; 1969 police mugshot of Van Houten; Van Houten during her murder trial with an X carved on her forehead. Leslie Van Houten, who went from a middle-class, fresh-faced, high school beauty queen to a key Charles Manson Family girl, convicted of murder. Notice Van Houten's innocent, happy-go-lucky, girl-next-door looks in her high-school pictures versus her photos after her arrests for crimes including murder.

The Manson Family had their healthy sense of society's rules altered by the massive abuse of drugs and alcohol. By changing his followers' state of consciousness with drugs, New-Age mumbo-jumbo lectures, and paranoid ranting and raving about Helter Skelter, Manson controlled his hangers-on and disciples.

Manson claimed he was not aiming to be a cult leader. However, once he got out of prison in 1967, he found that the "Summer of Love" atmosphere and hippie movement on the street was easy to exploit. He could live for free by manipulating his followers to support him.

By 1969, preaching Helter Skelter, getting them high and loaded on drugs, and manipulating his hippie devotees with hundreds of drug trips and sex orgies, he could control his cohorts to do crimes including a murder at his command.

Some clean-cut, girl-or-guy-next-door kids are pictured before they joined the Manson Family. Compare their innocent appearances with the photos of them after arrests. Police mugshots showed the impact of drug abuse and nightmare life in Manson's criminal cult.

Manson preyed on the vulnerable kids he found on the street and easily controlled them. But it eventually spiraled out of control. Arrests, jail, and prison sentences spoiled the fun. After giving his Manson Family admirers a lot of LSD, Manson was able to lead them further away from reality. Some of Manson's girls, like Leslie Van Houten, said that continuous acid trips led them further and further from the here and now.

So, Manson was able to turn his adherents' world upside down. He preached that good is evil, god is the devil, murder is love, and death is life. The Manson Family gang was not able to recover from the effects of drugs. There was little downtime; one dose of LSD was followed by another combined with other substances.

Police mugshots of the Manson Family after arrests showed the strain of drug abuse and the Manson Family's criminal lifestyle. Go back and compare pictures of them before they joined the Manson Family and these police mugshots after they entered the Manson cult. The drug abuse and criminal lifestyle Manson forced on them damaged all of them. They were mentally burned-out, sometimes murdered, turned into criminals, and murderers who often did severe prison time.

Manson controlled his cult via twisted, New-Age mind-control techniques such as those taught at Esalen or Silva Mind Control and some features of satanic cults. When Manson's supporters were not drugged, they were hypnotized or mesmerized by mind-control methods.

Chapter 4

SUSAN ATKINS (1948-2009): Susan Atkins
(aka: Sadie Mae Glutz, Sexy Sadie, Donna-Kay Powell, Sharon King) was proudly involved in the Tate and Gary Hinman murders. It was reported that Atkins either stabbed Sharon Tate to death or held her down while Watson killed her. Later, Atkins recanted and said she was only a bystander at the Tate murder scene. She was convicted of murder and died of cancer in prison in 2009. In 1967 Atkins met Charles Manson, joined the Manson Family, which went on the road for a time, and then settled at Spahn's Movie Ranch with the Manson pseudo-hippie criminal cult. She went to hide at the Barker Ranch and Myers Ranch in Death Valley after several murders.

Atkins was born on May 7th, 1948, in San Gabriel, California. Her parents were alcoholics, and she grew up in Northern California. She dropped out of high school to support herself because her mother died when she was 15, and her father abandoned his three kids. Atkins came from a very dysfunctional family. She was living with friends in San Francisco when she met Charles Manson. Susan took off with Manson, who named her Sadie Mae Glutz. When she had a baby, Manson called her baby Zezozose Zadfrack Glutz.

Left: Susan Atkins, 1970. Middle: Patricia Krenwinkel, 1970. Right: Krenwinkel after decades in prison.

Manson, who trusted Atkins to kill for him, brought Atkins along to help him rob and murder Gary Hinman. Manson slashed Hinman's ear and face with a sword while Bruce Davis held a gun on Hinman. Davis and Manson then left. Manson left Atkins, Bobby Beausoleil, and Mary Brunner to finish robbing and killing Hinman.

Susan Atkins shocked people when it was revealed she growled at Sharon Tate, "Woman, I have no mercy for you." Then Atkins stabbed the pregnant 26-year-old actress to death as Tate cried for her mother and begged to live to save her baby. Atkins and the Manson Family killer crew slaughtered five people the night of August 9th, 1969. She then went along the next night when they killed the LaBiancas. Years later, Atkins, in prison, recanted and claimed she could not stab Voytek Frykowski or Sharon Tate. Watson said she held Tate down while he stabbed her.

Susan Atkins, under arrest, during her murder trial, 1970.

Atkins came from troubled, agitated family background. Her father was an alcoholic. But many people come from broken, unhappy families and don't become killers. She escaped to San Francisco and hooked-up with the bad company at every turn.

Atkins led a wild, stormy life before she met Manson. She joined two ex-convicts and went on a tempestuous-robbery spree and ended up doing some months in an Oregon prison. She was in a topless show produced by the Church of Satan founder.

When she met Manson, his combination of keeping her loaded on drugs, LSD, pot, or whatever, his guru brainwashing, and free sex in the Manson Family turned her into a murdering robot under Charles Manson's control. She was always turned down for parole.

Pictured are Susan Atkins and Charles Manson during their murder trial. Atkins was convicted of seven counts of first-degree murder. Atkins died in the California Institute for Women at Frontera on September 24th, 2009, at age 61.

Susan Denise Atkins's mother died of cancer when she was a teenager. Because her father was an alcoholic, and she was continually in conflict with him, she dropped out of high school and moved to San Francisco. Charles Manson specialized in young girls with father-figure issues.

Atkins was a high-school dropout and could only find unpleasant, low-paying jobs such as a phone salesgirl selling magazine subscriptions. She rented a room, was lonely, depressed, and quit her telemarketing job. A local coffee shop hired her as a waitress where she met some dangerous company.

As a waitress, she met two escaped convicts and went on the road with them. The three of them committed thrill-seeking armed robberies along the west coast. Arrested in Oregon, the two men went to prison. Atkins served three months in jail and got probation.

Susan Atkins danced topless in a show called the Witches' Sabbath organized by Church of Satan founder Anton LaVey.

Released from jail, she came back to San Francisco and found work as a topless dancer. It was there she danced in a show called the Witches' Sabbath organized by Church of Satan founder Anton LaVey. Her next crazy adventure, after she quit the topless job, began when she met Charles Manson. She became a fervid follower. Atkins left San Francisco and traveled with the Manson Family to Los Angeles.

The Manson Family got fake IDs, and Manson gave her the name Sadie Glutz. She was a big cheerleader for Charles Manson's activities. Atkins enjoyed Creepy Crawlers' missions. Manson Family members dressed in black, snuck into random houses at night, while people were sleeping. Inside the homes, they'd creep around, steal items and rearrange things to spook the residents.

Atkins was an attention-seeking young lady who clashed with Manson, at times, because he demanded to be the star of the Manson-Family show. Atkins caused the Manson Family to contract sexually transmitted diseases such as the clap. Manson kicked her out of the Manson Family cult for a while.

Ukiah Daily Journal
June 24, 1968

Angry Mother Triggers County Marijuana Raid

An irate mother whose son returned home under the apparent influence of LSD, triggered a raid by sheriff's deputies Saturday night which led to the arrest of nine adults and three juveniles in the Navarro - Boonville area on charges of possessing dangerous drugs.

Seven of the adults, ranging in age from 18 to 24, were also charged with furnishing dangerous drugs to minors, after deputies raided a residence between Boonville and Philo.

Arrested for possessing dangerous drugs—principally marijuana and LSD — were Larry Whilhite, 18; Donald Blake, 18; Peter Hornbluth, 18; R o b e r t Bomse, 18; Mary Brunner, 24; Sadie Mae Glutz, 23; Suzanne Scott, 22; Ella Beth Snider, 23; and Cathran Smith, 20, all of the Navarro - Boonville area.

Only two of those persons could be termed "permanent" residents of the area, the others being "floaters" or "hippies," authorities indicated.

Three 17-year-old boys w e r e placed in juvenile hall after being picked up by sheriff's deputies on suspicion of possessing and using dangerous drugs.

A two and a half months old infant of Cathran Smith was placed in the custody of the welfare department.

Also on Saturday an 18-year-old youth, Mark Toepfer, 18, Sunnyvale, and a 17-year-old companion were arrested near Willits in a stolen car and charged with suspicion of possessing dangerous drugs.

Susan Atkins, Mary Brunner, and several of the Manson Family members were arrested for dealing drugs. Atkins and Brunner were among those the locals called the "Witches of Mendocino" for selling LSD and marijuana to young people in their town.

Susan and some of the Manson Family lived in Mendocino, California, for a while. There the Manson group was arrested after dealing LSD to a group of local kids. At their trial, they were called the Witches of Mendocino.

Atkins, Sadie Glutz in Manson's Family, gave birth to a baby boy in October of 1968. She named him Zezozecee Zadfrack. Atkins spent time recovering after Zadfrack's birth at the Fountain of the World, a nearby religious retreat.

Susan Atkins was an enthusiastic supporter of Charles Manson's murderous agenda. Atkins participated in both the Tate and Hinman murders. After Bobby Beausoleil fatally stabbed Gary Hinman, Mary Brunner and Atkins took turns smothering Hinman with a pillow.

Susan Atkins, aka Sadie Glutz.

At the Polanski-Tate home, Atkins stabbed Wojciech Frykowski and helped Tex Watson kill Sharon Tate. Using Tate's blood, she wrote "PIG" on the front door of the house on Cielo Drive. That was part of Manson's big Helter Skelter plan that was to blame the Black Panthers who were expected to start a white-black race war.

After a Death Valley police raid resulted in the arrest of many Manson Family members, Kitty Lutesinger implicated Atkins in the Gary Hinman murder. Susan Atkins, who always wanted the center of attention, bragged to her cellmates that she was involved in the Tate murders. The cellmates informed the police. Six Manson Family members, including Atkins, were indicted on the Tate-LaBianca murders.

Atkins, always an unstable girl, went before a Los Angeles Grand Jury and revealed all the Manson Family crimes. She was expecting to be the prosecution's star witness and avoid the death penalty. But before the trial started, Susan recanted, took everything she said back that she told the Grand Jury. She showed she was loyal again to Manson.

She was convicted of seven counts of first-degree murder and one count of conspiracy to commit homicide. Like the others, her death sentence was commuted to life in prison when California temporarily outlawed the death penalty. At the California Institute for Women, Leslie Van Houten and Patricia Krenwinkel shunned her for informing on the Manson Family killers.

Susan Atkins

Atkins' son, Zezozecee Zadfrack, was adopted by a doctor who changed his name to Paul. Bruce Davis, like Tex Watson, became a born-again Christian and inspired Susan Atkins to believe in Jesus. She then said Jesus had entered her prison cell, and she was born-again as a Christian. Too bad they didn't find religion BEFORE they committed serial murders.

Atkins, with Bob Slosser, wrote an autobiography called *Child of Satan, Child of God.* She has had few write-ups for bad behavior in prison. Atkins married a con artist named Donald Lee Laisure and then divorced him when she found out he had lied to her. He claimed he was a millionaire and was not. He was married 35 times.

She divorced him and in 1987, married James W. Whitehouse, a law student 15 years younger than Atkins. Atkins, like Tex Watson, has been busy with her prison ministry. She completed an Associate's degree via correspondence courses. When she was diagnosed with brain cancer in 2008, she applied for a "compassionate release" and was denied by the California Board of Parole Hearings. She died in prison.

INTERVIEW COMMENTS – SUSAN ATKINS:

Susan Atkins, 28, was interviewed in 1976:

Left: Susan Atkins, circa 1970. Right: Susan Atkins, Patricia Krenwinkel, and Leslie Van Houten, 1970. Atkins, along with Krenwinkel and Van Houten, lost sympathy with the public because of her joking and detached attitude during her murder trial.

Atkins: The night of the Tate murders, I remember getting in the car with Tex. Tex Watson and my co-defendants. Tex and I had our stash of cocaine and methadrine. We snorted some speed and got in the car. We were very, very wired. We drove to the Tate house with instructions from Charlie Manson to kill everyone in the house. And not just that. We were instructed to go on down and hit every house on the street and kill all the people in all the houses. We went into the house. A car came up, and I was in the bushes. Tex fired the gun while I was in the bushes. He killed Steven Parent. The people in the house were all brought into the living room and tied up. I remember that Voytek Frykowski, I tied his hands with a towel and then was instructed to kill him. I raised the knife, but I could not bring it down. There was a force that kept me from moving. He undid the towel on his wrists, and we began to fight. I was screaming for help. And he was screaming for help. Then Tex came and helped me. I was left to sit and watch Sharon Tate. All I can remember were people scattering in different places and running.

Left: Krenwinkel, Atkins and Van Houten, circa 1970. Right: Atkins, circa 1969.

Atkins: Sharon Tate was talking to me. I felt nothing for her. She begged for her life and the life of her baby. I remember when we first went in, people said who are you? And Tex said, "I'm the devil and I'm here to do the devil's business." My conscience was so alive in me. I remember I had gone so far, and there was no turning back. Even if I wanted to run, I couldn't. I was caught up in something I had no control over. No say so. I was just like a tool in the hands of the devil. I believe that it was by the grace of God that my hand did not go down to stab Voytek Frykowski's chest. Tex killed everybody.

Diane Sawyer interviewed Susan Atkins after she did 37 years in prison when Atkins had brain cancer and asked for a release from prison:

Sawyer: What about those eerie smiles you showed at the trial?

Atkins: It is really difficult to go back in time.

Sawyer: People say to do monstrous things you have to be a monster?

Atkins: That simply is not true.

(Cut to a clip when Atkins said, "I told Sharon Tate I didn't have any mercy for her when she begged for her life and the life of her baby.")

Atkins: You know a person by her behavior and my behavior in this institution speaks to the change that has occurred. I'm not the same person I was when I came here after 37 years.

Sawyer: Manson said he wasn't responsible. You did what you wanted to do.

Atkins: I can't answer for what Charles Manson said. I don't know what's in his mind.

Sawyer: Sharon Tate's father complained about your giggling behavior in court. What argument can you make to him?

Atkins: There's only the continued attempt to apologize to him every time I've gone to the parole board. Remorse and sorrow for hideous actions aren't calculated. It's not tangible. Remorse isn't sitting in a prison cell for the rest of your life crying over what you can't change. Remorse is genuine repentance. Turning away from the behavior. Manson is the one person who is the most difficult to forgive. I don't want to live a life with any unforgiveness in it. So many lost so much. The victims. The families of the victims who were involved. The community at large. The society at large. Everybody lost.

Film and TV portrayals of Susan Atkins:

- Mikey Madison played Susan Atkins in *Once Upon a Time in Hollywood*, a 2019 movie.

- Marianne Rendon portrayed Susan Atkins in *Charlie Says*, a 2018 film.

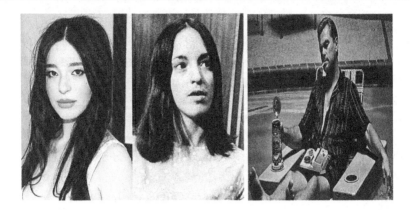

Left to right: Mikey Madison, Susan Atkins, and Leonardo DiCaprio. DiCaprio's character is attacked in his swimming pool by Mikey Madison playing Susan Atkins in Once Upon a Time in Hollywood, a 2019 movie.

- Sarah Paulson played Susan Atkins in *American Horror Story: Cult.*

- Ambyr Childers was cast as Susan Atkins in the 2015 TV series *Aquarius.*

- Devanny Pinn played Susan Atkins in *House of Manson*, 2014.

- Anjelica Scannura was cast as Susan Atkins in *Manson, My Name is Evil*, 2009.

- Marguerite Moreau was Susan Atkins in the 2004 remake of *Helter Skelter.*

- Maureen Allisse portrayed Susan Atkins in *The Manson Family*, 2003.

- Nancy Wolfe portrayed Atkins in the 1976 made-for-TV film *Helter Skelter.*

Summary of Susan Atkins: Atkins served approximately 40 years in prison because she was convicted of a series of murders and died in prison. She was never recommended for parole. She claimed to have been a born-again Christian while in prison. Atkins became better educated and participated in a prison ministry, helplng others.

I listened to some of her parole hearings, which included a district attorney and victims' family members who were against her release on parole. She had a history of changing her stories about her part in the murders.

At first, for example, she asserted that she stabbed Sharon Tate viciously. Later, she said Charles "Tex" Watson had committed most of the killing. Atkins held Sharon Tate down while Tex Watson stabbed her. Atkins, after she was in prison, claimed she had some moral reluctance to stick the Tate murder victims.

Susan Atkins, at her parole hearings and in interviews, came across as sincere in becoming a Christian, recovering from Charles Manson's brainwashing and her years of drug abuse. However, there seemed to have been a lingering doubt about her credibility and genuine remorse for the murder victims.

As a former chief correctional psychologist of a state prison system, I have had many psychopathic or antisocial criminals try to insight me to death about their remorse and rationalize their crimes. Did Atkins honestly change for the better? Susan Atkins appeared to have made an effort to change and reform herself.

But on another more profound level, she may not have deserved to be released on parole given her track record and conviction for committing eight murders. Atkins, unfortunately, came from a very dysfunctional family and combined with her antisocial tendencies, she spiraled out of control into criminal activity with the awful company. Atkins was the longest-serving female inmate in the state of California at the time of her death on September 24th, 2009, at age 61, at the Central California Women's Facility in Chowchilla, California.

Chapter 5

By selecting mostly girls with emotional and psychological issues, he made them feel better by making the Manson Family their home. He used sex and drugs, and New-Age jive talks to break the will of his hangers-on. Then Manson pressured them into identifying with his own sick goals. Because Manson had a weird charisma and streetwise-leadership quality, he could brainwash his devotees to do almost anything. Charlie was a god to his cohorts.

At first, like other cults, the Manson Family members were mostly given a lot of fake love, free sex orgies, and druggie trips. By the summer of 1969, Manson's cult entered a nightmare of violence and murder.

How did Charles Manson form his Manson Family? In 1967 Manson was released from prison and ended up on the streets of San Francisco where conveniently the hippie "Summer of Love" ambiance was happening. There was free food handed out in the parks for hippie-street people. It was hip, slick, and cool in that atmosphere to counter the "Establishment."

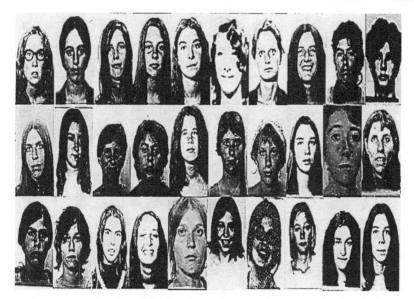

See the Manson Family abuse in the police mugshots of Charles Manson's girls: 29 females (1 male). Go back to the last chapter and compare the fresh, clean-cut looks they had before they joined the Manson Family with these police mugshots of them after the drug abuse and criminal activity in the Manson Family. Manson Family members all ended up with criminal records. Being a pseudo-hippie rebel in the late-1960s counterculture was initially a lot of fun and games for the Manson Family members. However, drug abuse, sexual promiscuity, unhealthy criminal lifestyle, and drop-out disadvantages caught up with them over the years.

Young adults and runaway-teen girls flooded the streets, ready to join the counterculture. Manson said he played the role of the father figure many of the young runaways and drifters never had.

Many of the girls were very attractive and came from modest, middle, or upper-middle-class homes in the suburbs. It was exciting to live on the wild side and escape their dull, boring life built on values of the 1950s.

Police arrested these key Charles Manson Family members for various crimes, yet most of them were from middle-class, educated backgrounds. After the Manson Family nightmare lifestyle of drugs, sex, and evil, they ended up convicted of murder, in prison for various felonies, drug addicts, and mentally burned-out, sometimes murdered or dead.

The kids wanted to follow the hippie-druggie doctrine, which was summarized by former-Harvard psychologist Dr. Timothy Leary: "tune in, turn on, drop out!" The hippie-obligatory lifestyle was getting loaded on drugs, getting into the occult and New-Age way of life, radical left politics (SDS, Weather Underground), free-sex and commune-style living. In prison, Charles Manson had studied New-Age thinking, mind-control methods, and occultism.

Because Manson had spent many years in prison, he was familiar with many types of crimes, con games, and pimp skills in handling women. Although Manson was short and skinny with a bearded-unkempt look, he managed to project a mysterious and charismatic vibe that attracted girls.

Manson played guitar and sang his bizarre-song lyrics, which entertained his Manson Family, who were too stoned on drugs to notice that he lacked any real talent. Right: Manson Family girls eating from a garbage dumpster. Slumming was fun for these middle-class girls. In the late 1960s, the hippie movement approved living like dogs. From left in the supermarket dumpster: Lynette "Squeaky" Fromme, Sandra Good, Mary Brunner, and Ruth Ann "Ouisch" Moorehouse eating stale garbage.

He played some folk-acoustic guitar and sang his enigmatic or strange lyrics for his female fans and guy admirers. His cryptic-songs seemed to have some mystical insight into life for his stoned troopers. He turned them into robotic devotees, ready to follow his commands.

Manson moved his growing Manson Family to Los Angeles on an old bus and planned on pimping girls and drug dealing. Manson and his gang began dealing drugs with Hollywood celebrities and players in the film and music industry. Charlie used the girls like hookers and pimped them out.

Manson is pictured aging through the years.

He was pimping out his hippie-girl disciples to Hollywood film actors and rock stars. Manson even pimped-out his young men to closeted, gay-Hollywood players. Manson and his Family hung out with Dennis Wilson of The Beach Boys.

Manson was at parties with Hollywood showbiz names like members of The Monkeys, Jane Fonda, Cass Elliot, Sammy Davis, Jr., Robert Conrad, Steve McQueen, Sharon Tate, Jay Sebring, Yul Brynner, Peter Sellers, and others.

The next stop for the Manson Family was Spahn's Movie Ranch, a desert film location for westerns, where the cult lived free by giving free sex to the owner of the ranch and doing some chores around his operation.

Susan Atkins, Patricia Krenwinkel, and Leslie Van Houten on March 24th, 1971, with X's on their foreheads, were copying Charles Manson. It took years for Manson Family members to recover from Charles Manson's brainwashing and the impact of drug abuse. Years later, in prison, Van Houten and Krenwinkel revealed that Charles Manson programmed and scripted their behavior at the Manson Family murder trial.

Manson kept his devotees under control by keeping them loaded on LSD and crystal methamphetamine. He broke down the psyches of his followers using drugs, sex orgies, and Charlie's New-Age-psychobabble lectures.

He used threats of violence and mind-control techniques. He demanded that his drugged cliques do singalongs of his bizarre-song lyrics. They listened to his incomprehensible-occult philosophies, strange slogans, twisted-songs, cult programming, and Helter-Skelter predictions. Many of his followers saw Manson as a Jesus Christ figure, a messiah and father figure combined, who they obeyed.

Chapter 6

PATRICIA KRENWINKEL (1947-): Patricia
Krenwinkel (aka Katie, Big Patty, Marnie Reeves, Mary Ann Scott, Cathran Patricia Smith), age 73 in 2020, was convicted in the Tate and LaBianca murders and has spent her life in prison. She was born on December 3rd, 1947, in Los Angeles, California. At 17, her parents were divorced.

After she graduated from high school, she moved to Alabama to live with her mother. She had taught Sunday school and had thought about becoming a nun. Krenwinkel went to a Catholic college for one semester and then dropped out. She moved in with her step-sister, Charlene, a drug addict, in Manhattan Beach, California. Krenwinkel got a job as a processing clerk.

In an unlucky twist of fate, in September 1967, Krenwinkel met Charles Manson at a nearby house where he was visiting with Mary Brunner and Lynette "Squeaky" Fromme. Manson charmed Krenwinkel by playing guitar, singing to her, and later telling her she was beautiful to get her in bed.

Left: Patricia Krenwinkel, 1970. Right: Recent Krenwinkel photo.

Because Krenwinkel had such low self-esteem and felt ugly, Manson easily manipulated her. After sex with Charlie, Patricia decided to go with him and the girls to San Francisco, leaving her car and final paycheck behind.

Patricia was kind of quiet but showed an intense personality in the Manson Family. She helped take care of the cult's children. Krenwinkel was too dedicated to Charlie Manson to the point of killing for him.

In the summer of 1968, Krenwinkel and Ella Bailey were hitchhiking in Los Angeles when the Beach Boy's drummer Dennis Wilson picked them up. Wilson invited them to stay at his Pacific Palisades mansion while he went to a recording studio.

Pictured is Patricia Krenwinkel, 1970, during her murder trial.

Wilson came back hours later, and Charlie and the Manson Family pseudo-hippie-cult crazies were there. Thus began the relationship between Wilson and the Manson cult followers. In 1968, Krenwinkel was arrested for possession of Marijuana in Mendocino, after she and some other Manson Family girls sold LSD to some local youths. Krenwinkel became known as one of the "Witches of Mendocino" to the locals.

Krenwinkel joined Manson and his followers on the road and tripped on LSD hundreds of times. Manson convinced his cult that he was Christlike and that they should worship him and comply with his demands. Brainwashed, Krenwinkel moved in with the Manson Family at Spahn's Movie Ranch in the desert.

Sex orgies, fake love, drugs, Manson's bizarre music, and Helter Skelter was Manson's agenda. Krenwinkel was sent by Manson to kill at Tate's and the LaBianca's homes. She stabbed Abigail Folger to death and participated in the murders the next night when she stabbed Rosemary LaBianca to death with Watson and Van Houten.

Krenwinkel was blood-thirsty during the infamous Tate/LaBianca murders. At the Tate house, she wrestled and chased Abigail Folger, eventually pinning her down on the lawn. She stabbed Folger repeatedly and mercilessly. According to Krenwinkel, Abigail begged her to stop stabbing and cried out, "I'm already dead."

Patricia Krenwinkel, 1970.

It was another blood-crazy murder the next night as Krenwinkel joined in at the LaBianca home stabbing, slaughtering Leon and Rosemary LaBianca. She enthusiastically helped Charles "Tex" Watson, and Leslie Van Houten kill Rosemary LaBianca.

Either Krenwinkel or Watson carved "WAR" into Leno LaBianca. Tex Watson said he was the one who did it. But apparently, Krenwinkel wrote, DEATH TO PIGS, RISE, and HEALTHER SKELTER (misspelled Helter) in Leno's blood in various places inside the LaBianca home.

Krenwinkel wrote DEATH TO PIGS on the wall of the LaBianca home because Manson instructed her to. It was assumed the Black Panthers would be blamed, and it would start the Helter Skelter race war according to Manson.

Krenwinkel was arrested with the Manson-cult gang in both the August 16th, 1969, Spahn's Movie Ranch, and the October 10th, 1969, Barker Ranch raids. In October, her father, Joseph Krenwinkel bailed her out of jail, and she went to go live with her mother in Alabama.

The Manson Family murder trials had a circus quality. Krenwinkel, Van Houten, and Atkins carved an X on their foreheads in unison with Charles Manson, who said he was Xing or crossing out the establishment with an X on his forehead.

Patricia Krenwinkel, 1970, during her murder trial.

Patricia was indicted on December 2nd, 1969, for seven counts of first-degree murder and one count of conspiracy-to-commit murder. She was arrested and extradited to California, where she stood trial with Susan Atkins, Leslie Van Houten, and Charlie Manson. After a nine-month trial at the Hall of Justice, she was convicted of all counts and sentenced to death.

Krenwinkel, Van Houten, and Atkins sang bizarre-Manson songs on the way to and from the court and often goofed on photographers by making faces and laughing. Manson's girls were so brainwashed they were detached or alienated from the murder-trial process.

She and the other women were sent to a brand-new, Death-Row facility built especially for them at the *California Institute for Women* at Frontera (CIW). In 1972, the Supreme Court briefly abolished the death penalty, and all death sentences were commuted to life imprisonment.

Today, Krenwinkel is living within the general population at CIW. She has a perfect prison record, not once has she received a write-up. Through correspondence classes, she received a B.A. in Human Services from La Verne.

She is active with prison programs such as Alcoholics Anonymous, Narcotics Anonymous, and one where she teaches other prisoners how to read. Krenwinkel, creative, writes both poetry and music, plays the guitar, and is athletic. She has played on a volleyball team and given dance lessons.

Left photo (left to right): Patricia Krenwinkel, Leslie Van Houten, and Susan Atkins. Right: Susan Atkins, Patricia Krenwinkel, and Leslie Van Houten. Because the three young women killers added to a circus-like atmosphere at their murder trial by laughing, singing, chanting, and copying Manson's X on his forehead and his haircuts, they lost sympathy with the public. Manson's giggling girls came across as shallow, cold, and psychopathic.

Krenwinkel, like Susan Atkins and Leslie Van Houten, bounced into her murder trial laughing, which caused her to come across as cold and not be sympathetic. Krenwinkel ran down Abigail Folger as she escaped Tate's home and stabbed her over and over to death. The next night, with Tex Watson and Leslie Van Houten, Krenwinkel helped viciously kill the LaBiancas.

Krenwinkel met and hopped into bed with Charles Manson in September 1967. From then on, she was Manson's puppet, committing everything from petty crimes to mass murder as Charles Manson directed. She's been in prison for about 50 years as of 2020. And she's in the California Institute for Women at Frontera.

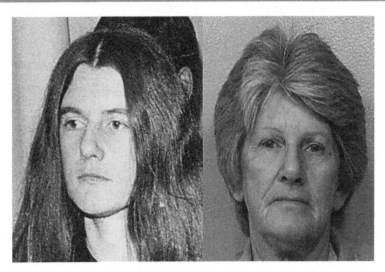

Left: Patricia Krenwinkel, circa 1970. Right: Krenwinkel, recent photo.

INTERVIEW COMMENTS – PATRICIA KRENWINKEL:

NY Times video My Life After Charles Manson interview in 2014 – 45 years after the murders:

Krenwinkel: I guess when I think about it, what a coward I found myself to be when I look at the situation. What and where I allowed myself to go. The thing I try to remember is that what I was at 19 is not what I am today. It all seemed so very simple in the beginning. And I can only say that what began with one woman and one man turned into one of the most disastrous, most horrendous, contemptible situations that could come out. By the time I was at the trial, I had given up every little bit of me to that man who demanded every little bit of me. I didn't realize I gave up the person who I could have been. I had to look at the discovery of how I got here. Where it started was, I was in a house where silence was golden by my parents. I had a sister seven years older than I was, and she was deemed incorrigible by the time she was 4 or 5.

Left: Patricia Krenwinkel. Right: Madisen Beaty. Madisen Beaty played Patricia Krenwinkel as "Katie" in Quentin Tarantino's film *Once Upon a Time in Hollywood*, 2019.

Krenwinkel: She was a half-sister. She ended up getting into drugs and had a child by 15. As I started to go to school, I never felt that I fitted in. I never had that sense of belonging. So I was watching my family fall apart, and I was watching my older sister, who was on a road to her destruction. And at that time, I was 18 or 19, and I'd started losing contact with friends. I decided to drop out of college, and I went to live with my sister.

I was drinking, using marijuana or hash, whatever my sister had around. I was looking for a way out. I found myself thinking there has to be more. Because I never developed a sense of knowing who I was and where I was going and what I wanted to do. Because I wanted to please, to love, I wanted to feel safe. I wanted to feel like someone was going to care for me because I hadn't felt that from anywhere else in my life. And in giving up and moving on with Manson was just throwing away the rest of my life.

Cheerleader. Prom Queen.
Manson Girl.

Leslie,
My Name is Evil

Left: Kaniehtiio Horn. Center: Patricia Krenwinkel. Right: Movie poster: Leslie, My Name is Evil. Horn played Krenwinkel in *Leslie, My Name is Evil.*

In popular culture, Patricia Krenwinkel has been portrayed in movies and TV:

- Madisen Beaty played Patricia Krenwinkel as "Katie" in Quentin Tarantino's film *Once Upon a Time in Hollywood*, 2019.
- Leslie Grossman was cast as Krenwinkel in the 2017 season of *American Horror Story: Cult.*
- Beaty again portrayed Krenwinkel in the 2015-16 TV series *Aquarius.*
- Olivia Klaus made a documentary short film on Krenwinkel, *Life After Manson.* The film was shown at the 2014 Tribeca Film Festival and included her first interview in 20 years.
- She was also portrayed by Leslie Orr in the film *The Manson Family* (2003), by Kaniehtiio Horn in *Leslie, My Name is Evil* (2009), by Vanessa Zima in *Manson Girls* (2013), and Serena Lorien in *House of Manson* (2014).
- Actress Christina Hart portrayed Patricia Krenwinkel in the made-for-TV film *Helter Skelter* (1976), and 28 years later in the movie's remake by actress Allison Smith.

Summary of Patricia Krenwinkel: She is 72 in 2020 and remains in jail. Krenwinkel is in the California Institution for Women in the Chino district of Corona, California. She had a parole hearing on June 22, 2017, and was denied parole. Krenwinkel has been denied parole 14 times.

Like some other Manson Family members who had been convicted of murder, Krenwinkel has recovered from Charles Manson's brainwashing, the drug abuse, and has taken affirmative steps in prison to improve herself. She has graduated from college, participated in Alcoholics Anonymous and Narcotics Anonymous, and taught other inmates how to read.

If you are in the "tough-love" camp, you may want her to remain in prison for life even though she's served nearly 50 years in prison. If you see the progress, Krenwinkel has made to recover, that she's made some amends, and her contributions to help other prisoners, you might support her parole and release.

Krenwinkel diminished her participation in the bloody mass murders by indicating her desperate need to be loved and approved of by Charlie Manson drove her to follow orders. She said, "I wanted this man's love, any time I saw something I normally would be against, any of the values I held, I began to justify it, rationalize it - the more I did that, the more I lost any values I held."

Also, in fairness, some other Manson Family members convicted of murder (Steve Grogan) or attempted assassination of President Ford (Lynette "Squeaky" Fromme) or accessory to murder (Nancy Pitman), have been released on parole from prison. Should Krenwinkel be released? Krenwinkel has been denied parole over a dozen times. She is the longest-incarcerated woman in the California penal system. Originally sentenced to death, the Supreme Court outlawed the death penalty for a time in 1972. So she serves nine life sentences instead.

Chapter 7

Manson's demands became increasingly bizarre. But his disciples usually followed his orders. Their lives consisted of getting loaded on drugs, sex orgies, scrounging for food, stealing, skinny-dipping, chanting, and singing Charlie's nutty song lyrics. In the context of the hippie values of love and total freedom, it seemed to make sense to most of his devotees. The Manson Family party was over by the early 1970s because many were arrested, jailed, and faced prison sentences.

Manson fed his Manson Family a steady stream of oddball quotes, counter-intuitive slogans, and weird mottos and mantras. Here are some of his quotes ranging from rationalizations for his insane-criminal lifestyle to apocalyptic catchphrases: "You know, a long time ago being crazy meant something. Nowadays, everybody's crazy." Or how about, "We're not in Wonderland anymore, Alice." On the way to murders, Manson would urge: "If you're going to do something, do it well. And leave something witchy."

Nancy Pitman (aka Brenda McCann), Sandra Good, Catherine Gillies, and Mary (Mary Theresa Brunner) dubbed "the girls on the corner." They shaved their heads to copy Charles Manson during his murder trial.

When confronted with his responsibility for ordering murders, Manson asserted: "These children that come at you with knives, they are your children. You taught them. I didn't teach them. I just tried to help them stand up!" Asked if he had any remorse for his crimes and murders, Manson snapped: "Remorse for what? You people have done everything in the world to me. Doesn't that give me equal right?"

Charles Manson blamed everybody but himself for spending most of his life in jails and prisons. And when Charles Manson didn't get his music deal and become a big rock star, it was time for mass-murder revenge and payback.

"The real strong do not need to prove it to the phonies," Manson said. And here's an example of one of his strange-apocalyptic proclamations, Manson said: "From the world of darkness I did loose demons and devils in the power of scorpions to torment!"

Pictured are the Manson's girls during the Manson Family murder trial (1970). Hardcore Manson Family members like these were puppets or robots following Manson's script, brainwashing, and drug abuse. From left to right: Lynette "Squeaky" Fromme, Sandra Good, Ruth Ann "Ouisch" Moorehouse, Catherine "Cappy" Gillies.

Manson had axioms and dictums to rationalize any behavior: "Pain's not bad, it's good. Pain teaches you things. I understand that."

However, as the druggie experience continued, there was a change from sex, drugs, and rock-and-roll to paranoia, violence, and crazy-apocalyptic predictions such as Manson's Helter Skelter. This dangerous, explosive, and volatile cocktail formed the framework for the Tate/LaBianca murders and further murders, including Donald "Shorty" Shea and Gary Hinman.

How could Charles Manson get young women, in their teens and twenties, to join his Manson Family cult and kill for him? Why follow Manson, a psychopathic ex-con? The Manson Family crazies followed down a crazy road. Charlie's path led to free sex, wild sex orgies, drug abuse, hustling to live rent-free, stealing to survive, dumpster diving for stale food, and ultimately committing murders.

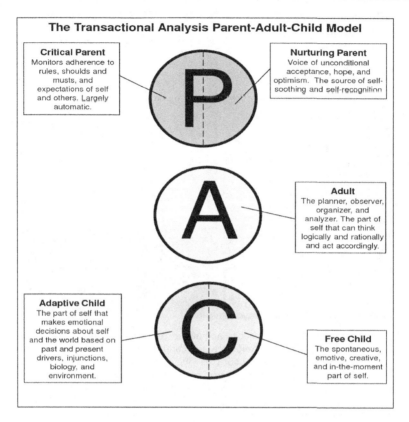

The Transactional Analysis Parent-Adult-Child Model

Critical Parent
Monitors adherence to rules, shoulds and musts, and expectations of self and others. Largely automatic.

Nurturing Parent
Voice of unconditional acceptance, hope, and optimism. The source of self-soothing and self-recognition

Adult
The planner, observer, organizer, and analyzer. The part of self that can think logically and rationally and act accordingly.

Adaptive Child
The part of self that makes emotional decisions about self and the world based on past and present drivers, injunctions, biology, and environment.

Free Child
The spontaneous, emotive, creative, and in-the-moment part of self.

Manson read Eric Berne's *Games People Play* and used this "Transactional Analysis" theory to manipulate his Manson Family and others. Manson used techniques and jargon from several sources. So, if one method didn't produce results, Manson would try another.

As I've discussed, both the Milgram and Zimbardo psychological experiments showed that most people would allow an authority figure to control them, and they will act against their morals and values to please the authority figure and play out a role. Manson was clever enough to use grooming and manipulation methods to recruit and control his disciples.

Manson studied these books and added concepts and advice to his bag of tricks he used to manipulate and control people. Heinlein's *Stranger in a Strange Land* was about free love and alienation. Dale Carnegie's book reveals some tried and true methods to get people to like you and influence them. Manson used techniques from Carnegie's book (*How to Win Friends & Influence People*) to recruit, control, and manipulate his cult members.

First, he had a magnetic and charismatic personality, which both attracted people and frightened those he threatened. Sometimes Manson would act crazy and seem to be a psycho. But it was part of his strategy to get people to cater to his desires.

Manson was in his early 30s when he was released from prison and began building his Manson Family. In jail half his life, Manson was prison educated by criminals on techniques to con, control hookers, and hustle people. Manson was streetwise, which was useful in manipulating his followers.

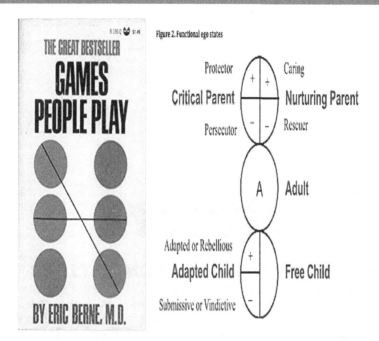

Figure 2. Functional ego states

Manson found Berne's *Games People Play* a handy way to control and manipulate his Manson Family followers. If this (Transactional Analysis jargon) didn't work, he had many other methods to use.

Chapter 8

LYNETTE "SQUEAKY" FROMME (1948-):

Lynette "Squeaky" Fromme (aka Squeaky, Red, Elizabeth Elaine Williamson), born on October 22nd, 1948, in Santa Monica, California, was one of the earliest members of Manson's Family. She attended Manson's murder trial and was known as a true believer in Charles Manson, and she still honors Manson in 2020. She is now 72 in 2020.

In 1975 she attempted to assassinate President Ford with a handgun and was convicted of the attempted assassination of President Ford and received a life sentence. Paroled in 2009 after serving 34 years, Fromme moved to Marcy, New York.

Lynette Fromme wrote a book, *Reflextion*, recently, and did an October 2018 radio interview. She said she started the book in 1970 and took a lot of notes. Fromme said a lot written on the Manson Family cases was not valid. So, she wanted to set the record straight from her viewpoint. She said some publishers wanted her to lie to make a better story. Squeaky was in denial and would not admit to the wild sex orgies, Charlie's sex assaults on girls and young women, and the series of crimes and killings by the Manson Family.

Sandra "Blue" Good und Lynette "Red" Fromme (left) – Manson cult girls. Charlie Manson pimped out his young women to stars like Dennis Wilson in hopes of getting a record deal and as payment for hanging out at Wilson's Pacific Palisades home. Right: The Beach Boys – Dennis Wilson is at the right rear.

Sex and violence on TV news turn her off. Squeaky said she is not allowed to go online. She said the environment, the ocean, and the air are essential. She spoke in platitudes, such as advising people to live in the moment. Fromme said people should not live their lives through celebrities. She favors recycling and does not want to carry items in a plastic bag. She warns that we must take care of the land, water, and air.

Fromme said that in the 1967 to 1969 time frame, that she met women who were energetic and improving things. She said people had been too negative. In listening to her radio interview, the radio hosts were keeping the conversation on a superficial level and agreeing with her clichés. Fromme put down materialism. They asked Fromme softball questions.

Pictured is a Charles Manson mugshot, 1969. Lynette "Squeaky" Fromme said it is very unfair to say Manson was some Svengali brainwashing people based on this wild-eyed photo taken by the cops.

She said Charles Manson had a delicate balance. She said Americans are spoiled. She questioned the delivery system, trucks using oil and gas polluting the environment. Fromme warned people not to order items from the market and get it delivered.

Fromme said she liked music videos on MTV. Squeaky wondered what happened to MTV? She said she had a friend in prison whose brother was in Great White, a band.

She said we fear what we've gone through and quoted a New-Age guru, Deepak Chopra. Fromme recalled a road trip with Charles Manson and Mary Brunner. She said there is magic and love in the world if we're silent. She wants to sit on the porch, watch birds, and smoke pot. She said she was not doing anything wrong using marijuana.

Manson Family members, including Lynette "Squeaky" Fromme (left). In the rear of the photo are convicted murderers Bruce Davis and Steve Grogan. Fromme claimed in a radio interview that the Manson Family was just completely innocent, doing harmless drugs and exploring the world. She said people <u>outside</u> the Manson Family were brainwashed.

Fromme said we should use things from nature instead of trying to kill it all. She said she cries when people want to destroy the environment. Squeaky, is it okay that the Manson Family murdered a series of people?

She commented on a picture of Charles Manson looking wild-eyed, which was taken by the cops. She said she was arrested with Manson and spent a night in jail. She said it was used to show Manson was a Svengali who hypnotized us. Fromme said she was brainwashed before, like people in general. She wanted to discover the world, unlike older generations.

Left: Lynette "Squeaky" Fromme, 1975. Right: Fromme holding a fist up to a media reporter, apparently in Marcy, New York, where she now lives. What happened to the 1960s peace and love generation? If you happen to be stopping at a Walmart near Marcy, New York, you might run into Squeaky talking peace, love, and the environment, and acting a little differently than her words. Fromme sugar-coats her criminal, ex-convict anger and aggression with chatter about love and protecting the environment.

Fromme said her father secretly admired her for going out and exploring the world. Her father was too focused on work and success. But she admitted she had conflicts with her father. She said Mike Love's book claimed Fromme wanted to get in the shower with him. Fromme said it was not her. She said Mike Love and Dennis Wilson were not friends.

Lynette "Squeaky" Fromme appeared, from the radio interview, to be in denial that Charles Manson or any of the Manson Family, including herself, had done anything wrong. She's typical of antisocials or psychopaths who rationalize and insight you to death about how innocent they are.

Squeaky now lives in Marcy, a rural village in Upstate New York, with a population of 9,000. She lives with her boyfriend, another ex-convict. The local district attorney said she is well known for scary reasons and that this should concern anybody. It's been over 40 years since she tried to shoot President Ford. So, maybe Squeaky has changed?

According to Lynette "Squeaky" Fromme, what Charles Manson, Squeaky Fromme, and the Manson Family were about was being open to exploring the world using hipster drugs. Marijuana was cool. Acid or LSD was okay. She didn't mention that she was convicted of the attempted assassination of President Ford or why. Charles Manson's serial killing was too insignificant to mention. Mass murders committed by the Manson Family wasn't worth discussing.

It's all about keeping the environment clean, the air, the land, the ocean should be respected and kept clean. The implication Fromme suggested was that the mass murders by the Manson Family members were a minor issue. The primary concern is the environment, doing mind-expanding drugs, and being open to the world, and Fromme's disdain for materialistic, greedy people. After all, she said Charles Manson was balanced about life.

Left: Squeaky after being captured trying to shoot President Ford.
Right: Squeaky seemed to enjoy publicity from her criminal activities.

I read a one-star, negative review of Fromme's book *Reflexions,* which seems to validate what I was saying about her radio interview. I assume the other reviews, which were four or five-star raves, were written by Fromme's friends or Manson Family survivors. Here is the objective and negative review:

Always is always.

After reading this, I realized that Spahn's Movie Ranch was a Boy Scout camp where everything was peaches and roses. They traveled up and down the coast, helping little old ladies across streets and taking in stray dogs and fixing up houses, grocery shopping for the elderly. Those Manson people were absolute angels and stellar humanitarians. There's no mention of murders and pointing guns at presidents, drug deals, and acid trips (that never happened) just living a good clean life for the rest of us to follow as an example.

Left: Squeaky was a high school junior in 1965. Middle: Squeaky with the Manson Family, 1970. Right: Fromme, under arrest, during her years of living dangerously as a criminal in the Manson Family.

Maybe we can get some clues as to what's going on in Squeaky's mind from her quotes:

"I co-counsel, and as co-counsel, I have the right to represent myself, speak for myself and conduct myself and my trial by myself in my best interests in order of due process." --Lynette "Squeaky" Fromme

I have found that psychopaths often demand to represent themselves in court. It is part of their grandiose sense of entitlement and ego-maniac personality. Besides Fromme, Ted Bundy, Charles Manson, Jodi Arias, and many other antisocials or psychopaths have demanded, at times, to represent themselves or get on the stand to testify in court.

Left: Lynette "Squeaky" Fromme sitting behind Charles Manson at Manson's murder trial. Right: Fromme with an X on her forehead. She copied Manson. Manson was Fromme's father figure and cult guru.

"My father had kicked me out of his house at the height of an argument over an opinion difference. He had become so enraged. He told me never to come back, and that was all the severance it took." --Lynette "Squeaky" Fromme

Charles Manson preyed on young women and girls with father issues. Manson then became the girls' father figure and authority figure. Fromme has never gotten over Manson as her father figure and has remained hypnotized by Manson even after Manson died in 2017.

"We all came from houses with doors, doors that were supposed to be closed when things were going on that we weren't supposed to see, and when our pants were down."

--Lynette "Squeaky" Fromme

Charles Manson and Lynette "Squeaky" Fromme, circa 1970.

It sounds like Fromme was justifying the Manson Family's crazy sex orgies. Manson was a sex addict and kept a 5-to-1 ratio of females to males in the Manson Family.

"Anybody can kill anybody." --Lynette "Squeaky" Fromme

"Well, you know when people around you treat you like a child and pay no attention to the things you say you have to do something."
    --Lynette "Squeaky" Fromme

"When the circumstances are right, everything becomes a dance."
    --Lynette "Squeaky" Fromme

Squeaky was justifying murders committed by the Manson Family, including her own attempted assassination crime.

Lynette "Squeaky" Fromme and her Manson Family friend Sandra Good (left, second from left); Squeaky under arrest. Fromme is sitting with a sad expression. Photos circa 1970-1975.

Squeaky was a former child performer. Maybe, if she'd gone straight, she could have become a working actress in Los Angeles. But Manson seduced her when he met her in Venice Beach. Unfortunately, she's been a loyal Manson follower even though Charles Manson is dead. She camped out outside the courthouse during Manson's murder trial.

Squeaky was released in 2009 despite a brief escape from prison in 1987. I guess part of the reason for the attempted assassination of President Ford was that she could go to jail like her idol, Charles Manson. Squeaky is a criminal trooper.

Born in Santa Monica, California, Lynette Alice Fromme grew up in Westchester, California, where her father William worked as an aeronautical engineer. Lyn was the first of 3 children, was a talented, well-liked child that toured throughout the United States and Canada in a song and dance troop called the *Lariats*. In Junior High School, Lynette was active with many after-school activities.

Lynette "Squeaky" Fromme; handgun is from her attempted assassination of President Ford.

She was a member of the *Athenian Honor Society* as well as the Girls Athletic Club. In her drama class, Lyn befriended a young Phil Hartman, who eventually gained fame on shows like *Saturday Night Live*, *The Simpsons,* and *Newsradio*. When her class gave out superlatives, Lynette was voted "Personality Plus".

As Lyn grew older, the relationship between her and her father was dysfunctional. Neighbors remembered William Fromme as a tyrant-like figure, who seemed to punish Lyn for little or nothing at all. In high school, Lynette became more rebellious, using drugs and alcohol. I'm sympathetic to her father, given Lynette's track record.

She worked in a shop where coworkers would see Lyn burn herself with lit cigarettes, and shoot staples into her forearm with a staple gun. She briefly dated Bill Siddons, who went on to be the road manager of *The Doors*. However, Siddons' mother felt that Lyn was disturbed, and talked Bill into steering clear of her.

After high school, Lynette bounced around, living with different people. She eventually moved back home and enrolled at *El Camino Junior College*. It wasn't long before Lyn and her father were fighting again. The two got into a fight over a definition of a word, and it was the last straw for Lynette. She hit the road again.

Lynette "Squeaky" Fromme, circa 1969-1975.

It was at this time that Lyn met Charles Manson on Venice Beach. Impressed by Manson, she quickly decided to leave Los Angeles to travel with Charlie and Mary Brunner.

Lynette had a special spot in the family; according to Paul Watkins, no one but Charlie was allowed to sleep with Lyn. At Spahn's Movie Ranch, Fromme spent most of her time taking care of the 80-year-old blind owner, George Spahn. Lynette would make squeak-like noises when George ran his hands up her legs, so he dubbed her "Squeaky."

Fromme was arrested with the family in both the Spahn's and Barker Ranch raids. During the Tate/LaBianca murder trial, Lyn was frequently arrested. The charges ranged from contempt of court, loitering, trespassing on county property, to attempted murder, for an LSD-laced hamburger given by Ruth Ann Moorehouse to Barbara Hoyt in Hawaii. Fromme was part of a small group of Manson Family crazies who tried to kill Hoyt to stop her from testifying against the Manson Family killers.

After Manson was convicted, Squeaky moved to San Francisco to be closer to *San Quentin prison*. She maintained contact with defense attorney Paul Fitzgerald and family members in and out of jail. However, prison officials were uncomfortable about her and wouldn't permit her to see Charlie. When Lyn wasn't petitioning to see Manson, she began writing a book about the Manson Family.

Left: Lynette "Squeaky" Fromme in 1975, under arrest for attempting to assassinate President Ford (right).

In September of 1972, Lynette was arrested in connection with the murders of James and Reni Willett. Authorities found she wasn't significantly involved with the killings; however, they were reluctant to let her go. Finally, on January 2nd, 1973, all charges against Lyn were dropped, and she was released the following day.

On her release, Lynette, arrested by LAPD, was accused of robbing a *7-11* convenience store in October of 1972. At the trial, Lyn's accuser, a 17-year-old *7-11* employee, admitted that the robber didn't have the X scar on her forehead.

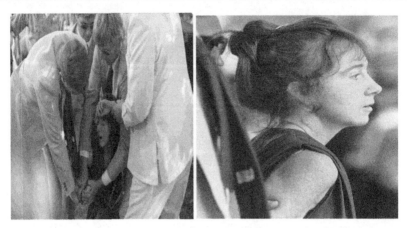

Pictured is Lynette "Squeaky" Fromme under arrest by the Secret Service for attempting the assassination of President Ford.

The charges were dropped after another woman was arrested and confessed to the crime. Freedom was bittersweet for Lyn; the Family was falling apart. Mary, Gypsy, Katie, Leslie, and Sadie all wanted nothing to do with Manson.

Later that year, Lynette moved to Sacramento with Sandra Good. The reason for the move was once again to be closer to Manson; Charlie had been moved from *San Quentin* to *Folsom Prison*. While walking in a park, Fromme befriended a 64-year-old man named Harold "Manny" Boro. According to Boro's daughter-in-law, the two were lovers.

In Sacramento, Lyn and Sandy became more preoccupied with saving the environment. Charlie Manson talked about the *Order of the Rainbow*, his religion in which Lyn and Sandy were to be nuns.

Left: Fromme under arrest after attempting to assassinate President Ford, 1975. Right: Fromme, circa the 1970s.

Each of the Manson girls was given a color; Lynette was dubbed "Red" and was given the duty of saving the Redwoods. Their Lifestyles would be very different compared to the Spahn's Movie Ranch days. The girls weren't allowed to smoke, have sex, or watch "movies with violence that sets thoughts to death and confusion."

From their P Street apartment, Lyn and Sandy started the *International People's Court of Retribution*, a fictitious terrorist group that would assassinate executives and CEO's of companies that polluted the Earth. The two sent out hundreds of threatening letters that claimed that there were thousands of members of the terrorist group just waiting to kill.

Pictured are Lynette "Squeaky" Fromme (left), Sandra Good, and Fromme, circa the 1970s.

While trying to get the local news to report the damage being done to the Redwoods from logging, Lyn was informed that the President of the United States was coming to town. On September 5th, 1975, Lynette headed down to Capital Park with a loaded Colt .45 automatic pistol (borrowed from Manny Boro) strapped to her leg.

When President Gerald Ford came walking down the path, Lynette pulled out her gun. Immediately Secret Service Agents wrestled Lyn to the ground, and the President escaped unharmed.

At her trial, Lynette followed Charlie's example and chose to represent herself. However, her presence in the courtroom was short-lived. When Lyn lectured about the Redwoods and her other environmental concerns, Judge Thomas McBride instructed Lyn to stick to things relevant to her case.

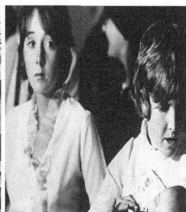

Left: Lynette "Squeaky" Fromme, 2018. Right: Fromme with Sandra Good, circa 1970.

As Fromme continued to talk about whales and pollution, McBride had her removed from the courtroom. Squeaky was returned to her jail cell, where she spent most of the trial, watching from closed-circuit television.

Later on, in the case, and nearly costing a mistrial, it was discovered that U.S. Attorney Dwayne Keyes had failed to turn over some exculpatory evidence. In late November of 1975, a jury convicted Lynette of Attempted Assassination of the President of the United States of America. Upon sentencing, an angry Lynette threw an apple at Dwayne Keyes' head, after which Squeaky was sentenced to life in prison.

Squeaky was sent away to the *Alderson Federal Corrections Institute* in West Virginia. She was eventually reconnected with fellow family member Sandy Good after she was transferred to a new prison in Pleasanton, California, where Good was serving time for sending threatening letters.

Left: Fromme, 1975. Right: Charles Manson, circa the 1970s. Fromme has remained loyal to Charles Manson.

In March of 1979, Lynette attacked a Croatian Nationalist named Julienne Busic, imprisoned from her connection in a 1976 airline hijacking. Squeaky hit Busic in the head with a hammer, got 15 months added to her sentence, and was sent back to the Alderson federal prison.

On December 23rd, 1987, Lyn got word that Charlie was dying of cancer, and escaped from Alderson. She was picked up two days later, having traveled only a few miles. Squeaky then bounced around the prison system: from Lexington, Kentucky, to Marianna, Florida, and finally to the *Federal Medical Center Carswell*, near Fort Worth, Texas, where she remained until her release on August 16th, 2009.

Pictured is Lynette "Squeaky" Fromme (left) circa 1970 with some Manson Family followers. At the rear are convicted murderers Bruce Davis and Steve "Clem" Grogan. Fromme has a romantic fantasy about the years of living dangerously with the Manson Family cult groupies.

INTERVIEW COMMENTS – LYNETTE "SQUEAKY" FROMME:

Squeaky Fromme interview 2/10/2019 on the radio with Rev. Moody and Sister Tracy on the Church of Rock radio show (Fromme plugs her new book, Reflexion):

I wrote down what I remembered from all the notes I collected over the years. I put them together. I hoped to leave the book behind in my passing. It feels good to have put it down there. I remembered conversations, little things about people. I lost some notes because I carried it through the prison system. When I got out of prison, I sat down and put it together.

(Fromme was asked about Dianne "Snake" Lake's book, which might have some inaccuracies.)

Dianne "Snake" Lake was about 14 when she joined the Manson Family, and she'd left her parents too early. She was confused. Her parents went on some other hippie route. We called her Snake. She was young and confused. Straight people think we were involved in sex and drugs. Everybody in San Francisco was, not just us in the Manson Family.

We weren't calling ourselves family or hippie or anything. We were living life and creating music. Just experiencing what we saw our parents give up. Because they seemed to be stuck in a lifestyle designed to acquire whatever they see on television or what people told them they should have.

(The radio hosts asked questions that were "deeper".)

I did not stalk Jimmy Page of Led Zeppelin. After 34 years, I got out of prison, and I didn't find anything different. The cell phone is amazing. The internet has been made into a garbage dump. ...Cappy Gilles passed away. In prison, I saw people get out after doing awful crimes. I wish the best for all of the Manson Family in prison. ...I didn't know Leslie Van Houten very well. The group got so big it was necessary to be in different places at different times. I turned 20 in 1968.

Sandy Good said she thought Charlie Manson favored me, that others were jealous of me. Leslie and Sandy were beautiful, so I felt lucky to be with them. ...Mary Brunner and I were with Charlie, and Manson would say, "Look at that beautiful girl." I look at people in terms of their spark, their joy in life. To me, it was about love.

...We realized what was happening about the Earth. Manson was very sensitive to what was happening to the Earth and natural things. Charlie said, "The animals run from me." He was ashamed of being human to scare wildlife. Charlie was tremendously sensitive.

Left: Dakota Fanning. Right: Lynette "Squeaky" Fromme. Fanning portrays Fromme in *Once Upon a Time in Hollywood*, 2019 movie.

Pop culture exposure of Lynette "Squeaky" Fromme:

- Along with John Hinckley, Fromme's story is one of nine told in Stephen Sondheim and John Weidman's musical *Assassins*. Their characters sing the duet "Unworthy of Your Love", Fromme to Manson, and Hinckley to Jodie Foster.
- Dakota Fanning portrays Fromme in Quentin Tarantino's film *Once Upon a Time in Hollywood.*
- Fromme is the subject of musician Shannon Beaty's song "Squeaky Fromme".

Lynette "Squeaky" Fromme was interviewed on Oxygen's *"Manson: The Women"* and asked what guilt or culpability do the Manson Family killers share for the 1969 murders of Gary Allen Hinman, Sharon Tate, Jay Sebring, Abigail Folger, Voytek Frykowski, Steven Parent and Leno and Rosemary LaBianca?

Left: Lynette "Squeaky" Fromme, 2020. Right: Fromme, ca 1970.

"Is Charles Manson responsible for anything about us? I don't feel that. We weren't raised by him. They weren't bloodthirsty. They were doing what they had to do. War is not murder."

Fromme discussed her jail experience after her assassination attempt against President Ford. In prison, Squeaky avoided suicide. She said, "About every five years I would wake up and see the bars and wonder if maybe I would want to put a plastic bag over my head or something like that. You think those things. You go through them, and you either do that or you quit thinking about it, you kick yourself in the butt and you do what you gotta do."

Summary of Lynette "Squeaky" Fromme: Fromme, who has continued to identify with Charles Manson, has followed a criminal lifestyle since meeting Charles Manson in the late 1960s. Will she stay out of prison? I'm afraid Lynette "Squeaky" Fromme is a couple of cans short of a six-pack.

Fromme may stay out of trouble, or if she seeks publicity, commit more crimes because she is antisocial or psychopathic. Fromme, to the present, is in denial about the Manson Family murders, the violent nightmare, wild sex orgies, Manson's sex assaults on the cult's women and girls, and drug abuse.

For example, if a new girl or young woman showed up at Spahn's Movie Ranch to possibly join the Manson Family, Charlie Manson would demand sex from her. If she didn't consent to Manson's sexual desires, he'd rape her.

But Squeaky, in 2020, still claimed Manson Family was all about ecology, saving the Earth, singing, dancing, and love. Lynette became Manson's second in command of his cult.

Since Charles Manson died in 2017, Squeaky seems to be the honorary leader of the Manson Family cult that unraveled since the many arrests and jail sentences in the 1970s. The Manson cult, as of 2020, is just a dark, strange, creepy legend like an old teen horror movie.

Chapter 9

His cult devotees and hangers-on were often from middle-class or even upper-middle-class families with some college education, and some were college graduates. He was about ten years older than his average follower. His big aim was to become a big rock star, and he used his Manson Family to support his goals and freeloader lifestyle.

Manson picked up girls who were emotionally damaged, which was a pimp tip he learned from criminals in prison. Then Manson could play the father-figure role, and he told girls that the problem was her parents. She was perfect and beautiful.

Manson hooked the girls and a few useful-idiot males by brainwashing them, drugging them, pretending to love them, and sexually abusing them. Charles Manson's control and power over his Manson Family cult resulted in Manson's sense of entitlement. The Manson trip went from wild fun to murder. Manson wiped his hangers-on's identity and morals away. He demanded his cult identify and mirror his commands.

Charles Manson was the focal point at all times. To stay in control, Manson either took little or no drugs while getting his followers to abuse drugs with hundreds of druggie trips on acid and other drugs. Manson, relatively sober, could then keep control over his drugged-cult hangers-on.

During the 1967 Summer of Love in San Francisco, scruffy, bearded New Age street gurus were on every corner, charming their followers. Since Manson had a guitar, he could play and sing to get girls. On the right is George Harrison of the Beatles playing for free during the 1967 Summer of Love.

For example, Patricia Krenwinkel, who was insecure about her looks and lost in an identity crisis, said: "I never developed a sense of who I was and where I was going and what I wanted to do... I wanted to please. I wanted to feel safe. To feel like someone was going to care for me. I hadn't felt that from anyone else in my life."

Manson read and studied books that could help him manipulate while he was in prison. He soaked up suggestions from Dale Carnegie (*How to Win Friends and Influence People*). He scrambled together jargon from various sources, including Scientology theories and Robert Heinlein (*Stranger in a Strange Land*).

Left: Susan Atkins (1969) and in 2001, after 30 years in prison. Right: Tex Watson (1969) and in 2014, still in prison for murder.

Heinlein's novel was about free love and alienation. Manson read up on *Games People Play: The Psychology of Human Relationships* by Eric Berne. He could chat about psychobabble theories and discuss "parent, child and adult" from Berne's theories.

His grandmother's fundamentalist church was the source of some of Manson's grandiose-apocalyptic revelations. He chattered about Helter Skelter, from a Beatles' record, and twisted that to fit his race-war revelations of doom.

Manson impressed his followers by "deep" interpretations of Helter Skelter's song lyrics. He wrote his bizarre song lyrics and claimed his words showed some great insights about the meaning of life. Manson's young, naïve, drugged disciples believed what he told them. Manson Family devotees swallowed New-Age slogans Manson fed them.

Berne's theory included naming various dysfunctional games such as 1) Life Games: Alcoholic; Debtor; Kick me; Now I've got you, you son of a bitch (NIGYSOB); See what you made me do (SWYMD). 2) Marital Games: Corner; Courtroom; Frigid Woman; Harried; If it weren't for you (IWFY); Look how hard I've tried; Sweetheart. Berne also included Party Games, Sexual Games, Underworld Games, Consulting Room Games, and Good Games.

I was once a participant in a group therapy session led by a psychiatrist who used Eric Berne's *Games People Play* as his therapy handbook to explain the behavior and problems of his clients. So, when a patient was anxious, he used Berne's "little people" concept and told them to have their "parent" lead their scared "child" out of the fear. How was one to do that? But there was no explanation of how your parent was to lead your frightened child out of fear.

But to naïve young people, psychological jargon can sound convincing and logical. Reduce life and psychology to tiny parent, child, and adult figures within your mind. Right? If one of Manson's verbal tricks didn't work with one young woman, he had other New-Age jargon to use, and he managed to brainwash and keep his cult members under a spell.

So, with all this psychobabble jargon, Manson had more ammunition to sell his cult members on what a genius Manson was. If anybody argued with Manson, he could con them by playing shrink and authority figures and point out the "games" they were playing. The only way was Charles Manson's way.

On every street corner, during the "Summer of Love" in 1967 in San Francisco, New Age street gurus were spouting mystical mantras. Gullible young people, who were alienated from their parents and rebelling against society, were easy picking for Charles Manson.

Manson became their authority figure substituting for their parents who did not seem to understand them. Added to this, Manson came across as hip, slick, and cool. Manson sang weird, strange-song lyrics, played the guitar and could mesmerize his followers with his slogans and philosophy of life.

Manson deflated the egos of his followers to control them. Manson did not allow romantic coupling. The girls did not belong to anyone except Manson. Manson and the few men in his cult enjoyed a 5-to-1 ratio of girls-to-guys. Charlie manipulated men he was using by offering them his Front-Street Girls, who were the prettiest girls he pimped out.

Years later, after his followers like Susan Atkins and Tex Watson had spent years in prison, his disciples no longer were under Manson's spell. They were no longer stoned on drugs and conditioned by Charlie's mind-control games. Atkins and Watson became born-again Christians. After Manson's followers were imprisoned or got away from him, they denounced Manson. Eventually, the fog lifted for most of his former cult members.

His brainwashed disciples hung out by the courthouse during the Manson Family murder trials. When Manson cut an X on his forehead and shaved his head, his followers did the same. The X was later changed into a Nazi swastika by Manson.

The X'ing symbolized the Manson Family exiting society. The irony was that by dropping out of the community, Manson and his robotic followers had traded a healthy society for an even more smothering system. Manson Family cult members could have no free choice or speech unless sick Charles Manson approved.

Even during the Manson murder trial, Manson scripted the behavior of the girls who were on trial for murder. Manson ordered them to sing his Manson songs, do stupid little behavior signals with their hands, or do other antics to disrupt the court process.

Chapter 10

MARY BRUNNER (1943-): Mary Brunner (aka Mother Mary, Mary Manson, Marioche, Linda Dee Moser, Christine Marie Euchts, Och), born December 17, 1943, a Manson Family member, was one of Charles Manson's first followers. Brunner is 77 in 2020. Shortly after she moved to California, at age 21, Brunner met Manson in 1967. He picked her up on the UC Berkeley campus, where she was working as an assistant librarian.

Manson crashed at her place and used her to support his activities, such as recruiting new girls for his Manson Family. She was easy for Manson to manipulate because she was homely looking and insecure. Brunner happened to be in jail for credit-card fraud at the time of the Tate/LaBianca murders.

She avoided serious murder charges because Manson might have sent her to the Tate/LaBianca homes to kill. However, she participated in the Gary Hinman murder. Mary quit her job at the Berkeley library. Brunner drifted up and down the West coast with Manson and some of his followers in his VW van.

Left: Mary Brunner under arrest. Right: Catherine Share and Mary Brunner under arrest after the Hawthorne shootout.

In April 1968, Brunner gave birth to Manson's son, Valentine Michael, nicknamed Pooh Bear. The legend is that the Manson Family delivered the baby. Manson cut the umbilical cord with his teeth.

Brunner lived with the Manson Family in Venice, San Francisco, and the secluded Spahn's Movie Ranch outside of Los Angeles. Brunner got full immunity for her testimony concerning the murder and attempted robbery of Gary Hinman.

Manson sent her, Susan Atkins, and Bobby Beausoleil to Hinman's place to take his money and murder him. Manson showed up with Bruce Davis and demanded money. Then Charlie cut Hinman's ear and face with a sword. Davis held a gun on Hinman. Then Manson and Davis left, stealing one of Hinman's cars. A few days later, Beausoleil stabbed Hinman to death. Beausoleil took his other vehicle. Beausoleil was arrested in San Luis Obispo, the cops found the bloody knife used to kill Hinman in the car.

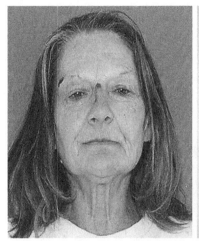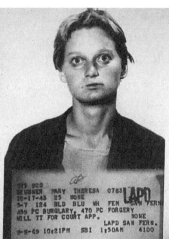

Left: Mary Brunner, 73, in a bloody police mugshot. Can't Brunner stay out of trouble? Right: Brunner in a police mugshot, 1969. Brunner has done prison/jail time for armed robbery, credit card theft, and indecent exposure.

The Manson Family members, who had bizarre ideas about life, came up with a scheme to spring Manson from prison. They planned a hijacking to force Manson's release. But it backfired, and the Manson Family crew was arrested and jailed. Brunner got out of jail in 1977.

The Manson Family, including Brunner, got the bright idea to hold up a surplus store, and they stole a lot of weapons. The plan was to hijack a commercial jet, hold the passengers as hostages, and kill one passenger per hour until the authorities released Charles Manson and the other Manson cult killers from prison.

But the big plan failed when the cops showed up at the surplus store. A shootout led to Brunner getting shot, and the Manson Family culprits were arrested. Brunner did about six years in prison.

Parents Seek Guardianship of Child

Mary Brunner Is Jailed; Fight Starts Over Her Baby

One of Charlie's girls, known only as Mary, holds her son, named Pooh Bear, Nancy.

Left: Mary Brunner holding Pooh Bear, Charles Manson's son (1971). Right: Brunner in the late 1960s and a recent photo.

Mary Brunner had the questionable honor of being Charles Manson's first Manson Family follower. She further honored Manson by giving birth to his son, Valentine "Pooh Bear" Manson. At Spahn's Movie Ranch, Brunner was a mother figure for the whole Manson Family.

While she missed the mass murders by being in jail, she did participate in killing Gary Hinman. It was reported she smothered Hinman with a pillow after Bobby Beausoleil stabbed him fatally to death. Brunner is a curious woman in that she was well-educated, a college graduate from the University of Wisconsin, and yet was an airhead moron in joining Manson's crew of murderers. And she was mixed up about her loyalty.

Mary Brunner, circa 1970.

She testified against the Manson Family members at the Hinman murder trial in exchange for immunity. Yet later, she joined the Manson Family in the Hawthorne robbery and shootout. They were caught stealing guns from a surplus-sporting-goods store by the cops, and shooting erupted.

In 1977, after her prison release, Brunner was reported to have changed her name. She was living below the radar someplace in the Midwest.

She was born and raised in Eau Claire, Wisconsin. George and Elsie Brunner were her parents. After graduating from the University of Wisconsin at Madison in 1965, she moved to Berkeley and became a library assistant at UC.

Mary Brunner, Bobby Beausoleil, and Susan Atkins, circa 1970.

She was 23 when she met Charles Manson who was 33 in 1967. She named her son Manson fathered Valentine Michael ("Pooh Bear") after the protagonist in Robert Heinlein's 1961 novel *Stranger In A Strange Land*, one of Manson's favorite books.

She gave birth in a condemned house in Topanga Canyon with the help of the Manson Family. She had several aliases and nicknames like other Manson Family members. Mary Brunner is aka Marioche, Och, Mother Mary, Mary Manson, Linda Dee Manson, and Christine Marie Euchts.

In 1967, she met and shacked-up with Charles Manson. Brunner has become known as the first member of what would become the Manson criminal cult. She left her job, hit the road with Charlie, and the Manson Family was born.

Mary Brunner with some Manson girls (left). Right: Brunner with her baby, Pooh Bear.

On April 1, 1968, Mary gave birth to Pooh Bear, the first baby of the family. Charlie abused baby Pooh Bear by scaring him, picking him up, and swinging him around while the frightened baby cried. In July of 1969, Mary witnessed Bobby Beausoleil stab Gary Hinman; she and Susan Atkins took turns smothering Hinman's face as he lay dying.

On the night of the Tate murders, Mary was in jail with Sandra Good. Brunner and Good were arrested earlier that afternoon for using a stolen credit card at a Sears department store. Danny DeCarlo later implicated Brunner in the Hinman murder. However, she turned state's evidence and was granted immunity.

On August 21st, 1971, the Hawthorne police department responded to a silent alarm set-off at a Western Surplus store in Hawthorne. They arrived in time to catch six Manson Family members, including Mary, in the middle of an armed robbery. After a brief shootout, cops busted the Manson Family crew.

Left: Mary Brunner under arrest. Right: Hawthorne shootout scene.

Along with Brunner, the HPD arrested Catherine Share, Charles Lovett, Lawrence Bailey, Kenneth Como, and Dennis Rice. The group had stolen close to 150 guns, which they intended on using in a plot to hijack a 747-jumbo jet, in which they would kill one passenger every hour until prison authorities released Charlie and Manson Family killers.

For her part in the Hawthorne shootout, Mary served six and a half years at the *California Institute for Women*, while Pooh Bear went to live with Brunner's parents. Mary has since used an assumed name and is last reported to be living in the Midwest.

INTERVIEW COMMENTS – MARY BRUNNER:

A reporter interviewed Mary Brunner while she was under arrest and walking outside court when she was 26-years old:

TV Reporter: What's your comment on being charged with murder? You say that Bobby Beausoleil, Susan Atkins, nor you killed Gary Hinman. Who did?

Brunner: Take Charlie Manson out of there also. Oh, take Bruce Davis out too.

Left: Mary Brunner in a recent photo. Right: Steve "Clem" Grogan and Mary Brunner, circa 1970. Grogan, a convicted murderer who escaped from a mental hospital, was released from prison in 1985. Brunner served six-and-a-half years after being convicted for the Hawthorne robbery and shootout.

TV Reporter: Who did kill Gary Hinman? Do you know who killed Hinman?

Brunner: You might say that.

TV Reporter: What was the motivation?

Brunner: That's more than what I want to get into.

TV Reporter: You know you may never see your baby again. Or at least for a long time. Does this have any effect on you?

Brunner: Of course.

TV Reporter: You're 26-years-old. Do you feel your life has been wasted at all?

Brunner: You gotta be kidding! (She laughed and walked off in handcuffs.)

Left: *Manson*, movie poster. Right: *Manson Girls* movie poster.

Mary Brunner filmography:

- 2007 *Inside the Manson Gang* (Documentary) Herself
- 2002 *Biography* (TV Series documentary) Herself - First Manson Family Member
- *The Manson Woman: An American Nightmare* (2002). Herself - First Manson Family Member
- 1973 *Manson* (Documentary) Herself
- 2019 *Mindhunter* (TV Series) Herself
- *Mindhunter* Episode 2.5 (2019). Herself (uncredited)
- 2019 *1969* (TV Series documentary) Herself
- *Manson Girls* (2019). Herself
- 2016 *Rare Manson Family News Footage*: Volume 1 (Documentary). Herself
- 1999 *Holy Smoke*. Herself - Manson Follower with X on Forehead (uncredited)

Summary of Mary Brunner: Brunner, who has a criminal record as a result of her association with Charles Manson and the Manson Family members, was significant in being the first member of Manson's crazy cult. She remained loyal to Manson for years and was the mother of a son with Charles Manson, named Valentine "Poor Bear" Manson.

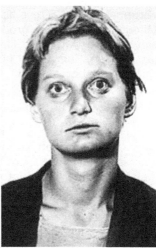

Left: Zarah Mahler. Right: Mary Brunner in a police mugshot, ca 1969. Mahler portrayed Brunner in *Manson Girls*. *Manson Girls* is about the female devotees who joined Manson's flock in the 1960s and helped carry out brutal killings meant to start an apocalyptic race war.

Because she testified against the others, she got immunity from the Hinman murder charges. She said she joined the Manson family because her life was too routine and boring. Even under arrest, she seemed to be having fun.

But apparently, she had some mixed feelings at times. For example, Brunner, who helped murder Gary Hinman, testified against the Manson Family members and associates at the Hinman murder trial in exchange for immunity.

Then, in a reversal, Brunner, who seemed to feel disloyal for getting immunity in the Hinman case, joined the Manson Family in the Hawthorne robbery and shootout. She then did 6.5 years in prison for the Hawthorne gun-store robbery and shooting.

Mary Brunner comes across as the poster-girl for how to destroy one's life. She is a college graduate who had a librarian job at UC Berkeley. Bored with her life, seduced by hardcore criminal Charles Manson, she joined his pseudo-hippie criminal cult that was exciting to her as part of the countercultural "Summer of Love."

Brunner participated in a variety of crimes with the Manson disciples – including theft, drug dealing, prostitution, and murder. Often arrested, Brunner spent years in prison. Brunner, using an assumed name, has faded into obscurity in the Midwest and cut ties to the Manson Family.

Chapter 11

The Summer of Love in 1967 turned negative by

the fall of 1967. The Diggers, an activist group, was providing free food in Golden Gate Park. The Summer of Love was a sort of idealistic concept providing free food, free love or at least free sex, free crash pads, free music concerts, stores with donated and gratis clothing and various items for free, and a free medical clinic.

Why work? Countercultural hippies in the 1960s were similar to radical leftists in 2019. Socialism or Communism – use other people's money until it runs out. The road leads to Venezuela's starving millions.

San Francisco's flower children, the anti-establishment hippies, were vulnerable to ex-convict Charles Manson. Manson was able to exploit and organize his Manson Family of hippie-cult criminals living for free by stealing or trading sex for whatever. The Summer of Love posters raved about: "A Gathering of the Tribes for a Human Be-in... Bring food to share, bring flowers, beads, costumes, feathers, cymbal flags."

But by late 1967, you had better bring a .45 or a .357 handgun in your belt. Because a darker, criminal, and druggie crowd with a hard edge had infiltrated the innocent, peace-and-love hippie, counterculture movement. For example, Charles Manson was the type of sick, psychopathic criminal exploiting the hippie movement by the late 1960s.

A bulletin board of teenagers reported missing, October 12, 1967. During the first six months of the year, 748 juvenile runaways were picked up by police in San Francisco.

Were you bored during the 1967 Summer of Love? Bands on stage in Golden Gate Park entertained crowds of hippies and random people. Many rock bands that were not yet famous appeared: The Grateful Dead, Jefferson Airplane, Janis Joplin's Big Brother and the Holding Company. I remember those bands who performed at San Jose State University when I was a student at SJSU.

Did you want to get into the New-Age vibe? Poets like Allen Ginsburg and Gary Snyder led Hindu chants. Rebel psychologist Dr. Timothy Leary spoke to crowds and urged them to turn on, tune in, and drop out. Free or cheap drugs, including LSD, pot, and hashish, were available to keep the hippies and runaway teens mellow, loaded, or shitfaced. Nobody cared about the long-term consequences of drug abuse. It was all about the Human Be-In.

Tired of providing free food and housing for newcomers in 1967, the Diggers proclaimed the Death of the Hippie with a parade through the Haight. The group left San Francisco before the end of the year.

Imagine, serial-killer Charles Manson, recruiting mostly teenage or early-twenties girls keeping to a 5-to-1 ratio of females to males he could use, scouting for talent. Manson wanted to find pretty girls he could pimp off and guys he could use for his criminal activities.

The Summer of Love was a bonanza of young, naïve teenage runaways and alienated drifters. Even the dangerous Hells Angels, the infamous biker gang, entertained and babysat lost kids until their mothers could pick them up. Crowds of 20,000 kids were usual at Golden Gate Park during the Summer of Love.

The Grateful Dead, an American rock band, played during the Summer of Love in Golden Gate Park. The Grateful Dead is known for mixing rock, folk, country, jazz, bluegrass, and blues.

Many of the young people were from middle-class and upper-middle-class homes looking for some excitement and an excuse to rebel. Being a druggie dropout was cool. The media labeled the Summer of Love scene as a love-in, a psychedelic picnic in an atmosphere of psychedelic drugs like LSD. It was a hippie happening Be-In. Radical social change was the aim.

Haight and Ashbury marked the crossroads in San Francisco of a neighborhood welcoming newcomers to the hippie movement based on love and freedom. Cheap crash pads could be rented in the Haight district. Hippie storefronts popped up like: The Psychedelic Shop, the Blue Unicorn Coffee House, Wild Colors Gift Shop, and the I And Thou Coffee House. The youth revolution embraced multiculturalism, freedom, and cultural renaissance.

Charles Manson charmed his followers by playing his guitar and singing his offbeat songs.

But, besides the Manson cult's formation, there were signs that some harmful or dark elements were coming. Peter Coyote, actor and Diggers activist, said, "I thought the Summer of Love was horseshit." Some did not like the self-righteous, radical leftists like SDS and the Weather Underground bombers.

Acid-heads could temporarily escape, but drug abuse always catches up on the abuser. And a rougher crowd of druggies, dealers, and bikers was using and selling harder drugs like heroin and amphetamines.

At first, it seemed to make sense. The hippies could take care of each other. There was even a free-medical clinic offering free health care. Who needed the boring life of working 9-5 and living in the suburbs. Hippie kids rejected the 9-5 routine.

Pictured is Ken Kesey's acid-filled school bus, accompanied by a group of Merry Pranksters in the late 1960s.

No need for marriage and jobs, have free sex, babies, and let the commune take care of the kids, food, clothing, whatever. The Diggers advocated freedom and free things. The problem with earning a living by working is that it limits mobility and spontaneity. How long could the freebie life work? Could everybody tolerate the ragtag existence?

Chapter 12

LINDA KASABIAN (1949-): Linda Darlene
Drouin Kasabian (aka Linda Christian, Yana the Witch, Linda Chiochios), age 71 in 2020, was born on June 21st, 1949, in Biddeford, Maine. Raised in Milford, New Hampshire, in New England, Linda is from a working-class family. Her father, Rosaire Drouin, was a construction worker. Her mother, Joyce Taylor, was a housewife or homemaker. She was a kind, shy, intelligent young woman. Linda was a bit of an impulsive, free spirit with a tendency to be a starry-eyed romantic.

When she was a young child, her father abandoned the family. Linda's parents remarried, her father moved to Miami, Florida. Her mother blamed herself for some of her daughter's problems. She said she did not have time to listen to Linda's issues and pay attention to her because she had young children and stepchildren.

Like a lot of Manson Family girls, Linda had an abnormal relationship with her father issue, which made her vulnerable to his angle of taking advantage of young women. Her answers to questions at Manson's murder trial reinforced her daddy issue, which Manson used.

Pictured is Linda Kasabian at the time of the Manson Family murder trials, circa 1970.

Q: "What conversation did you have with Mr. Manson while you were making love?"

A: "I don't recall the entire conversation but he told me I had a father hang-up."

Q: "Did this impress you when he said you had a father, hang-up?"

A: "Very much, so."

Q: "Why?"

A: "Because nobody ever said that to me, and I did have a father hang-up. I hated my stepfather."

And Linda's mother even admitted: "I didn't have time to listen to her problems. A lot of what has happened to Linda is my fault." Linda dropped out of high school and ran away from home at age 16.

Linda married Robert Peasley when she was 16 and then divorced him. She moved to Florida. Linda tried to connect with her father again, who was working as a bartender in Miami. But that didn't work out.

Linda Kasabian, circa 1970.

She moved to Boston, met and married Robert Kasabian, and had a baby with him in 1968. When her second marriage failed, she moved back to New Hampshire with her baby Tanya and moved in with her mother.

Robert Kasabian, her estranged husband, invited Linda to join him in Los Angeles. He wanted her to come along on a sailing trip to South America with his friend, Charles "Blackbeard" Melton.

Linda, with her daughter Tanya, moved to a hippie hangout in Topanga Canyon in the Malibu-Los Angeles area to live with Robert Kasabian. Her husband, Robert, left her behind and went on a trip to South America. She was pregnant a second time.

Melton knew Catherine "Gypsy" Share. According to Share, Spahn's Movie Ranch was a paradise, a sublime-ranch commune. Kasabian connected with the Manson Family after Share's introduction.

Linda tagged along with Catherine to the secluded Spahn's Movie Ranch in the Chatsworth region near Los Angeles. Linda, who brought Tanya along, then met Charles Manson on July 4th, 1969. Manson hypnotized Linda, she temporarily fell under his spell and agreed to his sexual demands.

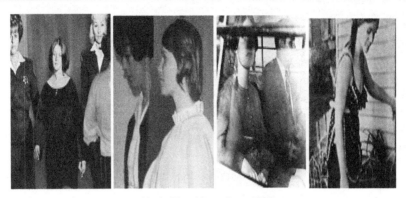

Linda Kasabian, circa 1970.

Manson sent her with some other Manson Family members on the nights of August 9 and 10, 1969, to commit mass murders. Linda served as a driver/lookout. She made a sort of passive effort to discourage the Tate home murders by telling the others that somebody was coming.

She did not do any of the stabbing and shooting of victims. Linda only served as a lookout for the other killers. Because of her status as a witness to the mass murders, the L.A. prosecutor, Bugliosi, offered her immunity in exchange for her testimony against Manson and the Manson Family killers.

As the prosecution's key witness against Charles Manson and the other Manson Family members, Kasabian had a significant role in helping to convict the killers.

She called Manson "a devil and not the wonderful man that I was led to believe." She quickly overcame Charles Manson's brainwashing.

Left: Linda Kasabian and Assistant District Attorney Bugliosi. Middle: Kasabian during the Manson murder trial. Right: Kasabian and a lover.

A couple of days after the murders, Linda took off for New Mexico and joined her estranged husband, Robert Kasabian. Vincent Bugliosi, the prosecutor at the murder trials, said he offered Linda immunity when she returned to Los Angeles. She then testified for 17 or 18 days and helped convict Manson and the others of murder for the Tate/LaBianca murders.

Linda Kasabian was born Linda Drouin on June 21st, 1949, in Biddeford, Maine. Kasabian is 71 in 2020. Linda's family was dysfunctional - her parents divorced and remarried when Linda was still young. At the age of 16, Drouin dropped out of high school and got married, and soon after, divorced. Linda married again, this time to a hippie named Robert Kasabian. The two traveled the country, enjoying the hippie lifestyle from commune to commune.

In March of 1968, Linda and Bob had their first child, Tanya. However, problems between the young couple led Linda and Tanya back to New Hampshire. To reconcile their marriage, Bob talked Linda into coming out to California. Bob was living in Topanga Canyon with a man named Melton.

Linda Kasabian is pictured during the Manson murder trial, circa 1970.

When things didn't work out with Bob Kasabian, Linda decided to go with Gypsy back to Spahn's Movie Ranch. After a day at the ranch, Linda returned to Topanga Canyon, retrieved her belongings, stole $5,000 from Melton, came back to Spahn's Movie Ranch, and joined the family.

On August 8th, 1969, Linda was selected to drive the killers to the Tate residence because she had the only valid driver's license. She witnessed Charles "Tex" Watson shoot and kill Steven Parent as he was trying to exit the property.

Linda was instructed to go back to the front gate and stand guard while the others went into the residence. As Linda heard people screaming for their lives, she ran to the main house. At the front door, she ran into a stabbed and beaten Wojciech Frykowski. Horrified, Linda looked him in the eye and said "sorry," just before he collapsed.

Linda Kasabian, circa 1970.

On the following day, Linda Kasabian once again drove a carload of killers around Los Angeles, finally dropping off Tex Watson, Krenwinkel, and Van Houten at the LaBianca residence. After this, Manson dropped Kasabian, Susan Atkins, and Steve "Clem" Grogan off at a Venice Beach apartment complex. The three were instructed by Charlie Manson to kill an actor who once picked Kasabian up hitchhiking. Linda purposely brought Atkins and Grogan to the wrong door, and the mission ended.

On August 11th, 1969, Manson instructed Kasabian to bring a message to the jailed Sandy Good, Mary Brunner, and Bobby Beausoleil. Kasabian saw it as an opportunity to flee the ranch (without Tanya). She drove straight to New Mexico, where her husband was living with another woman.

Linda explained what had happened and said that she couldn't have brought Tanya because it would've looked too suspicious. Bob Kasabian wanted to go back to Spahn's Movie Ranch to get his daughter. But Linda was too afraid.

Left: Linda Kasabian and a lover, 1976. Right: Kasabian in a recent photo.

After making a call to Spahn's Movie Ranch, Linda learned that Tanya was placed in foster care after the raid on August 16th. After talking to a social worker, Linda returned to Los Angeles and eventually got her daughter back. From there, Linda and Tanya flew back to New Mexico, only to hitchhike to her father's home in Florida and finally back to her mother in New Hampshire.

On December 2nd, 1969, Linda was indicted for the Tate/LaBianca murders. She turned state's evidence and received immunity in exchange for her testimony, which was, without a doubt, the most damaging to the family. In March of 1970, Kasabian gave birth to a baby boy, which she named Angel.

Linda took the witness stand in a series of trials and retrials. One defense attorney after the next tried unsuccessfully to punch holes through her testimony. And more than any other witness, Linda Kasabian's testimony helped convict Charles "Tex" Watson, Susan Atkins, Patricia Krenwinkel, Leslie Van Houten, and Charles Manson.

Pictured is Linda Kasabian, circa 1970-1971 during the murder trials.

After the trials, Linda escaped the public eye by going back to New Hampshire. She was last reported to be living with Tanya in Washington State. A car accident left Linda mildly disabled and unable to work. In late 1996, Linda, and one of her daughters were arrested in a police raid. The cops uncovered some drugs and a gun.

Linda's daughter, aka Lady Dangerous, arrested for possession of a controlled substance (both rock and powder cocaine), was sentenced to a year in state prison. Linda was found possessing methamphetamine and avoided a jail sentence by attending drug-counseling classes.

INTERVIEW COMMENTS – LINDA KASABIAN:

Larry King interview with Linda Kasabian in 2009 on the 40th anniversary of the Tate/LaBianca murders (Kasabian was in disguise); Vincent Bugliosi was also on the show:

Left: Linda Kasabian, ca 1970. Right: Kasabian in a recent photo. She now lives alone in Tacoma, Washington.

King: Do you think about the nights of the murders a lot? What are your memories of Charles Manson?

Kasabian: I don't think about it a lot. Charles Manson was a very charismatic, beautiful man.

King: How did you get involved with the Manson Family?

Kasabian: I was kind of left stranded with my daughter by my husband. I was physically and romantically involved with Charles Manson.

King: A month later, after you got involved with the Manson Family, the murders took place, right?

Kasabian: Yes.

King: Even though she was involved, she was not prosecuted?

Left: Linda Kasabian, ca 1970. Right: Maya Hawke. Hawke portrayed Kasabian in *Once Upon a Time in Hollywood*, 2019 film.

Bugliosi: Well, she was given immunity to testify against Manson, and if there ever was a star witness for the prosecution, it was Linda Kasabian. Without Linda's testimony, it would have been extremely difficult for me to convict Manson and his co-defendants. Even with Kasabian's testimony, the jury was out for a week and a half deliberating. Because if Manson had gotten off he would have continued to kill.

King: Linda, were you involved in other crimes with Manson besides the murders?

Kasabian: No. I think the worst thing I ever did was steal money.

King: Well, that's a criminal activity.

Kasabian: Yeah, okay.

King: How many people were in the Manson Family. Did Manson have sex with all the girls?

Kasabian: About 20 girls in the commune. Yeah, Manson had sex with them all. But it didn't bother me. It was a free-love kind of commune.

King: What happened the night of the murders?

Kasabian: I was told to go get a change of clothing, a knife, and my driver's license. And meet back.

King: Did Manson explain why you needed a knife?

Kasabian: No.

Bugliosi: Well, Linda was looking for Jesus. She had been to the Haight and Taos, New Mexico. Looking for a Christ-like figure. She thought Manson was Jesus. She found out eventually that he was the devil. But he got them to the point where they were willing to kill for him. He had total command over them. Linda thought it was just another creepy-crawly mission.

King: What's a creepy crawly?

Kasabian: That's where you kind of sneak around somebody's property to steal possessions.

Bugliosi: I'm convinced that Linda was a true hippie, a flower child. The reason Manson asked her to go along was that she was the only person in the Manson Family who had a driver's license.

King: Didn't you ask Manson why he was asking you to kill people?

Kasabian: When I was told to kill, I looked Manson in the eyes and told him I am not you. He said, "Sure, you can." He showed me how to cut a person's throat. He sent me and a couple of others to kill an actor I knew. Manson took off. I then knocked on the wrong door.

King: Were you going to kill somebody?

Kasabian: No.

Bugliosi: She frustrated the 8th murder by deliberately knocking on the wrong door.

Left: Billie Lourd. Right: Linda Kasabian. Billie Lourd portrays Kasabian in *American Horror Story: Cult* episode *"Charles (Manson) in Charge."*

Linda Kasabian in pop culture:

- In the book *The White Album*, Joan Didion wrote of her meetings with Kasabian during her stay in custody while testifying.

- Kasabian has been portrayed in various movies by the actresses Clea Duvall, Marilyn Burns, Maya Hawke, Erin Marie Hogan, Michelle Briggs, Tamara Hope, MacKenzie Mauzy, and India Ennenga.

- Kasabian, a British band, is named after Linda Kasabian.

- Billie Lourd portrays Kasabian in *American Horror Story: Cult* episode *"Charles (Manson) in Charge."*

- In the Death Grips album *Year of the Snitch*, the track "Linda's in Custody" is named after her, and the album's name itself is a reference to her role during the Tate-LaBianca murders. The album was also released on June 22nd, a day after her birthday.

- In the 2019 Quentin Tarantino film *Once Upon a Time in Hollywood*, Kasabian is portrayed by Maya Hawke.

Summary of Linda Kasabian: Kasabian, aka Yana the Witch, was reported to be living in the State of Washington near her daughter, Tanya (aka Lady Dangerous). Arrested for possession of illegal drugs, Kasabian and her daughter have had legal problems.

It was reported Kasabian now uses the last name of Chiochios. After she escaped a prison sentence for the Tate/LaBianca mass murders by turning witness for the prosecution during the 1970 Manson Family trial, she led an unstable life. Kasabian was arrested for indecent exposure, DUI, and meth possession.

She moved from state to state after cutting ties with the Manson Family cult. Kasabian now lives in a rough, high-crime part of Tacoma, Washington, reserved for low-income tenants.

Kasabian appeared to be one of those 1960s-hippie romantics who drifted into the Manson-criminal cult. Hopefully, she'll stay away from bad company, set a better example for her four children, and continue to fade away.

Chapter 13

Month after month, the Diggers had been

scrounging for free food items to make soups and stews, baking bread in church soup kitchens, and feeding thousands of hungry people in 1967. Lines at soup kitchens were multicultural: prostitutes, runaway teens, school kids, black, white, Native Americans, gays, bisexuals, cross-dressers, college professors, and people from every walk of life looking for something for nothing. But some Digger women were heard to complain that the men were out fighting the good fight for the revolution while they were making goddamn dinner again! A sign of trouble ahead?

The Diggers had some trust-funders to help pay the rent on crash pads they rented for runaway kids. The Diggers' Free Store tried to be all things to all people. Their motto was, "It's free because it is yours!" People were encouraged to donate items they did not need. The Diggers' Free Store offered tie-dye lessons, medical check-ups, and legal advice besides free clothing and other things.

The Grateful Dead was performing during the Summer of Love.

The word was going out across the United States. San Francisco's Summer of Love started a myth of the city as an urban utopia offering runaway teens and poor people free food, free sex, and free housing or at least crash pads to hang out overnight temporarily. Crowds between 50,000 and 200,000 came to the Summer of Love. The Diggers and other groups could not feed for free, provide free shelter and clothing for everybody.

It's like today's open borders crisis caused by politicians who want the voters and business interests who want cheap labor. The problem is that millions of illegal aliens cost taxpayers billions of dollars for welfare, medical treatment, free housing, food stamps, legal, schools and colleges, police and jails, or prisons. At some point, the USA is not only bankrupt like Venezuela but destroyed and overrun by crime. It's a childish fantasy that everything is free.

The Beach Boys. Left to right: Al Jardine, Mike Love, Carl Wilson, Bruce Johnston.

When Charles Manson and his followers invaded Los Angeles and settled at Spahn's Movie Ranch, it sounded great to hippies, runaway kids, and criminal drifters. Live for free, free sex sort of spoiled by sexually transmitted diseases. If you need a car, steal a car. Need gas? Steal credit cards. Need food? Do some dumpster diving. Bring decayed garbage back to the ranch and chow down.

Colleges let students out for spring break in March and April of 1967. The Haight-Ashbury area streets were overflowing with college kids and runaway teens. Hippies were panhandling, begging passersby for money on every street corner. Kids were desperately crashing in groups of strangers where they could beg or con a night's sleep. It seemed that by the summer when schools were out, there would be a tidal wave of youth and wannabe hippies storming San Francisco.

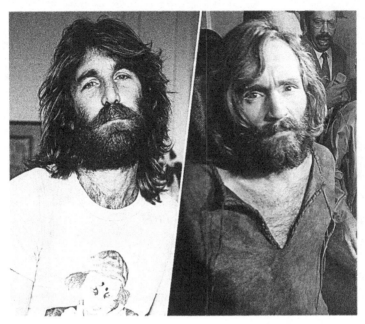

Left: Dennis Wilson of The Beach Boys. Right: Manson.

There was a dark side to the coming Summer of Love and the tsunami of teenagers, drifters, and criminals coming to San Francisco. The song "If you're coming to San Francisco, you're gonna meet some gentle people there..." did not tell the dark-side: hunger, violence, rape, gangbangs, gonorrhea, syphilis, theft, shoplifting, filth, and a lack of sanitation. People were urinating and defecating on the street or in parks.

The Fillmore, a music venue, was expected to be open six nights a week because millions of teens and twenties visitors to the Summer of Love would want to hear rock music and dance. Tour buses took tourists on a tour of the Haight-Ashbury district and pointed out the hippie sights and informed them of the hippie jargon: teeny boppers, speed, stoned, weed, etc.

But when the streets were overflowing with Summer of Love visitors starting in June, buses could not get through the streets, and the tours ended. City officials were not motivated to pay for extra services such as food, housing, and medical costs because the kids, drifters, and various criminal bums were coming to San Francisco by choice. The 25-block square area comprising the Haight district had a five-fold population increase as over 100,000 young people charged into San Francisco.

Rock music drew fans to the Fillmore and the Avalon Ballroom for standing-room-only-rock shows. The Haight Ashbury Free Medical Clinic treated 250 hippies daily who had contracted the clap, pneumonia, hepatitis, and other diseases, including malnutrition. The many months of work the Diggers put in providing free food, free housing, and complimentary clothing was burning them out.

The Diggers' solution was to leave town by the end of the year and start communes outside the city. So, Charles Manson's move to Spahn's Movie Ranch and set up the Manson Family there mirrored the trend.

Charles Manson arrived in the San Francisco Bay Area in April of 1967 after being paroled from Terminal Island prison in late March. He cruised the University of California at Berkeley campus and managed to pick up a lonely, kind of homely-looking twenty-three-year-old Mary Brunner. He sang her some songs while he picked his guitar and dropped hints that he needed a place to stay.

Mary offered to let Manson crash at her apartment. He got her into bed and moved in permanently. She was working at the UC Berkeley library and supported Manson. He slept at her place at night and began exploring the San Francisco neighborhood of Haight-Ashbury, which was on the east side of Golden Gate Park. Manson was eager to exploit the coming Summer of Love and began imagining some angles he could work to get over.

The free-love generation was popular during the Summer of Love, which killed Manson's pimp game. Nobody needed to pay for hookers when hippie girls would give out free sex. Drug dealing was a challenge. Everybody had easy access to LSD and pot. Manson lacked the contacts and finances to deal with hard drugs like heroin and speed.

He noticed New-Age gurus on every street corner who were attracting naïve, insecure young people who were hungry for a unique guru to tell them how to live their life, what to do, and what philosophy of life to follow. The teens and twenties seeking a Summer of Love were usually in some identity crisis. They wanted an authority figure to tell them how to live, what to think, and how to be happy.

Manson, a fast-talking hustler, streetwise, was perfect to be a crazy guru. He was an egomaniac and was skilled at manipulating young people by seeing their weaknesses and telling them what they wanted to hear. He had read enough Dale Carnegie (*How To Win Friends and Influence People*), Eric Berne's *Games People Play*, Scientology, various New-Age books, and observed Haight-Ashbury gurus.

Thus, Manson knew how to throw around buzz words, prison-jive talk, and psychobabble to impress alienated, wannabe-hippie girls and disaffected, young-male drifters he could use. He began playing his guitar, singing and lecturing young people on the street or in Golden Gate Park. Soon he was picking the better-looking girls and useful males to form his Manson Family.

Manson followed the Diggers around and noticed how they scrounged food from supermarket dumpsters. Then the Digger women collected the discarded food, cooked up soups, and stews that were semi-edible. And even tasty if one was hungry enough. He got his Manson Family girls out picking through supermarket dumpsters as a way of eating regularly.

Chapter 14

Dianne Lake (1953-): Dianne (aka Snake, Dianne Bluestein), born February 28, 1953, age 67 in 2020, was one of the youngest Manson Family members because Manson met her when she was only 14. At first, she was under Charlie's spell. But she later, at age 17, testified at the Manson murder trial against Manson and his killers. She was not involved in the infamous murders in August of 1969.

Lake wrote a book entitled *Member of the Family: My Story of Charles Manson, Life Inside His Cult, and the Darkness that Ended the Sixties.* The book is a memoir about her exciting days living with Manson's criminal-hippie cult. She discussed some of Charlie's brainwashing techniques. One, while she was loaded on LSD, acid, involved her facing a mirror with Manson. She said:

"Charlie had this ability to make sense out of nonsense. I have this memory of being on acid and standing in front of a mirror with him. He was showing me how many different people he could become, just by moving his facial muscles and smiling a certain way, shifting his hair or wearing a different hat. He was a chameleon, and he could find our weaknesses that way. He preyed on them, and he wanted to teach us how to do it too."

Lake, age 14, met and joined Manson's crazy cult.

Lake was placed in foster-child care after testifying in court at Manson's murder trial. Her parents were somewhat irresponsible in enabling her to join Charlie's cult when she was only 14. They had dropped out and joined the counterculture-hippie movement in the 1960s. She has said that she has tried to distance herself from the Manson Family experience. Writing the book was therapy for her.

In 2008, police had been investigating a cold case related possibly to the Manson Family killers. She said: "It all came back because of a police officer and his cadaver dog. I got a call saying the police had permission to dig for human remains, and if they found new bodies, I'd be the go-to witness in an investigation."

Pictured is Dianne Lake (second from left), 17, at court during the Manson murder trial.

She said she felt guilty about reliving the Manson Family nightmare by writing the book: "The front was going to collapse under the weight of my former life and the shame I'd concealed for years. Now I would have to tell my children what happened during those two treacherous years in California."

Eventually, she went back to school, met her husband, and had kids. She said her parents made a big mistake in letting her join Manson's group of drugged-out hippies and criminals. Her parents enabled her to get loaded on marijuana and LSD. Now she realizes that Manson was a predator. As she concluded regarding the warning signs:

"If someone is gushing too intensely over you when they meet you. Something's wrong. Charlie made me feel exceptional and meeting him, and his girls were like magic. This is how people are drawn into communities like the Manson Family."

Pictured are Dianne Lake, 14, and her father, who joined the 1960s psychedelic-hippie counterculture.

So, she says her book is a cautionary tale about young people who are vulnerable to be seduced into a destructive cult. Lake pointed out that, today, gangs and militant groups target young people who are vulnerable because they are lonely and alienated.

"These people you see doing horrendous things on the news...at some point, they were lonely, they wanted to belong to something and make a big splash, and people don't feel comfortable talking with other people about how they're feeling. If they're introduced to a delusion, it just builds and builds."

Lake said that initially, Manson didn't sound so crazy. He was talking like the typical, garden-variety-hippie-commune guru. He was a struggling musician with a collective of wannabe hippies who were doing the Dr. Timothy Leary thing of dropping out, tuning in, and turning on with drugs. They were talking about peace, love, free sex, and the usual 1960s doctrine.

Dianne Lake, 14, right, with her biological family shortly before they joined the hippie counterculture and let Dianne run off with Manson.

But later, she noticed Charlie Manson got a harder edge and began ranting and raving about starting a race war, that he was Jesus Christ. She had the insight to see that Manson had a rough childhood, parent issues, and was institutionalized.

But now she looks back and realizes that Manson was insane and a master manipulator. Lake also has the insight about Manson to see that: "You can't get a straight answer out of him. I've seen enough interviews to know that he's still trying to play with people's minds."

Left: Recent photo of Dianne Lake. Right: Police mugshot of Dianne Lake during her Manson Family criminal days, circa 1969.

Lake was lucky to escape the Manson Family, survive, and ended up leading a healthy family life. She said the nurses at the hospital where she stayed after she was removed from the Manson cult had helped her heal mentally. And her pastor, her husband, and her foster family helped her recover from Manson's brainwashing and all the drugs. She said her parents should have treated her as the child she was and taken better care of her.

In an interview to promote her book, Lake said: "People who have been victimized as children can carry that shame around like an awful weight as adults, and they don't have to. I also want my story to help parents with teenagers. You have to keep lines of communication open no matter what."

Left: Dianne Lake getting married. Right: Lake, 17, during the Manson murder trial.

Lake complained that Manson fans or acolytes had contacted her since she went public: "There are so many troubled people, hangers-on who claim to have been a part of the Manson Family, and I have no idea who they are. And other people are just obsessed with every nuance, and it's those wackadoodles who make me cautious."

"I've had a few encounters with them online, and one man even showed up and knocked on my door, but that was many years ago. The story overcomes the people, and it almost strikes me as a perversion. I fear people like that."

Left: Charles Manson's VW van. Right: Charlie's bus, Barker Ranch.

Lake put down true crime stories in the media. Yet she recently wrote this true crime book herself. She said: "I don't think the surge in those stories is good. People's morals are being eroded, and there are video games and films and television programs, giving you this imagery. Something horrible happens in the world now, and you can watch it on television over and over within a few minutes."

She revealed that she protected her children as they grew up: "When my kids were growing up, their friends would sleepover at our house, or they'd come over to play in the pool. I didn't allow them to play shoot-em-up games or anything." Lake laughed. "I'd say, 'Why don't you throw apples and pears around outside? Collect coins or something. Anything else.'"

Left: Manson Family bus abandoned in the desert. Center: Charlie's VW van. Right: Manson dune buggy.

Dianne Lake was arrested with some other Manson Family members in Ventura County, which is north of Los Angeles and includes part of Malibu. You can see from the following article in the Los Angeles paper that Lake lied about her age. The Manson Family bus broke down, and they camped out nude around a bonfire:

Nine Nude Hippies Arrested; Found Huddled Around Bonfire
The Los Angeles Herald Examiner. April 23, 1968.

Nine hippies were arrested, and five others were released after they were found sprawled nude around a bonfire near their disabled bus above Little Sycamore Canyon in the Bass Rock area, sheriff's deputies said.

Deputies said they found the group of hippies Sunday night after spotting their bus stuck in a deep ditch along Deer Creek Mountain Road, just above Bass Rock, located about five miles south of Point Mugu.

Dianne Lake, circa 1969-1971.

The 1952 bus had been reported stolen in San Francisco on April 12, according to deputies. One of the hippies, identified as Mary Brunner, of Topanga Canyon, was booked on suspicion of endangering the life and health of a child after deputies said they found her week-old son, Steven (Michael Brunner), improperly dressed and shivering in the near-freezing temperatures.

Miss Brunner claimed she delivered the child on the floor of a home with the help of a friend. The infant was placed in the protective custody of Ventura County General Hospital, where his condition today was reported satisfactory.

The alleged driver of the bus, Charles Manson, 34, whose address was unknown, was booked on suspicion of grand theft auto and having two driver's licenses in his possession.

Three others, Brenda McCann (Nancy Pitman), 18, Ella Sinder (Ella Jo Bailey), 23, and Mark Damion, 21, all of Topanga Canyon, were jailed on a charge of disorderly conduct and not having proper identification.

Booked on a charge of possessing fictitious and fraudulent prepared driver's licenses were Sadie Glutz (Susan Atkins), of Los Angeles; Diana Bluestein (Dianne Lake), 20, of Malibu, Susan Scott (aka Stephanie Rowe), 23, and Bruce Van Hall (Bruce Hall), 22, both of Hollywood.

Left: Dianne Lake, circa the 1970s. Center: Lake in a recent photo.
Right: Teenage Lake.

Deputies said the group was driving back into the canyon when the bus became stuck in the deep ditch along the roadway about a quarter-mile east of Highway 1.

Dianne Lake was born in December of 1953. Her parents were prominent members of Wavy Gravy's Hog Farm commune. From an early age, Dianne was subject to both group sex and hallucinogenic drugs. In 1967, just before her 14th birthday, Dianne met the Manson Family at The Spiral Staircase house in Topanga Canyon.

With her parent's permission, Lake left to travel with the Manson Family. Charles Manson seemed to have it out for Snake (Dianne's alias in the Manson Family), often beating her in front of others. When police raided Spahn's Movie Ranch on August 16th, 1969, Dianne, along with Tex Watson, was hiding out at a ranch in Olancha.

It was there that Tex laughed at a newspaper headline about Sharon Tate's murder. "I killed her. Charlie asked me to. It was fun," Watson told Snake. He told her to keep quiet, and she did.

Left: Dianne Lake, recent photo. Center: Recent photo of Charles Manson. Right: Manson, circa 1970.

In October of 1969, Dianne was arrested with the Manson Family in the second Barker Ranch raid. In December, Lake testified that she knew nothing about the murders. She remained silent even after LAPD interrogated her for hours, threatening her with the gas chamber.

She finally broke her silence when she was befriended by Jack Gardiner, an Inyo County officer, and his wife. After this, she provided the District Attorney with loads of incriminating evidence against the Manson criminal cult.

In January of 1970, Dianne was admitted to Patton State Hospital, where she was labeled "schizophrenic" due to emotional trauma combined with drug abuse. She spent six months there and even began attending high school. She made good progress and was eventually declared competent to testify at the murder trials.

Left: Dianne "Snake" Lake. Right: Sydney Sweeney. Sydney Sweeney portrayed "Snake," Dianne Lake, in *Once Upon a Time in Hollywood*. "Snake" was Diane Lake's nickname. Lake rolled around on the grass, pretending to be a snake. She told others, and Manson gave her the nickname.

After being released from Patton State, Dianne was taken in by Jack Gardiner and his wife. Dianne went on to graduate both from high school and college. Today she is reportedly happily married with three children.

INTERVIEW COMMENTS – DIANNE "SNAKE" LAKE:

Dianne Lake was interviewed on the *Crime Watch Daily* TV show in 2015:

TV interviewer: What was it like to live with Charles Manson in the commune?

Left: Diane "Snake" Lake in a recent photo. Right: Lake, ca 1970.

Lake: Manson threatened to hang me upside down and skin me alive. ...I was the youngest of the girls in the Manson Family at age 14.

TV interviewer: Manson had a harem? Did he sexually assault you?

Lake: Yes, we shared Manson and had sex with him. I was lonely and felt I didn't fit. I was jail bait. The Manson Family accepted me and loved me.

TV interviewer: Your parents gave you a sugar cube of LSD and told you could be an emancipated minor.

Lake: I heard God's voice say it was time to leave home. I talked to my parents about it. And they gave me permission at 14.

TV interviewer: You bounced around different hippie communes, and how did you meet Charles Manson?

Lake: These hippies took me to a party, and that's where I met Charles Manson. He was happy to have me in his group. He offered me a root beer. And I listened to his songs. He made you feel like there was no one else that he loved more. He could make everybody feel that way.

TV interviewer: Did he sexually assault you?

Lake: I had sex with him. I submitted to Charlie's sexual demands. I didn't feel like it was an assault. It was very loving, very gentle. And instructive. I remember some good times at Spahn's Movie Ranch. I also remember some scary times.

TV interviewer: For two years Manson controlled his cult with drugs and group sex. How many others were you involved with?

Lake: We shared sex with Charles Manson. There were a few other men in the group we also shared sex with. But Manson was our center.

TV interviewer: Did Manson physically abuse you?

Lake: He did beat me. He did rape me. He had sex with me in a way that I did not want. There were a few parties we went to where Manson wanted me to have sex with the host of the party. ...Dennis Wilson saw Charlie as this love guru or whatever. ...Charlie wasn't happy with the Beach Boys changing his music. He had a blow-up with Dennis Wilson.

TV interviewer: Helter Skelter?

Lake: Manson predicted Helter Skelter, a race war, and we had to prepare for it. I was shocked that these people I loved emotionally and physically were capable of perpetrating such a horrendous crime as the Tate/LaBianca murders. I was scared for my life. Totally overwhelmed. The motive was they had to start Helter Skelter.

Lake experienced an unhinged, erratic trip in her teen years. For example, she traveled to and lived in abandoned houses, hippie communes, and ranches in the desert. Lake revealed that part of the Manson cult moved in with Dennis Wilson of the Beach Boys.

Charlie did not want to overwhelm Wilson, so he sent Sadie (Susan Atkins), Mary Brunner, Ella Jo Bailey, Big Patty (Patricia Krenwinkel), and Stephanie Rowe up to Mendocino in a black bus to check out some connections up there. Later the Manson cult was reunited at Spahn's Movie Ranch – after Dennis Wilson kicked them out of his mansion in Pacific Palisades.

Summary: Dianne Lake, who joined the Manson Family when she was 14, was one of those hippie-wannabe kids who left home too early. Lake was ceaselessly moving as a young teenager with her biological family and later with the Manson Family cult.

She went through an identity crisis that Manson exploited like many of the others in the Manson Family. She testified against the Manson Family killers, later got an education, married, and went straight in life. When asked recently about the share of guilt the Manson Family cult killers had for the mass murders, Lake said, "I was totally traumatized by the murders."

Chapter 15

Manson had been arrested and convicted of various crimes, including car theft, forging checks, probation violation, pimping prostitutes, breach of the Mann Act – the White Slave Act, and violation of Title 18 Section 2421 – Transportation of Women in Interstate Commerce for Purposes of Prostitution. He had been arrested, found guilty of various crimes, and imprisoned for years in California from October 1955 until he was released from Terminal Island prison in San Pedro, California, in March of 1967.

Two psychiatric assessments in the 1950s did not recommend him for parole. The psychiatrist who examined him both times concluded that he was a sociopathic personality without psychosis. Other terms for sociopath include antisocial-personality disorder or the hardcore version of antisocial personality, the psychopath. Manson was a hardcore psychopath. From a series of petty crimes, he graduated to being convicted of mass murders after his release in 1967.

Manson claimed he never had parents. That was not accurate. His mother, Kathleen, was a struggling hooker and petty criminal. She moved to Los Angeles from West Virginia. Charlie's ex-wife, Rosalie, was caring for their son, Charles Jr. She lived with Manson's mother in the mid-1950s while he was doing time in Terminal Island Penitentiary.

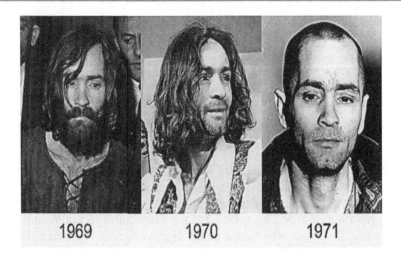

1969   1970   1971

Kathleen then moved back to West Virginia. She remarried and wound up living in Spokane, Washington. She wrote to a judge and offered to put up her house as security for Manson's release from McNeil Island Penitentiary. The judge turned the offer down because he did not have jurisdiction in the case. So, he had a mother who stuck her neck out for him, and Manson took advantage of her. He led a psychopathic life of crime.

Manson got into various types of mind control, new-age-buzz words, and guru jargon, which could appeal to the alienated-young people of the 1960s counterculture. The airhead-hippie druggies, runaway-teenage girls, and assorted-criminal hustlers were vulnerable to Charles Manson's pitch.

He studied occult topics, magic, warlockry, hypnosis, astral projection, Scientology, the "power of positive thinking," subliminal motivation – posthypnotic suggestions, Masonic lore, T.A. – Eric Berne's *Transactional Analysis*, and *Games People Play*.

Recent Charles Manson photo (left), Manson turned 80 in 2014. The right photo is from the late 1960s.

Another book that influenced him was Robert Heinlein's *Stranger in a Strange Land,* which is the story of a power-hungry, sex-obsessed, telepathic Martian wandering the earth with a harem of women who are proselytizing for a new-religious movement.

Kind of sounds like Manson's Helter Skelter race-war paranoia when he was preaching to his druggie cult of over a dozen young women who followed him around like hippie-hooker robots. I don't believe Manson believed the Helter Skelter nightmare story. Helter Skelter was Charlie's excuse to commit murders to get revenge for not getting a record deal.

Manson lacked or remorse or guilt. Zero empathy. Deceitful and manipulative. His psychopathy enabled him to commit a string of murders. Manson ordered his killer crew, the hardcore-Manson-Family-cult-killer faction, to do mass murders.

Charlie Manson twisted the Beatles' Helter Skelter into his Manson Family apocalyptic vision he preached to his drug-muddled, madcap, and scatterbrained cult of pseudo-hippies he ordered to commit mass murders starting in the late 1960s.

Chapter 16

Ruth Ann Moorehouse (1951-): Ruth Ann
Moorehouse (aka Ouisch, Ruth Ann Huebelhurst, Rachel Susan Morse) was born in Toronto, Canada, on January 6th, 1951. Ruth is 69 in 2020. She was a member of the Manson Family. Her father, a preacher, had picked Charles Manson up when he was hitchhiking with Lynette "Squeaky" Fromme and Mary Brunner.

He brought them to his home and preached to them over dinner. Manson was checking out 14-year-old Ruth Ann for his Manson Family. Dean gave Manson a piano he later traded for a VW microbus. Manson took Ruth Ann with him to Mendocino.

When Dean found out he took Ruth Ann, he was ready to kill Manson. But Charlie gave Dean some LSD and convinced Dean to let him stay at his house for a few weeks. Dean's wife left to go live with her sister because she did not like Manson and his cult followers.

Left to right: Ruth Ann Moorehouse, circa 1969. Moorehouse in a police mugshot on a Grand Theft Auto charge (aka Ruth Ann Smith). A recent photo of Moorehouse.

Manson told Ruth Ann she could live with them if she got married. So, she married some random guy, a bus driver, and left him to live with the Manson Family at Spahn's Movie Ranch outside Los Angeles.

Manson put Ruth Ann to work on the usual Manson Family activities:

1) going on garbage runs; 2) dumpster diving behind supermarkets to get food for free; 3) panhandling or begging for money from strangers; 4) taking care of the Manson Family children; 5) getting high and abusing drugs; 6) and enjoying sex orgies; 7) committing crimes with the Manson Family members; 8) working as a prostitute to manipulate men for Charlie.

On August 16th, 1969, Ruth Ann and the Manson Family were arrested at Spahn's Movie Ranch in a police raid.

Ruth Ann Moorehouse, circa 1969-1970.

She began living with the Manson Family at various residences, including Spahn's Movie Ranch. The ranch's owner, George Spahn, gave her the nickname Ouisch, pronounced *üsh*. Charlie pigeonholed Ruth Ann as one of his "front street girls" - the prettiest women and girls in his cult he used for prostitution and to manipulate men. Dean, her father, also spent time with Charlie and the girls and practically worshipped Manson who supplied him with drugs.

Months later, she was again arrested with the Manson Family on October 10th, 1969, in a Barker Ranch raid. "Just before we got busted in the desert", Ruth Ann said, " there were twelve of us apostles and Charlie." Quisch had swallowed Charlie's Kool-Aid and was brainwashed.

Left: Ruth Ann Moorehouse, Catherine Gillies, Mary Brunner, circa 1970. Center/right: Moorehouse.

After the mass arrests and getting released, Ruth Ann lived with her mother. Moorehouse was naïve and believed in Manson's guru-fairy tales. She reconnected with the Manson Family during the Tate/LaBianca murder trial and became a regular fixture on the corner of *Temple and Broadway*. While being questioned by authorities, Ruth Ann remained loyal to the Manson Family and maintained that she knew nothing about the murders.

Ruth Ann had become indoctrinated by Charlie. While they were traveling in Death Valley, Susan Atkins told Ruth Ann about the murders of Sharon Tate and Abigail Folger. Ruth Ann shrugged it off, and it did not bother her. Ruth Ann told Barbara Hoyt that she knew of 10 other murders committed by the Manson Family in addition to the Tate murders.

Left: Ruth Anne Moorehouse, circa 1970. Center: Sandra Good, Moorehouse, and Lynette "Squeaky" Fromme. Right: Moorehouse.

She then got back with the Manson Family during the Tate/LaBianca murder trial and was a fixture as one of the "girls on the corner" at Temple and Broadway. Ruth Ann and several other girls were sitting in a vigil in support of the killers on trial. Ouisch was devoted to the Manson Family and claimed she knew nothing about the Manson Family murders when questioned several times by the police.

In the fall of 1970, Ruth Ann was part of a plot to stop Barbara Hoyt from testifying at the Manson murder trial. She flew with Barbara Hoyt to Hawaii. Ouisch laced a hamburger for Barbara with ten tabs of acid to either disable or kill Barbara Hoyt and stop her from testifying against Manson. Hoyt freaked out and ended up in a hospital emergency room. Ruth Ann flew back to Los Angeles.

Left: Ruth Ann "Ouisch" Moorehouse & Steve "Scramblehead" Grogan, two of five charged with the attempted murder of Barbara Hoyt. Grogan, convicted of murdering Donald "Shorty" Shea, served 15 years in prison, released in 1985. Ouisch fled and never served her jail sentence. Center: Ruth Ann "Ouisch" Moorehouse, 1970. Right: Moorehouse. Ruth Ann is a cautionary tale – a 14-year-old girl joins a destructive cult and suffers the consequences of various crimes, drug abuse, sexual assault, and brainwashing.

The Hawaiian-psychedelic-hamburger incident caused Los Angeles prosecutor Vincent Bugliosi to go after the Manson Family members involved in hurting or attempting to murder Barbara Hoyt.

The prosecutor Vincent Bugliosi came up with charges like Conspiracy to Prevent and Dissuade a Witness and Conspiracy to Commit Murder. A judge dismissed the latter charge by the time Moorehouse was arrested in December 1970, a pregnant Ruth Ann was arrested and then released.

Left to right: Catherine "Gypsy" Share, Ruth Ann "Ouisch" Moorehouse, Lynette "Squeaky" Fromme, ca 1970.

She fled to stay with her sister in Carson City, Nevada. Ruth Ann was then pregnant. However, the D.A.'s office thought it was too much trouble to extradite her and didn't pursue the matter. Eventually, the D.A.'s office dropped the matter.

INTERVIEW COMMENTS – RUTH ANN MOOREHOUSE:

Ruth Ann Moorehouse was interviewed by two cops, Detective Sartuche and Detective Nielson on December 30, 1969, in Inyo County:

Left: Ruth Ann Moorehouse. Right: Moorehouse in jail with Catherine "Gypsy" Share, and Lynette "Squeaky" Fromme.

Cops: How are you? I am showing you some mugshots. This one is you.

Ruth: That's not me. That's Sherry Cooper. How about some cigarettes and a Milky Way bar?

Cops: What's your nickname?

Ruth: Ouisch.

Cops: A lot of people have been talking since we saw you last time. Let's talk about the LaBianca case, two people murdered. Shorty Shea murdered. The Black Panther shot.

Ruth: They told me nothing.

Left: Ruth Ann Moorehouse, circa 1969-1970. Far-right: A recent photo of Moorehouse.

The cops tried to get Ruth Ann Moorehouse to reveal her knowledge of the Manson Family murders. She giggled her way through the interview, denying knowing anything, or talking in vague terms. She had a charming way of ducking questions.

Left: Pussycat portrayed by Margaret Qualley in *Once Upon a Time in Hollywood*. Right: Gypsy, Pussycat, and Brad Pitt's character. Pussycat's persona and looks represent Ruth Ann "Ouisch" Moorehouse. "Pussycat" is a composite character, with her nickname based on Kathryn Lutesinger's, "Kitty Kat," yet modeled after Ruth Ann Moorehouse.

Left: Recent photo of Ruth Ann "Ouisch" Moorehouse. Right: Pregnant teenage Ruth Ann Moorehouse under arrest. A parents' formula for child abuse: enable your 14-year-old daughter to join a sick cult, get sexually abused, pregnant, commit various crimes including attempted murder, eat out of garbage cans, work as a prostitute for an ex-con mass murderer, abuse drugs, and get brainwashed.

The *Sacramento Bee* reported on October 8, 1975, that Ruth Ann Moorehouse, 22, was arrested by police on October 7th, 1975, on several charges including burglary and conspiracy to commit murder. Ruth Ann, known to Manson followers as Ouisch, was arrested at an apartment at 2453 Rio Linda Blvd. in Sacramento. She was served with a Los Angeles warrant. She offered no resistance.

The FBI said that her Sacramento address was learned during investigations following Lynette "Squeaky" Fromme's alleged attempt to assassinate President Ford. In 1971, Moorehouse was convicted of feeding an overdose of LSD in a hamburger to a prosecution witness in the Tate-La Bianca murder trial.

Left: Ruth Ann "Ouisch" Moorehouse with Susan Atkin's son. Center: Ruth Ann, ca the early 1970s. Right: Moorehouse at Spahn Movie Ranch, ca the late 1960s.

The prosecution, in that case, said Ruth Ann Moorehouse, Lynette "Squeaky" Fromme, Catherine "Gypsy" Share, Steven Grogan, and Dennis Rice lured Manson Family member Barbara Hoyt to Honolulu and fed her the LSD to keep her from testifying against Manson and the Tate-LaBianca killers. Nine months pregnant, she disappeared before her four codefendants, including Lynette Fromme, were sentenced to 90 days in jail.

The manager of the apartment complex where Ruth Ann was arrested said Moorehouse had lived there since April 18th. She had given the name Ruth Fowler and was living with two small children and a man who was identified as Ray Bones. Asked if he had ever seen Lynette "Squeaky" Fromme or her roommate Sandra Good at the apartment, the manager said, "They haven't had any visitors like that." He said, "They didn't leave the apartment that much. I never saw anything unusual."

Before coming to Sacramento, Moorehouse had been living in the Carson City, Nevada area authorities said. Investigators in the Tate-LaBianca case had known of her whereabouts then but didn't think it was worth trying to extradite her. She was expected to be transferred to Los Angeles on October 9th or 10th, 1975. Charges against Moorehouse in Los Angeles were later dismissed.

Summary: Ruth Ann Moorehouse, who was involved and charged in the attempted murder of Barbara Hoyt and other Manson Family crimes, fled and managed to avoid jail time.

She had a slick way of giggling her way out of trouble and then running away. I listened to tapes of her police interrogations. Moorehouse had a talent for getting cops to crack up laughing, she giggled and joked to evade questions, and escaped consequences for her crimes.

Manson seduced Ruth Ann at age 14 into the Manson Family, sexually assaulted her, brainwashed her, pushed her to abuse drugs, used her as a prostitute, and conned her into criminal activities.

Ruth Ann Moorehouse was enabled by her mother and sister to escape from the Manson Family criminal problems. Moorehouse had plastic surgery to remove the "X" from her forehead. She changed her name. She was last reported living under the radar in Minnesota with her businessman husband and three kids.

Chapter 17

Manson ordered murders and participated in some savage homicides. Convicted of first-degree murder and conspiracy to murder seven people, Manson received a life sentence. In prison, Manson worked on his music and songwriting. He even made some contacts in jail, such as Phil Kaufman, who gave him a connection at Universal Studios in Hollywood. At Universal, in 1967, he recorded his songs as a demo tape.

Then through some strange connections, he hung out with Dennis Wilson of The Beach Boys and got an audition with Terry Melcher, Doris Day's son, The Beach Boys' record producer. Melcher was not impressed with Manson's music. Neil Young, a rock star, said Manson was a good songwriter who was out of control.

When word got back to Melcher and others that Manson was threatening people with knives and guns, shot a drug dealer, and possibly was murdering people, it turned off people in the entertainment industry – he and his music got rejected. Success in Hollywood requires a pleasant personality and discipline, which means Manson was not going to make it.

Charlie Manson, using sex, drugs like LSD, and apocalyptic philosophy, brainwashed and directed his Manson Family to commit mass murder. Some key Manson cult killers included (top row from left) Manson, Leslie Van Houten, Patricia Krenwinkel, and Susan Atkins. Bottom row from left: Charles "Tex" Watson, Bruce Davis, Steven "Clem" Grogan, and Bobby "Cupid" Beausoleil.

The Beach Boys used a song Manson wrote on a record – but they had to revise and rewrite the song to make it commercially acceptable. Manson did not get credit.

However, The Beach Boys paid Manson cash and gave him a motorcycle for the song. His revised song on the B-side of The Beach Boys' record was not a hit. Later, Manson would claim the record people stole his music.

It was that paranoid perception which led him to murder a series of innocent people. If Hollywood were not going to make him a rock star, then people in Hollywood would die!

To an experienced forensic-clinical psychologist or forensic psychiatrist, Charlie would be understood to be manipulating or brainwashing by using strange and colorful language. To potential followers such as naïve young women, he could seem like some spiritual wonder spouting new-age philosophy and using profound cosmic metaphors.

What are Charles Manson's criminal psychopath symptoms?

What's a psychopath?

The APA (American Psychiatric Association) has developed a sort of psychopath-light diagnostic category called APD (Antisocial Personality Disorder). APA's **antisocial personality disorder (APD)** is diagnosed as follows:

A) There is a pervasive pattern of disregard for and violation of the rights of others occurring since age 15 years, as indicated by three or more of the following:

1) Failure to conform to social norms concerning lawful behaviors as indicated by repeatedly performing acts that are grounds for arrest.
2) Deception, as indicated by repeatedly lying, use of aliases, or conning others for personal profit or pleasure.
3) Impulsiveness or failure to plan.
4) Irritability and aggressiveness, as indicated by repeated physical fights or assaults.
5) Reckless disregard for the safety of self or others.

6) Consistent irresponsibility, as indicated by repeated failure to sustain consistent work behavior or honor financial obligations.

7) Lack of remorse, as indicated by being indifferent to or rationalizing having hurt, mistreated, or stolen from another.

B) The individual is at least age 18 years.

C) There is evidence of conduct disorder with onset before age 15 years.

D) The occurrence of antisocial behavior is not exclusively during schizophrenia or a manic episode.

Psychopaths are much more hardcore-criminal personalities than antisocials. What theoretically defines a **psychopath**? Hare (*Without Conscience*) has developed a test or measure (*Psychopathy Checklist*) to determine levels of psychopathy. Hare's *Psychopathy Checklist* (PCL-R) in a 20-item version includes the following items:

1) Glibness, superficial charm.

2) Grandiose sense of self-worth.

3) Need for stimulation, proneness to boredom.

4) Pathological lying.

5) Cunning, manipulative.

6) Lack of remorse or guilt.

7) Shallow affect.

8) Callous, lack of empathy.

9) Parasitic lifestyle.

10)   Poor behavioral controls.

11)   Promiscuous sexual behavior.

12)   Early behavioral problems.

13)   Lack of realistic, long-term goals.

14)   Impulsivity.

15)   Irresponsibility.

16)   Failure to accept responsibility for your actions.

17)   Many short-term marital relationships.

18)   Juvenile delinquency.

19)   Revocation of conditional release.
20)   Criminal versatility.

Key Symptoms of Psychopathy Can be Categorized as Either:

A) Emotional/Interpersonal.
B) Social Deviance.

A) **Emotional/Interpersonal   Symptoms   of   Psychopathy Include:**

1) Glib and superficial.
2) Egocentric and grandiose.
3) Lack of remorse or guilt.
4) Lack of empathy.
5) Deceitful and manipulative.
6) Shallow emotions.

B) **Social-Deviance Symptoms of Psychopathy Include:**

1) Impulsive.
2) Poor behavioral controls.
3) Need for excitement.
4) Lack of responsibility.
5) Early behavioral problems.
6) Adult antisocial behavior.

In my opinion, the *Psychopathy Checklist* is a good start as a measure or test of psychopathy. However, an assessment of psychopathy – the hardcore version of Antisocial Personality Disorder (APD) – would be much improved with an individualized profile such as I have developed in my Interself Profile.

Here's a sample Interself Test Personality & Self-Concept Profile form which can be used for the 10-minute short-cut or the 100-item Interself Test:

Stage/ Trait	Dynamic	Objective	Mirror	Actual	Ideal	Naïve	Social
Growth							
Transition							
Conflict							

For example, if the psychopathy symptoms were assessed trait-by-trait in stages, a profile could be individualized, which would be more useful for psychotherapy and discussion of individual cases.

Hare's basic approach is to determine if a person is a psychopath according to his scale or not. He does divide the psychopath in general into mild, moderate, or severe.

For example, create a three-stage, individualized profile of psychopathy. Use the emotional & interpersonal symptoms of psychopathy. Similar profiles could be produced for the social-deviance symptoms of psychopathy:

Stage/trait	Glib or superficial	Egocentric & grandiose	Lack of remorse/guilt
Growth/mild			
Transition/ moderate			
Conflict/ severe			

Stage/trait	Lack of empathy	Deceitful & manipulative	Shallow emotions
Growth/ mild			
Transition/ moderate			
Conflict/ severe			

J. Fallon (*The Psychopath Inside*), a professor and neuroscientist at the University of California, Irvine, claimed that there were no significant scientific tests available to measure psychopathy, which would hold up in court.

Fallon wrote: "This could be dangerous in a courtroom. Going from a useful clinical tool and a nice parlor game to determining someone's life or death, that's a big jump - using this stuff when deciding guilt would be jumping the gun. I have nothing against it ethically, but scientifically we're not ready."

Fallon is not a forensic-clinical psychologist or a forensic psychiatrist and thus has zero experience doing psychological assessments of criminal suspects. Clinical tests and observations assess criminal suspects routinely, and the written results – the clinical reports - are accepted in court. What has Fallon been smoking on campus?

He compared some neurophysiology to Freudian theory. Fallon discussed parts of the brain in psychoanalytic language:

"The **Ego** (dorsal prefrontal cortex) adjudicates the conflict between **Id** drives (amygdala) and the moral context of the **Superego** (orbital/ventromedial cortex). Onto this reductionist view of the brain as a machine, we might say that the dorsal prefrontal cortex sees the dualistic nature of the conflict between drives and social context, and makes a decision."

Chapter 18

Barbara Hoyt (1951-2017): Barbara Hoyt, born December 27th, 1951, in Seattle, Washington. She died on December 3rd, 2017. Hoyt was a witness for Los Angeles prosecutor Vincent Bugliosi in his prosecution of Manson and his killer associates in the Tate/LaBianca murder case. Barbara was a Manson Family member and later became a nurse. She lived with the crazy Manson Family cult at Spahn's Movie Ranch.

Because Hoyt was going to testify against Charles Manson, Susan Atkins, Leslie Van Houten, and Patricia Krenwinkel at the Tate/LaBianca murder trial, some of the Manson Family members hatched a crazy plot to kill Hoyt to prevent her from testifying.

Five Manson Family members were charged with attempted murder when they planned and tried to kill Barbara Hoyt. The aim was to stop her from testifying at the Tate/LaBianca murder trial. The five charged: 1) Catherine "Gypsy" Share; 2) Lynette "Squeaky" Fromme; 4) Steve "Clem" Grogan; 5) Ruth Ann "Ouisch" Moorehouse.

Pictured is Barbara Hoyt, circa 1970-1971, during the Manson Family murder trials. Hoyt was hiding her face from the press.

Barbara Hoyt was lured to Hawaii and accompanied by Ruth Ann "Ouisch" Moorehouse. If Moorehouse could not convince Hoyt not to testify, she was to kill Hoyt. So, as they waited for the flight back to Los Angeles on September 9th, 1970, from Honolulu, since Hoyt intended to testify, Moorehouse gave her a hamburger laced with a huge overdose of LSD or acid. Hoyt freaked out after eating it, ran off, and collapsed on a street corner.

Moorehouse flew back to California. In a hospital emergency room, Hoyt survived. Hoyt then returned to Los Angeles to testify. Prosecutor Bugliosi charged Share, Fromme, Rice, Grogan, and Moorehouse with attempted murder.

Later, the charge was reduced to conspiracy to dissuade a witness from testifying. The plotters (Share, Fromme, Rice, and Grogan) served a 90-day jail sentence at the Los Angeles County Jail. Moorehouse, who failed to show up at the sentencing hearing, never served her sentence.

Pictured are Barbara Hoyt, 1970; Hoyt in a recent photo.

Barbara Hoyt is a compelling case that shows the fighting among the Manson Family members over the consequences of the various Manson Family murders and crimes. Hoyt wrote a letter against Leslie Van Houten getting released on parole based on her experience living with Van Houten and other Manson Family members at Spahn's Movie Ranch.

Hoyt read a letter at Leslie Van Houten's 2007 parole hearing that was attended by Los Angeles Deputy District Attorney Patrick Sequeira:

"Dear Board of Prison Terms: My name is Barbara Hoyt. I testified in many Manson related trials against these defendants for seven years. I also testified before you on 10/20/06 against Bruce Davis. I lived with the Manson Family for six months when I was seventeen years old."

Pictured is Barbara Hoyt, circa 1969-1970s.

"One of the ways I have to judge whether or not a particular defendant has changed or is sorry is by how truthful they are in the present about their roles in the past. If they are lying or minimizing their actions, I know it because I was there."

"I was struck by Leslie Van Houten's 2006 parole hearing because she made that task more difficult by refusing (like Sadie – Susan Atkins) to discuss the crime events at all. She not only murdered these poor people, but she is now playing Mansonesque games, i.e., demanding that their memory cease to exist."

"This is a major red flag for me. In none of Van Houten's prior parole hearings that I have watched has she ever owned up to how aggressive she was, or how aggressive her participation was in these crimes. If there was something she wanted and you got in her way, she could be quite abusive."

Left: Barbara Hoyt, Debra Tate (Sharon Tate's sister). Right: Hoyt and prosecutor Bugliosi.

"Her demeanor never changed after the murders. Her affect was never sad to me. According to Sadie (Susan Atkins), who I overheard talking about the murder to Ouisch (Ruth Ann Moorehouse), Leslie forced Mrs. LaBianca into her bedroom, put a pillowcase over her head, and wrapped a lamp cord around her neck, and shoved her onto the bed and held her down so Katie, Patricia Krenwinkel, could stab her. Krenwinkel stabbed her, but her knife bent on the victim's collarbone."

"When Mrs. LaBianca overheard her husband being murdered, she jumped up from the bed with superhuman strength, screaming, 'What are you doing to my husband?' She managed to keep Leslie and Katie at bay by swinging the lamp at them with the cord still around her neck."

Barbara Hoyt, circa 1969-1971. Even intelligent teenagers are vulnerable to cults because they can be emotionally impulsive and rebel against their parents and authority figures. Hoyt was lucky to turn her life around.

"So, Leslie got Tex. She knocked the lamp from Mrs. LaBianca's hands, and Tex, with a large knife, stabbed her, bringing her to the floor. Several people lived with the Manson Family, who, despite believing that Charlie was Jesus Christ, that despite fearing the coming of the end of the world and Helter Skelter, despite the cult techniques of indoctrination, chose not to harm others, even if it meant not surviving Helter Skelter."

"There was also a group of Manson Family members who could not wait to kill. Leslie was in the latter group. I believe that even without Charlie, she would have harmed others in some capacity. I saw an interview with Leslie's father, and he stated that he has never asked her about the murders. She has never commented about it, that he has not lost any sleep over this entire – over this crime and that he doesn't think about the victims, and that he forgave Charles Manson a long time ago."

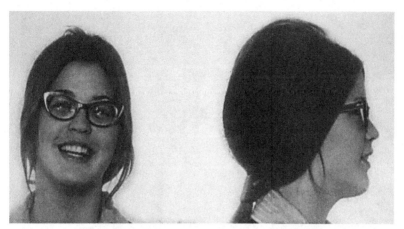

Pictured is Barbara Hoyt, circa 1969, police mugshot.

"It must be nice. If my child had murdered, I would have asked a lot of questions, and I would have lost a lot of sleep. Leslie's ability to kill – or excuse me – Leslie's ability to feel no concern for others isn't a trait she learned from Charlie but from her father. Charlie just gave her a place to express herself."

"She chose to kill. She asked to kill. She wasn't a mindless, drug-crazed zombie soldier for Charlie, as she described herself in an earlier parole hearing. She had lots of fun. She played games, camped, sang songs, raced in dune buggies, had casual sex with favorite partners."

"She enjoyed herself. She was not an innocent who was abducted from her home. She came to the Manson Family with her group, including Bobby Beausoleil and "Gypsy" Share, who were both involved in another murder and attempted murder. Leslie, also at the time, knew what she did was wrong."

Left: Barbara Hoyt, circa 1970. Right: Hoyt with Brooks Poston.

"On the morning following the LaBianca murders, I entered the back house of the ranch to find Leslie on the bed, counting coins. A call came from the field phone that a man was on his way looking for Leslie. She told me the man had given her a ride last night from Griffith Park and for me to hide her, which I did. In 1977 Leslie was out of prison for a few months."

"I feel from her statements that the only person she feels is a victim is herself. I compare the Manson story with that of Hitler because there are so many similarities. Both groups consisted of antisocial people who, in their blood-thirsty quest for personal power, were willing to kill innocent people to get it."

Left: Sharon Tate, murder victim, her husband, Polanski. Center: Patricia Krenwinkel and Leslie Van Houten, laughing during the Tate/LaBianca murder trial. Right: Hoyt during the Manson Family trials. She testified against the Manson Family members.

"At least Hitler's cronies were held responsible for their murders despite pleas that they were only following orders, and so should the Manson followers who chose to kill. Both groups have left behind a legacy of evil that haunts us still today."

"I believe that if Leslie were truly and deeply sorry, she would stop these parole hearings and let the victims' families have some peace and serve her time in silence and dignity. In closing, I would like to say to Leslie that there is a fact that you seem to be unaware of, and that is, that murder is something that you can never recover from or make right."

Left: Manson Family murder victims. Right: Manson Family convicted murderers (clockwise): Charles Manson, Leslie Van Houten, Susan Atkins, Charles "Tex" Watson, Patricia Krenwinkel (lower photos are pictures after decades in prison).

"The victims never get their lives back. The families never get to stop mourning. The witnesses never again get to live without fear, and the killers spend the rest of their lives in prison. You demanding to be able to leave prison would mean that you would be the only one to be able to walk away from the carnage you caused, and that would be a travesty of justice. Thank you. Barbara Hoyt."

You can judge for yourself. But in my opinion, while Barbara Hoyt suffered and had personal experience with the Manson Family, her viewpoint is subjective and colored by her angry feelings, which she has a right to have. She was the victim of a Manson Family murder conspiracy.

Left: Steve "Clem" Grogan. Middle: Lynette "Squeaky" Fromme. Right: Nancy Pitman. All three of these Manson Family members were involved in murders and have been released from prison. Grogan was convicted of murdering Donald "Shorty" Shea and released in 1985. Lynette "Squeaky" Fromme was released in 2009 after serving time for the attempted assassination of President Ford. Pitman participated in the two Willett murders – a young couple shot and buried. She did only 18 months in prison for a 5-year sentence for the accessory to murder two people.

She did see Leslie Van Houten before and after committing murder about 50 years ago. But Leslie Van Houten has been recommended for parole several times. Some of the Manson Family members involved in murders or attempted killings have been released from prison or did short sentences or did no time in jail or prison.

Steve "Clem" Grogan, convicted of murdering Donald "Shorty" Shea was released from prison in 1985 – 35 years ago in 2020.

Ruth Ann Moorehouse (left) attempted to murder Barbara Hoyt (center), so she could not testify against the Manson Family killers. She laced a hamburger in Hawaii with a massive overdose of LSD. Hoyt freaked out, was taken to a hospital emergency room, recovered, and was a witness against Manson and his cult killers. Moorehouse did not show up for sentencing in the attempted murder and never was punished.

Nancy Pitman only served 18 months for involvement in the two Willett murders. For the attempted murder of Barbara Hoyt, several Manson Family members (Fromme, Rice, Share, and Grogan) only did 90 days in jail.

Ruth Ann "Ouisch" Moorehouse avoided serving any time because she fled. Other Manson Family members committed murder and got away with killing Donald "Shorty" Shea, Zero (John Haught), Ronald Hughes, and others. If you take a look at the Patty Hearst case, you can see parallels to Leslie Van Houten. They both had exciting adventures with killers, were involved in murder, and because Hearst was a billionaire with political connections, she got pardoned and only did a couple of years in prison.

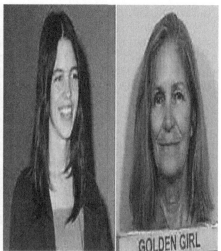

Left: Barbara Hoyt, circa 1970-1971. She testified against the Manson Family killers. Right: Leslie Van Houten, circa 1970; Van Houten after nearly 50 years in prison. Hoyt was against parole for Van Houten based on her experiences with Van Houten during their time in the Manson Family and Leslie's lousy behavior.

The justice system is far from perfect. Steve "Clem" Grogan and Ruth Ann "Ouisch" Moorehouse and other Manson Family members get away with murder and attempted murder. They are free today after serving either short sentences or no time at all. Maybe the other Manson killers should be let out of prison after nearly 50 years. If they then commit crimes or violate parole, send them back to prison.

Barbara Hoyt began living with the family at Spahn's Movie Ranch in April of 1969. On the night of the Tate murders, Susan Atkins instructed Hoyt to retrieve three sets of dark clothing from the Manson Family's garment pile. Upon her return, Barbara was greeted by Charles Manson, who told her that Atkins and crew had already left.

The following day, Barbara became suspicious when some family members watched television reports of the Tate murders with delight. Hoyt was arrested with the family August 16th, 1969, in a Spahn's Movie Ranch raid. A week later, she was awoken by the screams of Donald "Shorty" Shea, as other family members were killing him behind Spahn's Movie Ranch.

In Death Valley, Barbara overheard Susan Atkins tell Ruth Ann Moorehouse that she had killed Sharon Tate. After this, Hoyt, along with a girl named Sherry Cooper, fled the family.

Charles Manson eventually caught up with the pair at a restaurant in the town of Ballarat. After a short conversation, Manson gave the girls enough money to get back to Los Angeles. It was rumored, that Manson later sent three family members to L.A., to retrieve or kill the two girls.

In the fall of 1970, Hoyt was unsure if she wanted to testify in the Tate/LaBianca murder trial. The Manson Family offered her an all-expense-paid trip to Hawaii in return for not testifying. Barbara agreed to the deal and flew to Hawaii with Ruth Ann Moorehouse.

On September 9th, Moorehouse flew back to Los Angeles after feeding Hoyt a hamburger laced with ten tabs of acid. When the drug kicked in, Barbara freaked out, ran for several blocks, collapsed, and was rushed to the emergency room. Hoyt's mother flew to Hawaii the following day and brought Barbara back to California.

Several Los Angeles newspapers reported on the LSD-hamburger incident in Honolulu. Here is the detailed summary:

In Los Angeles on December 19th, 1970, secret grand jury indictments were returned Friday against members of the Charles Manson cult in the case of the LSD-laced Honolulu hamburger. Three of the five named, Catherine "Gypsy" Share, Lynn "Squeaky" Fromme, and Ruth Ann "Ouisch" Morehouse, waited for an arrest near Los Angeles Civic Center. Sheriff's deputies showed up about an hour later and took the three into custody.

Pictured are the crazy Manson cult LSD-psychedelic Honolulu hamburger conspirators who were charged with the attempted murder of Barbara Hoyt. Left to right: Ruth Ann "Ouisch" Moorehouse, Catherine "Gypsy" Share, Moorehouse, Lynette "Squeaky" Fromme, Dennis Rice, and Steve "Scramblehead" Grogan.

The indictment, returned by the Los Angeles County grand jury after a half-day inquiry, reportedly also named Steve "Clem" Grogan, 19, and Dennis Rice. Grogan had been in custody in Inyo County, Calif.

These five of the Manson clan trooped into the Los Angeles County Hall of Justice with officers. The five were indicted on charges of conspiracy against Barbara Hoyt, 18, a former member of the Manson criminal band who testified in the Tate-LaBianca murder case.

The tall, dark-haired teenager said she had been given a massive overdose of LSD in a hamburger last September. She told authorities that members of the Manson Family cult had convinced her to go to Hawaii to keep from testifying and had secured a credit card for her and Ouisch to make the trip.

Hoyt said she became extremely sick after seeing her companion, Ruth Ann "Ouisch" Moorehouse off at the airport, where she had been encouraged to eat a hamburger Moorehouse had secretly laced with at least ten hits of acid or LSD.

She said she became terribly ill on a bus, ran down Honolulu streets, collapsed, was taken to a hospital emergency room, and ended up in the psychiatric ward of a Honolulu hospital. As she left the grand jury room, the young woman was asked whether she thought someone had tried to kill her. "Yeah," she replied.

After the indictments were returned, members of the Manson Family gang gathered outside the Hall of Justice. They sat lightly clothed in the cool wind of an approaching storm, singing Charlie Manson's songs and waiting for police officers.

Summary of Barbara Hoyt: Barbara was eager to testify against the family after some in the Manson Family attempted to murder her. She provided loads of damaging testimony at the Manson Family murder trials. Hoyt joined Debra Tate, Sharon Tate's sister, and testified against some Manson Family killers at their parole hearings.

Hoyt returned to high school, graduated, and then pursued a nursing degree in college. She worked as a nurse, married and divorced, lived in Washington State with her daughter, and died in 2017.

Chapter 19

I was a student of Dr. Sarnoff Mednick, who was a professor of psychology at The New School for Social Research, Graduate Faculty, New York City, while I was completing my Ph.D. in psychology. Mednick conducted some ground-breaking, pioneering-prospective, high-risk-longitudinal studies. He investigated the etiology - the causes of psychopathy and other mental disorders such as schizophrenia.

Mednick set up an Institute in Denmark – I can verify that because I visited his Institute while I was a graduate student in psychology. Denmark was selected for Mednick's longitudinal, high-risk for schizophrenia and psychopathy study because Denmark has a central-mental-health register, adoption register, death register, and various means of tracking subjects across generations. Also, because Denmark has a homogeneous and stable population, it was easy to trace topics over time.

Over twenty years – from 1962 until the early 1980s – Mednick predicted subjects who later broke down with schizophrenia as well as psychopathy and other mental disorders. The cause of brain abnormalities in schizophrenia and psychopathy subjects was early environmental factors such as pregnancy and birth complications (PBCs) or in-utero insults. Some experimental groups received prevention treatments.

So, for instance, a mother of a psychopath who had PBCs in birthing her child might damage the Amygdala, hippocampal cortex (animal drives, emotions, psychoanalytic ID location). Thus, a lack of inhibitory factors could lead to psychopathy. Mednick and associates conducted other studies of criminal behavior. An article in *Science* (1984) revealed Mednick's findings - that antisocials and psychopaths had a genetic component.

Charles Manson and Possible Genetic/Neurological Factors:

I would speculate that perhaps Charlie could have broken down with psychopathy as a result of either a genetic predisposition or as a result of his mother's possible PBCs (pregnancy and birth complications). As Mednick and others have found from longitudinal-genetic studies, there often is a genetic-neurological component which in interaction with environmental factors, can result in psychopathy. The genetic-neurological factors are more significant than environmental stress as a cause of psychopathy.

Mednick used an adoption paradigm, and no correlation was found between criminal conviction in the adoptive parents and their children. But there was a correlation between **biological**-father-criminal conviction and child-criminal conviction. **Genetic factors were significant,** while environmental stress was not significant in causing breakdowns of psychopathy and a consequent track record of criminal offenses.

These Mednick findings argue against the usual sob story psychopaths, and antisocials frequently use as an alibi: "I'm a violent murderer because my mother and my father beat and abused me."

In Charles Manson's case, he has blamed not having an intact family with two parents as causing his problems leading to his prison terms. He denies murdering anybody and claims that if his friends killed anybody, it is the fault of society for shaping them into murderers. Manson excused himself from any guilt or responsibility for the murders he was convicted of and his other crimes.

Genetics only partly controlled antisocial behavior – the point was that there was a genetic component. Earlier in Mednick's career, he had hypothesized that autonomic under-arousal might be a genetic factor predisposing to antisocial/psychopathic behavior because under-arousal slows the socialization process.

Meloy (*The Psychopathic Mind*) reviewed several of Mednick's studies, which validly showed a genetic and neurological predisposition for psychopathy. Mednick has also published books and articles on the causes of criminality. His studies explored: 1) the psycho-biological, genetic basis of criminality; 2) psychopathy; 3) other conditions such as schizophrenia.

CHARLES MANSON'S TEST PROFILE
INTERSELF TEST & THEORY

As I was completing my Ph.D. in psychology at The New School for Social Research, Graduate Faculty, New York, I developed a personality and self-concept theory. I called it the Interself personality and self-concept theory. **I've included the 100-item Interself profile of Charles Manson in this section, which breaks out his personality and self-concept according to the Interself theory based on Manson's test performance.**

Besides the theory, I developed a 100-item personality & self-concept test or measure and a profile format -- the Interself profile chart showing the test results. I'll discuss the Interself theory in the context of an Interself group psychotherapy workshop I created.

Fast & simple 10-minute ice-breaking interview aid or conversation enabler:

Stage/ Trait	Dynamic	Objective	Mirror	Actual	Ideal	Naïve	Social
Growth							
Transition							
Conflict							

Instead of spending time with a client or friend taking the 100-item personality & self-concept Interself Test, you can take a simple and fast shortcut. In about 10 minutes, you can ask the person or client to assess which stage he or she would estimate each of the seven parts or selves of his personality and self-concept would rank currently.

For example, Dynamic Self refers to energy, self-assertion, motivation, and there are three stages: Growth, Transition, and Conflict. Let's say your client or friend estimates he/she is in the mid-range. Then you list him in the Transition Stage. You continue across all seven parts or Seven Selves and mark or rate them on one of the three stages. Then you can discuss their reasons for making these choices.

Another advantage is that the Interself Test Personality & Self-Concept Profile is a non-threatening way of discussing personality and self-concept. I've avoided trying to come up with a negative, stigmatized, or pathological mental disorder or a series of diagnostic categories from the DSM.

If a client or friend's personality is ranked on several of the seven parts or selves in the Conflict Stage, they may need some crisis-intervention psychotherapy. What if they can't afford therapy with a state-licensed psychologist or psychiatrist? They could find a Twelve-Step program such as A.A., N.A., Al-Anon, or other programs best fitting their issues – Twelve-Step programs are free and do work.

If a person uses the 10-minute shortcut method to assess their profile and they score in the Conflict Stage on several parts or selves of their personality and self-concept, they should take the 100-item test to cross-validate their profile.

Outside of the clinical setting, you can use it as a way to stimulate some social interaction with friends. Nobody needs to feel put down or diminished or sick because they fall into one stage or another. If they're in the Conflict Stage on any of the seven parts of selves, then this can be addressed in psychotherapy or a Twelve-Step program like Alcoholics Anonymous, or another program fitting their issues.

Here's a sample Interself Test Personality & Self-Concept Profile form which can be used for the 10-minute shortcut or the 100-item Interself Test:

Stage/ Trait	Dynamic	Objective	Mirror	Actual	Ideal	Naïve	Social
Growth							
Transition							
Conflict							

INTERSELF PERSONALITY & SELF-CONCEPT THEORY:

All kinds of new options in psychotherapy are opening up these days. This proliferation also has created some confusion and frustration. People are increasingly aware of personal problems and the availability of a vast range of psychological-help systems. But to find one's way around the various theories and choose one which is relevant can be bewildering.

The layperson can help himself. But people are more complicated than they think. The frequent difficulty of predicting oneself shows the need for acceptance when things don't go your way. People tend not to take cognizance of *all* of themselves. There is more to them than they realize.

"How can I say what I really mean? How can I come across to the people who matter to me -- lover, friend, offspring, parent, boss, and associate -- to make myself understood and accepted? How can I really accomplish the things I truly want to do?"

To meet any of these questions which all of us put to ourselves, we first need to know ourselves: our *whole* selves, *all* of our selves.

This new self-concept is embedded in the classical psychology of which all current theories are heirs. It draws upon and synthesizes the vital contributions of psychologists holding distinctive self-concepts.

Added to this integration is the particular innovative factor of the *Dynamic-Self*, representing a force in the personality I came to regard as pivotal -- motivation.

William James, perhaps America's greatest psychologist, derived a theory of self embodying two primary entities: the self-as-known (*the empirical Me*) and the self-as-knower (*the Ego or I*).

Pertinent to the Interself theory is James' social aspect of the *empirical Me*, which multiplies with each recognition received from others. The fluid element of the Social-Self and Mirror-Self in Interself group therapy program is analogous to James' social point of the *empirical-Me* concept.

Sigmund Freud initiated a tripartite theory of id, super-ego, and ego. Freud's ego concept is parallel to the self-concept of the Interself system in terms of awareness.

Much of Freud's theory, of course, was based on pre-scientific and mythological, empirically untestable, instinct formulations from the nineteenth century. But Freud's impact is rendered in my Naïve-Self viewpoint of the unconscious. Self-image is vital in Interself.

Kurt Lewin's concept of life-space relates to self-concept in that he is talking about psychological space known in one's experience. Lewin's life-space parallels my Objective-Self, and spotlights the need for my Dynamic-Self innovation.

George Mead, the sociologist, stressed self-awareness as a significant influence on perceptions and behavior. My "Mirror-Self" is directly derived from the early twentieth-century sociological theory.

For instance, Daniel Kulp, an educational sociologist summarizing earlier discoveries, wrote of *five* selves. I have taken the five names for various selves Kulp discusses (Objective, Mirror, Ideal, Naïve, Social), and to these have added Dynamic.

Also added is the Actual-Self from Cattell's theory of self. Kulp's use of the Mirror-Self was based on Cooley's looking-glass-self-concept.

However, there is a degree of difference between my definition of the six selves Kulp and Cattell reveal. The present Interself theory considers the conscious and unconscious to be directly linked in continuous interaction.

Counter-opposed to this formulation is Carl Rogers' self-concept approach, which asserts a discontinuity between conscious and unconscious. But Rogers likewise perceives the importance of positive self-feelings in awareness for productive behavior.

Cattell segments the self into 1) awareness; 2) sentiment; 3) names an Actual-Self and an Ideal-Self. These latter two are generally parallel in significance to Interself's Actual and Ideal distinction.

Allport theorized that self was both object and process, which is in alignment with the present theory. His concept of the functions of the person or personality coincidentally includes seven features, which he discusses developmentally in terms of childhood-growth stages. In Allport's view, by the end of adolescence, an individual has acquired the seven aspects of self.

Interself group therapy theory is based on four views of consciousness derived from self and influenced by communication theory:

1) Selves known to the individual and others (Dynamic-Self, Social-Self):

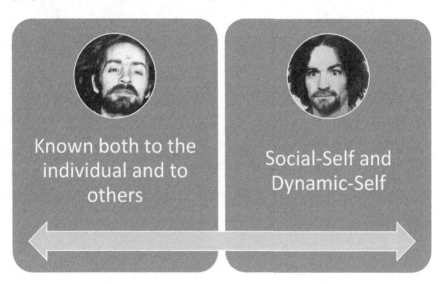

Known both to the individual and to others

Social-Self and Dynamic-Self

The first quadrant comprises the Social-Self and the Dynamic-Self. Dynamic-Self, my particular innovation, is the self of motivation, drive, assertion, and aggressiveness. For example, if you have intense energy and desire, you can accomplish a specific goal in life. Social-Self refers to conscious feelings and a sense of identity in Interself theory.

2) The self only others know is the Objective-Self -- as others see you:

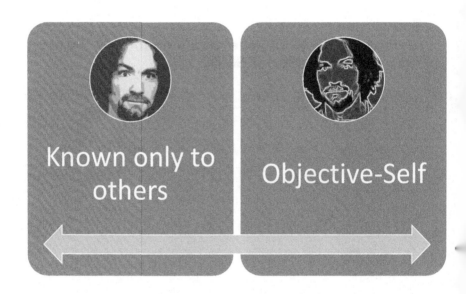

Objective-Self includes social image, reputation, what others think of you.

3) Selves that only you know -- Actual-Self, Mirror-Self, Ideal-Self:

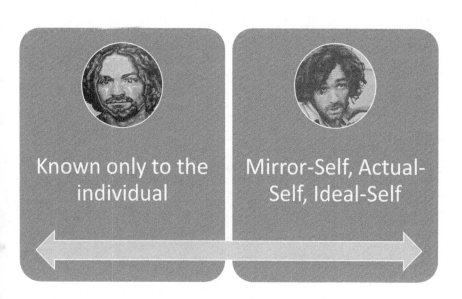

Actual-Self is the way I am now, my present reality, problem-solving ability. Mirror-self addresses the interpersonal, how you get along with others, what you think they think of you. Ideal-Self is the way I would like to be, conscience, future goals.

4) The self nobody knows is the Naïve-Self:

Known neither to the individual nor to others

Naive-Self

Naïve-Self, the self nobody is aware of, is the unconscious -- habits and emotions out of awareness.

You can use a helpful acronym: D-O-M-A-I-N-S, a word with the first letter of each of the seven-selves -- the DOMAINS of your personality and self-concept. For further information on the Interself Test & Profile, see my other books (TED BUNDY'S SEX LIFE; MASKS OF PREDATORS; PSYCHOPATHS; PRINCESS DIANA'S THERAPIST; etc.).

Charles Manson's Interself Profile:

Stage/ Trait	Dynamic	Objective	Mirror	Actual	Ideal	Naïve	Social
Growth							
Transition	■			■			■
Conflict		■		■			

I interviewed Charles Manson while he was in San Quentin prison in September of 1988. Besides the prison interviews, I tested him and did a psychological assessment and diagnosis.

I concluded he was a psychopath. I rated Charles Manson as having the above Interself profile based on his completion of my 100-item Interself Test. Charlie could not fake my test because it has a built-in lie scale, which counters psychopathic tendencies to appear socially acceptable or to answer dishonestly.

1) DYNAMIC-SELF: Charlie is in the transition range in motivation and energy. The problem is that he lacks motivation and has misused his energy and motivation resources. I diagnosed him as a Psychopath with a serial-killer track record.

2) OBJECTIVE-SELF: Obviously, Manson's social image and reputation have been destroyed, and so he scored in the Conflict Stage on this trait.

3) MIRROR-SELF: He was in the Conflict Stage on this interpersonal trait. Charlie has had significant problems getting along with others as a function of his psychopathy. He comes across as a pushy-control freak, a manipulator, and a cold-blooded killer.

4) ACTUAL-SELF: Charlie scored in the Transition Stage in terms of his problem-solving ability. While Manson has the intelligence to solve problems and cope, he has wasted his skills in a crazy-mass-murder scenario. Her psychopathic narcissism spun him off track. As an arrogant psychopath, threatening and killing people, he demanded record deals in Hollywood. Instead of becoming a rock star, he became notorious as a mass murderer.

5) IDEAL-SELF: Manson rated in the Conflict Stage in terms of his lack of conscience. He has no moral compass and ended up convicted of first-degree murders.

6) NAÏVE-SELF: Charlie tested as having major-unconscious conflicts that put him in the Conflict Stage as far as his unconscious mind and emotions.

7) SOCIAL-SELF: Manson scored in the Transition Stage in terms of his unstable feelings and fractured sense of identity.

Chapter 20

Nancy Pitman (1951-): Nancy Pitman (aka Brenda Sue McCann, Brindle, Cydette Perell), 69 in 2020, was born in Springfield, Illinois, on January 1, 1951. Nancy Pittman grew up in a wealthy household in Malibu, where her father was a successful engineer, and her mother was a society matron. She and her two younger brothers wanted for nothing materially, and her childhood years were devoted to school and surfing. However, the wealth didn't bring her happiness. Or she was bored with the soft, easygoing, and indulgent life in Malibu and itching for adventure with bad boys and wild girls – the Patti Hearst syndrome which I'll discuss later in more detail.

At 16, she befriended some slightly older girls who were living with an older man whom they spoke of glowingly. The teenage Pittman convinced them to introduce her to him. The man was Charles Manson. She was immediately taken with him and ran away from home at the age of 16 to be with him. She quickly became one of his most ardent backers and traveled with him to various parts of California.

Ultimately, they moved to a deteriorating film set, Spahn's Movie Ranch. She stayed loyal to Manson after hearing about the murder of Gary Hinman and Manson's role in it. Pitman got a thrill out of murder.

Nancy Pitman, circa 1969-1971.

She was also present at the ranch when Manson sent Charles Watson, Susan Atkins, Patricia Krenwinkel, and Linda Kasabian to commit murders at a house formerly occupied by producer Terry Melcher and actress Candice Bergen.

Manson's business with Terry Melcher had gone badly. Melcher's rejection of a record deal with Manson was a critical factor in the murders. Manson, who knew Melcher had moved out, seemed to want to kill the new occupants to send a message to the establishment and successful Hollywood people.

Pitman, Manson, and others drove to the house later than night to tamper with the crime scene according to a rumor. After the arrest of Manson and his family for the Tate/LaBianca murders, she was one of his most conspicuous supporters, singing and handing out placards to passersby.

After the trial, she drifted into the Aryan Brotherhood and moved to a house in Stockton with a few other members. Two house-mates, James and Lauren Willett, were subsequently murdered by Manson Family members who lived there. Pittman ultimately was convicted of being an accessory after the fact to the Willett murders.

Left to right photos: Nancy Pitman, circa 1970, with the Manson Family. A recent photo of Pitman enjoying herself at the beach. Steve "Clem" Grogan happily singing with his band. Both Pitman and Grogan were convicted and did prison time for murder. Pitman, released after 18 months. Grogan walked out of prison in 1985, 35 years ago, in 2020. These Manson Family members got light sentences for murder and have been living happily ever after. Yet Tex Watson, Leslie Van Houten, Patricia Krenwinkel, Bruce Davis, and Bobby Beausoleil, convicted of killings, rot in prison 50 years later.

She served 18 months in prison and wound up marrying one of the co-conspirators. They subsequently divorced, and she moved to the Pacific Northwest with her children and changed her name. She has renounced Manson and keeps a low profile, striving to shield her children from any fallout from her past.

Like many in the Los Angeles area, her father was employed in the aerospace industry, working as an aeronautical engineer designing guidance systems for missiles. Growing up in Malibu, California, Nancy and her brothers were surrounded by the rich and famous.

She was first introduced to Charles Manson and the family through her friend Deirdre Lansbury, daughter of the famous actress Angela Lansbury. Deirdre hung out with the family from time to time and even had a note from her mother, stating it was okay for her to travel with them. Nancy, on the other hand, wasn't getting along with her parents. She had been kicked out of her house. The Manson criminal cult welcomed her to stay with them, and she happily accepted.

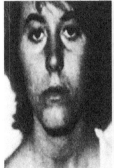

Nancy Pitman, circa 1969-1970.

In March of 1968, Nancy, who often went by the name Brenda McCann, accompanied Manson and other family members to a party at the home of Harold True. True's house was located at 3267 Waverly Drive, right next door to the LaBianca residence.

A year later, on the night of the Tate murders, Nancy was present when Charlie instructed Susan Atkins, Patricia Krenwinkel, and Linda Kasabian to go do "what Tex said." After the four killers returned, the legend is that Nancy and Charlie drove to the Tate house and inspected the crime scene. I doubt that happened because Manson avoided murder crime scenes to avoid taking responsibility for murders.

Nancy was arrested with the family in both the August 16th, 1969, Spahn's Movie Ranch, and October 10th, 1969, Barker Ranch raids. During police questioning, she stayed loyal to the Manson Family and maintained that she knew nothing about the murders.

She returned to her parent's home after being released from jail but rejoined the Manson Family when the murder trials began. She was arrested in 1971 for aiding in the escape of Manson Family associate Kenneth Como, but charges were dropped due to lack of evidence. Like Ruth Ann Moorehouse, Pitman played dumb about the Manson cult murders – and she avoided punishment or managed to get a slap on the wrist, little jail time for participating in murders. Her rich parents hired top lawyers.

Left: Nancy Pitman, November 2014. Middle/right: Pitman, circa 1970.

Following the Tate/LaBianca murder trials, the Manson Family slowly began to break up. Nancy lived with Sandy and Squeaky for short periods, but it wasn't long before they too were going in different directions. Nancy ended up living with a couple of convicts that escaped from a prison in Northern California.

She fell in love with one of them, a man named Michael "Red-Eye" Monfort, aka: "Red-Eye". Together with three other couples: James "Spider" Craig & Priscilla "Tuffy" Cooper, Billy Goucher & Maria "Crystal" Alonzo, and James & Reni Willett with their infant daughter Heidi. Nancy and Red Eye moved into a cabin in Guerneville.

It was there that Red-Eye, Spider, and Billy decided to kill their roommate James Willett. They brought him to a wooded area on the outskirts of town and told him to dig a hole. After Willett was done, Red-Eye, Billy, and Spider took turns firing bullets into him. The group then buried Willett's body in the hole he had just dug.

Left: Nancy Pitman, March 1970, still hypnotized by Charlie Manson. Center: Pitman in a more recent photo – happily socializing about 45 years after getting out of prison on a murder conviction. Right: Pitman in jail with Squeaky Fromme in the good old days of living dangerously with Manson Family criminals.

Because she continued to travel with the group, authorities believe that James' wife Reni approved of her husband's murder. However, they would never get the chance to talk with her.

Monfort ended up shooting her in the eye and buried her in the basement of the group's Stockton, California home. It happened, supposedly by accident, but many believe that Reni had found out about her husband's murder and was going to snitch on the group.

Nancy Pitman and Lynette "Squeaky" Fromme appeared in a video that was shot in the 1970s. Pitman rationalizes the Tate/LaBianca murders just like Charles Manson has done:

"Every show we ever watched was all killing. All those old-time gangster movies where it was all exciting...they were in the cars with the low hats, and they were cruising, and they were shooting out the windows. We are what you made us..."

HELD WITHOUT BAIL — Michael Monfort, 24, (left) and James Craig, 33, Monday, were arraigned in Municipal Court at Stockton, Calif., as suspects in the killings of an ex-marine, James Willett, 26, and his wife, Lauren, 19. Also arraigned were three female members of the "Manson Family," Lynnette Fromme, 24, Nancy Pitman, 24, and Priscilla Cooper, 21. Their hearings were continued until Nov. 27. All were ordered held without bail. (UPI Telephoto)

Left: Nancy Pitman under arrest for the two Willett murders. Right: Michael "Red-Eye" Monfort and James Craig, arrested for the Willett murders. Pitman was in love with Red-Eye.

"...Exactly. So, what's the big deal? Five or six people get killed, and you all freak-out and put it on us. We're just reflecting you at yourselves," Nancy Pitman said.

Authorities eventually caught up with the group, and they all went to jail. For the murder of Reni Willett, Nancy Pitman was convicted of being an accessory after the fact and did 18 months in prison. She and Monfort had a jailhouse marriage and stayed together until 1990.

Summary of Nancy Pitman: Nancy Pitman, who was a hardcore Manson Family member, was rumored to be Charles Manson's female assassin. She did prison time for accessory to murder. She continued a criminal lifestyle for 20 years until 1990.

Left to right: James Willett, Lauren Willet, and her baby, Squeaky Fromme, Nancy Pitman, Michael "Red-Eye" Monfort, and James Craig. Pitman, Fromme, Monfort, and Craig were arrested and charged with murder. Both James and Lauren Willett were shot to death. Nancy Pitman and Michael "Red-Eye" Monfort, were married while Red-Eye was in jail, and after their release from prison for the Willetts murders, they lived together. Nancy's parents purchased a home in Napa, California, for the couple to live in after Nancy was released from prison. It is so beautiful to have wealthy, tolerant parents. Pitman was later divorced from Red-Eye. The Manson Family girls were suckers for murdering ex-convicts.

Pitman struck me as a girl who followed the Patty Hearst pattern. I compared and contrasted Nancy Pitman to Patty Hearst in my book *Charles Manson's Girls*. For some rebellious teenagers in Malibu, such as Nancy Pitman, who lack gratitude for their privileged life of luxury, they seek stimulation on the wild side. The Manson Family's mass murders were fun to Pitman. She married an ex-con named Red-Eye who was on the run and participated in cold-blooded killings. She loved to hang out with criminals.

Pitman came from a wealthy family in Malibu and seemed to get a kick out of the bad company, bad boys, and murdering criminals. Pitman was reported to have moved on from her criminal past with the Manson Family and criminal associates after 1990. She was last reported to be living in the Pacific Northwest with her four children.

Chapter 21

Charles Manson used mind-control techniques like other cults use to influence, brainwash, thought reform, and remold his Manson Family followers. By coercive persuasion, drugs, free sex, and wild orgies, Charles Manson broke down his cult disciples' sense of self.

In 2019 there are still hundreds of destructive cults operating in the United States. The lure of dangerous cults is a reason to study the evolution of the Manson Family from a hippie commune based on sex, drugs, and petty crime to a darker stage involving serial-killing and mass murder.

Some of the Manson Family members who have gotten an education in prison and have had decades to recover from the Manson Family cult discussed Manson's methods in interviews. Leslie Van Houten and Patricia Krenwinkel have been very articulate about Charles Manson's cult techniques. For instance, Manson isolated his cult members, pressured them to live in the moment, the "now" or a moment-to-moment existence.

Left: Bhagwan Shree Rajneesh, a guru who set up a nutty-sex cult in Oregon under the pretense of a spiritual journey. Right: Charles Manson, a con artist and serial-killer who recruited a criminal-sex-druggie-hippie-commune cult in the late 1960s.

Leslie Van Houten admitted, "I knew there would be killing. The violence in us was nurtured and remolded by Charles Manson. Manson remolded middle-class girls into killers. My father left our family, and I had a space for a father figure. Charles Manson had the answers. I had met someone by being around him would be a positive change. Helter Skelter was going to be a racially motivated revolution. I robbed my father's house for Manson…"

Van Houten: "You could not talk about your past at all. Manson would stop you and move his hands and make faces, and your exercise was to copy and mirror him. He used the girls for sex, and you had to have sex with who he said. Manson asked, 'Would you die for me?'."

Van Houten: "Manson ordered us around like saying, 'Bow like sheep!' Manson told Tex not to scare the LaBiancas like the panic that happened at Tate's home. When the killing was the real thing, I was torn in half. I stabbed Mrs. LaBianca about 16 times. I realized for a brief moment that these are people that love each other as her husband was dying."

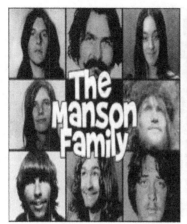 

Charles Manson scripted his destructive Manson Family cult's behavior even during the Tate/LaBianca murder trial. Like other cults, Manson programmed, brainwashed, and manipulated his cult followers.

Patricia Krenwinkel said, "I was using a lot of drugs... Hashish, marijuana, LSD. I had hundreds of LSD trips... That night Charles Manson and I slept together, and he said I was beautiful... It wasn't so strange to give up everything in 1967 and join the Manson Family..."

Krenwinkel: "I didn't contact my parents... I cut off my past. It was about becoming like Manson. Group sex was a means of control. To bring a man into the group, you had to have sex with him. Manson would throw hatchets at you as you stood by a tree to prove you trusted him. We ran on fear with more knives and guns at Spahn's Ranch. I followed Charlie's orders to kill in the Tate/LaBianca murders..."

Charles Manson: "I don't live in anticipation... I live in now..." Manson denied any responsibility for ordering the murders. "When I stand on the mountain and say, do it! It'll get done! If it don't, I'll move on it! And that is the last thing you want to happen!"

Left: Reverend Jim Jones at Jonestown. Right: Destructive cult gurus.

How were old fears and anxiety handled? The Manson Family suppressed and repressed fear and anxiety by singing Manson's songs with bizarre lyrics, by chanting and meditation. The Manson Family commune at the Spahn's Movie Ranch was a daily magical mystery tour. Dress up in costumes, play-act at being a pirate or a gypsy or a cowboy. Forget your past, and don't think about your future.

Manson cut his Manson Family hangers-on, admirers, and adherents off from their families except to pump them for money. The maturity and psychological growth healthy people experience stopped. The abuse of drugs and the restrictive mind control locked Manson's Family in an adolescent stage at best.

Love bombing. Charles Manson's love-bombing technique. Manson identified a girl with some father-figure issue, an identity crisis who was looking for love in the wrong places. For example, Lynette "Squeaky" Fromme first met Manson in Venice Beach, where she was sitting sadly on a bench. She was an emotionally vulnerable target, stressed-out because her father had kicked her out of the house.

Charles Manson isolated his Manson Family cult at remote desert ranches, including Spahn's Movie Ranch (left) and Barker Ranch in Death Valley (right), Paul Watkins, Brooks Poston.

He then flooded Fromme with affection, flattery, and validation. Manson became the father figure and authority figure many alienated, drifting, runaway young people were seeking. Patricia Krenwinkel had said in interviews that she was overwhelmed when Manson made love to her and told her how beautiful she was. Krenwinkel and Mary Brunner were rather plain looking or homely young women who craved loving, flattering attention.

Manson then trapped his Manson Family robots in an approach-avoidance conflict. The Manson Family commune provided a haven at Spahn's Movie Ranch. But simultaneously, Manson kept cult members off-balance by scaring them with his demands and threats and apocalyptic visions of Helter Skelter. This was illustrated by the mixed feelings his Manson cult members experienced because of both the positive and negative effects of Charlie's mind control techniques.

At one moment, they'd disloyally testify against the Manson Family criminals, and in the next moment, they'd do some crazy stunt aimed at helping Manson Family killers who were in prison. Mary Brunner is a good example. She testified against the Gary Hinman killers who were convicted: Charles Manson, Bobby Beausoleil, Susan Atkins, and Bruce Davis.

Left: Catherine "Gypsy" Share & Mary Brunner arrested after the Hawthorne gun store robbery and shootout. Middle: Barbara Hoyt at court to testify against the Manson Family killers after they tried to kill her in Hawaii with a drug OD. Right: Brunner at court to testify against the Gary Hinman killers, including Charles Manson, Bruce Davis, Susan Atkins, and Bobby Beausoleil. Manson cult members showed mixed feelings and approach-avoidance conflicts.

Then Mary Brunner joined the insane faction behind the Hawthorne robbery and shootout, which was intended to hijack a 747-jumbo jet, kill passengers, and force authorities to free the Manson Family killers from prison. Similarly, some Manson Family members ran away from the cult and then returned later.

Barbara Hoyt went through a similar approach-avoidance process of accepting an all-expense-paid trip to Hawaii with Ruth Ann Moorehouse to avoid testifying. Then, after Moorehouse laced her hamburger with massive quantities of drugs to kill her, Hoyt luckily recovered in a hospital emergency room and then was motivated to testify against the Tate/LaBianca killers.

Left: Charles Manson's cult activities ranged from playing guitar, singing songs with his followers, to sex orgies, drug abuse, and ordering murders. Innocent singing, drugs, and sex orgies led to various crimes, serial killings, arrests, and police mugshots.

Charles Manson was streetwise and sharp enough from his prison experiences to spot vulnerable young women and girls and alienated young guys who were good candidates for his Manson cult.

People who are susceptible to mind control techniques have identifiable characteristics. For example, the young girls and guys who were dependent and unassertive were vulnerable.

His Manson Family members often had a low tolerance for ambiguity – they want answers right now! They don't want to be uncertain. Idealistic hippie drop-outs with a strong desire for spiritual meaning were very vulnerable to Manson's cult pitch.

Manson's cult robots often had an impaired or no ability to be critical of Charlie's brainwashing or mind control techniques. Barbara Hoyt gave an example.

Manson ordered Susan Atkins to go get him a fresh coconut, and he yelled at her, "I don't care if you have to go to Jamaica to get one!" Atkins rushed off to get Manson a fresh coconut. This blind obedience is why Atkins was dependable to join in mass murders Manson ordered.

Chapter 22

Catherine Gillies (1950-2018): Catherine Gillies (aka Cappy, Capistrano, Cathy Myers, Patricia Anne Burke, Patti Sue Jardin), born August 2, 1950, was a Manson Family member. She died on June 29, 2018.

Catherine Gillies was a native of Southern California. She was reportedly a Buffalo Springfield groupie before she joined the Manson criminal cult sometime in 1968. As Charlie and the family looked for a new home, they learned that Catherine's grandmother, Arlene Barker, owned a ranch in Death Valley.

In Charlie's eyes, Myers Ranch and the neighboring Barker Ranch seemed to be the perfect home. In November of 1968, Manson gave Mrs. Barker a Beach Boys gold record, in exchange for permission for the family to stay at the ranches.

Catherine Gillies, circa 1969-1970, with the Manson Family.

The Manson criminals lived at Barker and Myers Ranch on-and-off throughout 1968 and 1969. Manson wanted to own the Barker Ranch but didn't have the money. At one point, there was an attempt to kill Arlene Barker for the ranch. As the story goes, a bunch of cult members was on route to kill Mrs. Barker, but the mission was aborted due to a flat tire.

Cathy, or Capistrano, as George Spahn called her, was arrested in both the Spahn's Movie Ranch and Barker Ranch raids. Venice Police also listed Gillies present when family member Zero (John Haught) committed "suicide" or was murdered. At the Tate/LaBianca murder trial, Catherine was a regular on the corner of *Temple and Broadway*.

During the sentencing phase, Gillies testified that the murders were copycat killings committed in an attempt to get Bobby Beausoleil out of jail. Like Pitman and Moorehouse, Cappy Gillies was a hardcore Manson cult criminal.

Left: Catherine "Cappy" Gillies, 1969. Middle/right: Recent photos of Catherine Gillies, who is now dead. Cappy appeared to have led a rough life as a result of the Manson Family and motorcycle gang criminal lifestyle.

She went on to say Charlie had nothing to do with the murders, and stated that she wanted to go with the killers on both nights, but was told that she wasn't needed. Cathy testified that the killings didn't upset her, and she would willingly commit homicide to get a brother out of jail. After the family broke apart, Gillies reportedly joined a motorcycle gang. She married, then divorced, and for many years, lived near Death Valley with her four children.

A recorded phone conversation between Catherine "Cappy" Gillies and a documentary maker, Bill Nelson, was released in 2016. Mostly they discussed a Julian, who was posing for a time as the son of Paul Watkins and Ruth Ann "Ouisch" Moorehouse. Nelson was trying to get close to ex-members of the Manson Family.

Summary of Catherine Gilles: Catherine "Cappy" Gillies was a hardcore member of the Manson Family who had bonded not only with Manson but also Lynette "Squeaky" Fromme and Sandra Good. Since Gillies died in 2018, we won't have to worry about "Cappy" getting back together with "Squeaky" and Good to commit more crimes.

Left: Josephine Valentina Clark. Center/right: Catherine "Cappy" Gilles. Clark portrayed "Happy Cappy" in *Once Upon a Time in Hollywood*. Her character is based on Gilles. Catherine Gillies was nicknamed "Capistrano" by George Spahn, owner of Spahn's Movie Ranch, but called "Cappy" for short. Gillies died during the film's production.

"Happy Cappy" was a cold-blooded criminal at heart. She came up with the idea of murdering her grandmother, Arlene Barker, to inherit her ranch for use by the Manson cult. After the Manson groupies scattered, following many arrests and jail sentences, Gillies moved on to join a motorcycle gang. Cappy was comfortable with criminals and killers.

Chapter 23

Charlie Manson's horrifying charisma, his magnetism, fueled his infamous image as a counter-cultural icon of evil. Charlie's dark allure attracted predominantly middle-class, educated young women and girls with dysfunctional-father issues who were love-starved or sexually promiscuous.

Charlie was a magnet for 1) antisocial-wannabe-hippie males; 2) criminal losers and drug dealers; 3) teenage drug addicts and alcoholics looking to get loaded or shitfaced drunk; 4) licentious-motorcycle-gang bikers; 5) sex addicts; 6) pimps; 7) sex perverts who escaped from a mental hospital; 8) ex-convicts.

Charlie exploited runaway or drifting teens and twenties in the late 1960s. Manson played on their identity-crisis anxieties, abusing their passive need for approval, and pushing their mental disorder buttons. Charlie forced his cult to abuse drugs, traumatized girls with sexual assault, and physical abuse that may have triggered various syndromes including borderline personality disorder, drug-induced insanity, bipolar disorders, and mental burnout.

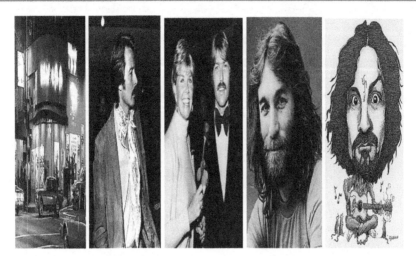

Left to right: Whiskey a Go-Go, the late 1960s; Gregg Jakobson; Doris Day & Terry Melcher; Dennis Wilson; Charles Manson. Charles Manson made a big splash when he went to the Whiskey a Go-Go nightclub with Dennis Wilson, Terry Melcher, and Gregg Jakobson.

As is typical with dangerous psychopaths, they first come off as charming, charismatic, perhaps enchanting, persuasive, and captivating. Charlie had some traits similar to cult leaders such as harmful or hurtful narcissism based on Manson's self-love, egotism, sense of self-importance, and self-centered perception of Charlie's entitlement.

Charlie was very intuitive and could scan people, which is common among psychopaths, antisocials, and ex-convicts who survived in prison by assessing the strengths and weaknesses of other inmates and the prison staff. Charlie created chaos to keep a balance of power in his favor.

Manson was unpredictable. His cult members never knew if Charlie was going to love-bomb some new girl? Get a wild sex orgy going at Spahn's Movie Ranch? Harass them with some crazy Helter Skelter ranting and raving? Suddenly get paranoid? Or order his followers to assault or kill one of his perceived enemies?

Left: Charles Manson under arrest during a police raid at Spahn's Movie Ranch. Right: Beach Boys and Charles Manson. Manson's criminal lifestyle interfered with his rock star dreams.

Charlie demanded that the Manson Family members must be isolated from former friends and family. Why? Because they won't get or approve Helter Skelter or Charlie's semi-hippie commune or cult rules of behavior. Charlie told them how to dress, how to speak, how to sing his eccentric songs, and to believe his zany Helter Skelter master plan.

Because the Manson Family, while functioning with a core of about 20 hardcore members, became bigger at times with possibly up to 100 individuals drifting in and out of the cult, Charlie set up a hierarchy and tasked some followers to be enforcers-by-proxy. Charlie used Tex (Charles "Tex" Watson) to assault and kill people at times.

Steve "Clem" Grogan, Bruce Davis, and Bobby Beausoleil were also Manson underlings Charlie used to commit assaults and murders. Charlie got very paranoid about snitches or police informers and sometimes murdered them with his cronies or sent his enforcers to do the dirty work.

Donald Shea

From left to right: Charles Manson, Donald "Shorty" Shea, John "Zero" Haught, Sandra Good & Joel Pugh. Manson participated in murdering Donald Shea. Manson was suspected of ordering the murder of Haught and Pugh. Charlie suspected them of being police informers or snitches who knew too much about Manson Family crimes.

Charlie joined several of his cult followers and murdered Donald "Shorty" Shea who Charlie said was a snitch. Charlie is suspect of ordering the murder of other possible snitches or people who knew too much about Manson Family crimes such as John "Zero" Haught, Joel Pugh, and others.

Charlie picked some hardcore loyal or obedient robots to discipline, lead, assault, and kill by proxy. Lynette "Squeaky" Fromme was the leader of the Manson Family when Charlie was in prison. Charlie selected girls who would execute or support his murderous aims.

Hardcore Manson Family females who would commit murder or rubber stamp and endorse Charlie's-killer commands included 1) Lynette "Squeaky" Fromme, 2) Nancy Pitman, 3) Mary Brunner, 4) Sandra Good, 5) Patricia Krenwinkel, 6) Susan "Sadie" Atkins, and 7) Leslie Van Houten. Ruth Ann "Ouisch" Moorehouse attempted to murder Barbara Hoyt with a drug overdose, was charged with attempted murder, and avoided a jail sentence by running away.

Left to right: Hardcore Manson Family girls including Mary Brunner, Susan "Sadie" Atkins, Catherine "Gypsy" Share, Lynette "Squeaky" Fromme, Sandra Good, Ruth Ann "Ouisch" Moorehouse, Patricia Krenwinkel, Atkins, Leslie Van Houten, and Nancy Pitman. All of these young women were involved in murders, attempted murder, and convicted of felonies resulting in jail and prison sentences.

All of these women, except for "Ouisch" Moorehouse, who giggled in denial when police questioned her and fled, ended up doing years or decades in prison. And as of 2019, Krenwinkel and Van Houten are still in prison nearly 50 years later. Atkins died in prison.

Manson used his pimp experience and skills to manipulate not only pretty young women and girls but also to manipulate men he wanted to use. Charlie ordered his Front Street Girls or the best looking and sexiest Manson Family girls to have sex with guys he tried to influence, such as Dennis Wilson of The Beach Boys.

Charlie and his Manson Family, mostly the girls who outnumbered the guys in the cult 5-to-1, had managed to temporarily move into Dennis Wilson's mansion in Pacific Palisades for several months during the summer of 1968. The Manson Family were parasites leeching off Wilson in exchange for Wilson and his celebrity friends getting sexual favors from Manson's girls.

Charles Manson had an impact on the music industry. Unfortunately, Charlie's significance and higher profile resulted from his dark side and murder convictions. Manson's criminal way of life interfered with the development of his raw talent as a songwriter and potential success in rock music.

Charlie invited himself along when Dennis Wilson and his music-industry players went out partying at clubs on the famous Sunset Strip, which was known for rock music, sex hookups, and mind-altering drugs.

One summer of 1968 night, Dennis Wilson and his buddies went out to party at the Whiskey a Go-Go nightclub. Wilson's pals were 1) Terry Melcher, a music producer and son of Doris Day; 2) Gregg Jakobson, a talent scout, and rock/pop recording session organizer; 3) Charlie Manson. The Whiskey a Go-Go nightclub was on the Sunset Strip. Charlie rode with Wilson in his burgundy Rolls Royce.

Of course, while long lines were waiting to get into the Whiskey, Wilson, Melcher, and Jakobson were waved past the queue with Charlie Manson following them inside. Wilson, Melcher, and Jakobson went to a VIP section. Soon they noticed a commotion on the crowded dancefloor where Charlie had slid into the crowd dancing. Suddenly the dance crowd moved out of Charlie's way and circled Manson.

Manson demonstrated his unique power to hold the center-of-attention and not just as a flaky-New-Age guru spouting psychobabble and spiritual-jive talk. Gregg Jakobson remarked on Charlie's horrible-charismatic trait years later: "That was when we realized that he was something different, that time at the Whiskey. Anytime, anywhere, that Charlie decided to be the center of attention, he could be. At the Whiskey, everybody thought that they had seen it all. Until that night, when they saw Charlie."

At the center of the uproar and upheaval on the Whiskey dancefloor, was Charlie Manson doing a whirling-dervish number, gyrating, madcap dancing, spinning frantically, throwing his arms out and tipping his head back. Charlie's strange charisma had mesmerized about 300 jaded people who circled the dance floor, enabling Charlie to show-off. Charles Manson, who came across as a Mephistophelian guru, devilish, and diabolical was partly effective in brainwashing his followers because he could command the center of attention.

Chapter 24

Sandra Good (1944-): Sandra Good (aka Sandy, Blue, Sandra Collins Pugh), age 76 in 2020, was born February 20th, 1944. Good was the youngest of three girls. Her father was a San Diego stockbroker, and her mother divorced when Sandy was only four years old. She attended both the University of Oregon and San Francisco State College. Sandra Good was a hardcore member of Manson's cult and had the criminal record to prove it.

Good joined the family in April of 1968, and a month later, she found a new home for them at Spahn's Movie Ranch. Sandra was in jail with Mary Brunner on the night of the Tate murders but was back at the ranch in time to get arrested on the August 16th raid. On September 16th, 1969, Sandra gave birth to her son Ivan.

Almost a month later, she was arrested with the family during the October 10th Barker Ranch raid. On December 1st, 1969, a man named Joel Pugh was found murdered in England. Good denied Pugh was her husband. But he was her lover, at least. In October of 1971, Good was arrested while aiding family associate Kenneth Como in a botched escape from the Hall of Justice.

Sandra Good, circa 1969-1971.

After Manson's conviction, Good moved to Oregon with an ex-con and Aryan Brotherhood member named Steve Bekins. In July of 1972, Sandra was arrested for trying to hide Bekins after he had robbed a supermarket. After Bekins was caught and sent back to prison, Sandy skipped town.

She was picked up in San Francisco in December 1972 and was brought back to Oregon, where the charges against her were eventually dropped. Good then moved to Sacramento with Lynette Fromme, where the two women became nuns in Manson's newfound religion, the Order of the Rainbow.

Sandy led a drug-free life of abstinence and took on the new name of Blue. Both Blue and Red (Fromme) became obsessed with the environment and started the International People's Court of Retribution, a fictitious terrorist group that would assassinate executives and CEOs of companies that polluted the earth.

The two sent-out hundreds of threatening letters that claimed there were thousands of terrorists in the IPCR just waiting to kill. Good enrolled at Sacramento State University and majored in Ethno-botany.

Pictured is Sandra Good, circa 1969-1970, with some Manson Family members.

In December of 1975, Sandra was arrested along with Susan Murphy for conspiracy to send threatening letters in the mail. She was later convicted on all five counts and served ten years in prison. She began her sentence at Terminal Island Prison, then moved to Pleasanton, California, and was finally moved to Alderson in West Virginia, where she met up with Lynette Fromme again.

She was released in 1985, and for some time, lived in Vermont. Little is known about Good's son, Ivan. However, it has been reported that he went to college on a football scholarship.

In the mid-'90's, Good and a man named George Stimpson started the website Access Manson (no longer online) on which they claimed to have the real source of Manson thought.

Throughout the years, Sandy has stood by Manson's side. Although she isn't allowed to visit him herself, she continues to claim that Charlie had nothing to with ordering the murders.

Sandra Good, circa 1969-1970s, with her Manson Family girlfriends and a guy, Pugh, Good's lover or husband who either committed suicide or was murdered. Getting involved with Manson Family criminal girls can be hazardous to a guy's health. Bruce Davis and Sandra Good are suspects in Pugh's murder.

INTERVIEW COMMENTS – SANDRA GOOD:

Sandra Good was interviewed at her home in Vermont in 1990 in a video:

Sandra Good: Charlie Manson is inside all of us. He's our soul. To me, nature is God. And when you destroy your air, your water, your animals, and your trees, you're destroying God. Los Angeles will burn to the ground.

(Sandra Good claims to be on the same ecology crusade as Lynette "Squeaky" Fromme is. And she defends Charles Manson like Squeaky.)

Good: Charles Manson is whatever you want to make of him. A mirror actually.

Reporter: What do you mean by a mirror?

Good: A reflection of yourself.

Reporter: If you had your way, where would Charles Manson be?

Good: Charlie would be in the United Nations. He could help put order back into this country. He's a mind. A great mind. He has the heart to go with it.

Pictured is Sandra Good aging: left in 1996, 52, middle in 2010, 66, right in 2013, 69.

He has the awareness. He has the experience. Unlike any mind you have. Especially in the White House. I have absolute respect for Charles Manson. I've never met anyone like him. He doesn't lie.

Sandra "Blue" Good was interviewed on Oxygen's "Manson: The Women" and asked what guilt or culpability do the Manson Family killers share for the 1969 murders of Gary Allen Hinman, Sharon Tate, Jay Sebring, Abigail Folger, Voytek Frykowski, Steven Parent and Leno and Rosemary LaBianca?

"Just because a person kills does not make them evil and bad. I knew these were warm, good people. How can you point the finger at us and call us evil for being good soldiers and doing what needed to be done?" Good has always asserted that the Manson cult crimes were valid and blamed Hollywood and the American culture.

Left: Sandra "Blue" Good, 2020. Right: Good, ca 1969.

Were the Manson Family crimes "evil"? Good replied, "You want to talk about devils and demonic and immorality and evil, go to Hollywood. We don't touch the evil of that world. We don't even skim it. However, we *did* skim it. It needed to be touched." Why did Good stay with the Manson cult? "I had to have a feeling of safety. Safety has always been a big issue with me."

Summary of Sandra Good: Sandra Good, 76 in 2020, who has a criminal record, is still crazy after all these years and continues to worship Charles Manson's memory. Sandra Good and Squeaky Fromme have gotten into a lot of trouble together. Maybe her parole restrictions will keep her away from the surviving Manson Family members.

Sandra Good has made some creepy, spooky statements about the Manson Family cult murdering a Manson Family defense attorney, Ronald Hughes. Good, antisocial or psychopathic has proven to be a die-hard Manson Family member with criminal tendencies.

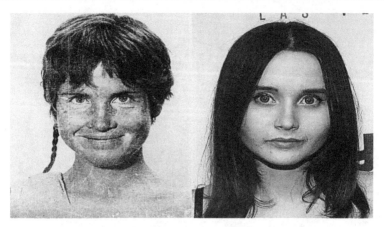

Left: Sandra "Blue" Good. Right: Kansas Bowling. Bowling portrayed "Blue" in *Once Upon a Time in Hollywood* based on Sandra "Blue" Good.

Sandra Good has quite a criminal record. In December of 1975, Sandra was arrested along with Susan Murphy for conspiracy to send threatening letters in the mail. She was later convicted on all five counts and served ten years in prison.

She began her sentence at Terminal Island Prison, then moved to Pleasanton, California, and ended up at Alderson in West Virginia, where she met up with Lynette "Squeaky" Fromme again.

After her release in 1985, she lived in Vermont. Sandy has stood by Manson's side. Sandra "Blue" Good, like "Happy Cappy" and Lynette "Squeaky" Fromme, claimed that Charlie Manson had nothing to do with ordering the murders.

Chapter 25

Dr. Dawson: Charlie, from my research you've been arrested, convicted of various crimes including car theft, forging checks, probation violation, pimping prostitutes, violation of the Mann Act – the White Slave Act, and violation of Title 18 Section 2421 – Transportation of Women in Interstate Commerce for Purposes of Prostitution. You had been arrested, found guilty of various crimes, and imprisoned for years in California from October 1955 until you were released from Terminal Island prison in San

Pedro, California in March of 1967. Two psychiatric assessments in the 1950s did not recommend you for probation. The psychiatrist, who examined you both times, concluded that you were a sociopathic personality without psychosis. Other terms for "sociopath" include antisocial personality disorder or psychopathy. From a series of petty crimes you "graduated" to being convicted of mass murders after your release in 1967. Are you a criminal psychopath?

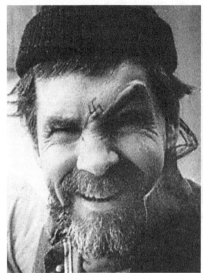

Charles Manson as he appeared in 1988 interviews.

Charles Manson: Whatever the hell it means, society made me what I am! I was raised in jail. Prison's my home. I never had parents to take care of me.

Dr. Dawson: Charlie, that's not quite accurate. Your mother, Kathleen, who was a struggling hooker at one time, moved to Los Angeles from West Virginia, and your ex-wife, Rosalie, who was caring for your son, Charles Jr., lived with your mother in the mid-1950s while you were doing time in Terminal Island Penitentiary. Kathleen then moved back to West Virginia. She remarried and wound up living in Spokane, Washington.

She wrote to a judge and offered to put up her house as security for your release from McNeil Island Penitentiary. The judge turned the offer down because he did not have jurisdiction in the case. So you had a mother who stuck her neck out for you and you took advantage of her. You led a psychopathic life of crime.

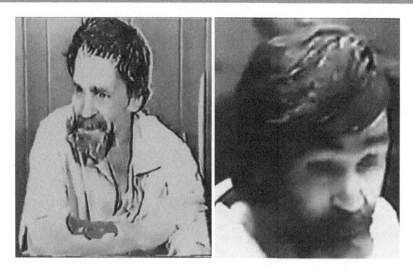

Left: Charles Manson in a 1988 interview. Right: Manson at a parole hearing, 1992.

What did you expect was going to happen? Let's talk about what a psychopath is. I'll run psychopathic traits by you and you tell me if they apply to you. Let's start with symptoms in the arena of emotional and interpersonal such as being glib and superficial. Are you glib and superficial?

Charles Manson: No, I'm deep and profound. Glib and superficial? Is that supposed to mean I'm psycho?

Dr. Dawson: Glib and superficial refers to your shallow, frivolous, and cursory dismissal of being guilty of mass murder, for example. Part of your jailhouse education was in learning from old convicts in prison the ways to control a group of prostitutes. Pimp talk.

Left: Charles Manson, 1968. Right: Manson, 2017.

Charles Manson: (laughs) Yeah, we'd rap about training whores in the slam. Like the "main old lady" who controls the other bitches in your stable of hookers.

Dr. Dawson: You also got some self-help training in various types of mind control, new age buzz words, and guru jargon which could appeal to the alienated young people of the 1960s counterculture – the airhead-hippie druggies, runaway-teenage girls, and assorted-criminal hustlers.

You studied occult topics, magic, warlockry, hypnosis, astral projection, Scientology, subliminal motivation – posthypnotic suggestions, Masonic lore, T.A. – Eric Berne's Transactional Analysis, and Games People Play. Another book that influenced you was Robert Heinlein's Stranger in a Strange Land which is the story of a power-hungry, sex-obsessed, telepathic Martian wandering the earth with a harem of women who is proselytizing for a new religious movement.

Kind of sounds like Charlie Manson's "Helter Skelter" race war paranoia when you were preaching to your druggie cult of over a dozen young women who followed you around like hippie-hooker robots. Any comment?

Charles Manson: Yeah, Doc. I put together a bag of tricks in prison and I watched some gurus on the streets of San Francisco. So what?

Dr. Dawson: So what? Your psychopathic foundation included some parts such as being glib and superficial. You were egocentric and grandiose which drove you to want to lead a crazy-druggie-murder cult.

Your lack of remorse or guilt, your lack of empathy combined with the fact that you're deceitful and manipulative and you have shallow emotions. The psychopathic result was you committed a string of murders along with your killer crew, the Manson Family. Right?

Charles Manson: I wasn't even there when those psychos killed people.

Chapter 26

Kathryn Lutesinger (1952-): Kathryn
Lutesinger (aka Kitty, Catherine Lynn Drake, Katy), 68 in 2020, born on August 14th, 1952, was introduced to the Manson Family via Bobby Beausoleil, her boyfriend. She was pregnant with Beausoleil's child.

It seemed that Kathryn Lutesinger was frequently in conflict with Charles Manson because he suspected she was trying to get Bobby Beausoleil to cut ties with the Manson Family. Beausoleil considered himself an associate and not a member of the Manson Family.

Manson kept threatening Lutesinger for trying to take Beausoleil away from the Manson criminal clan. Finally, she ran away from the Manson Family, left Spahn's Movie Ranch on July 30th, 1969.

Lutesinger reported Manson to the police and went home to her parents' horse ranch. Beausoleil was arrested for the murder of Gary Hinman while Lutesinger was away. She called Spahn's Movie Ranch asking about Beausoleil, but nobody would tell her what happened to him.

Pictured are Kathryn Lutesinger with other Manson Family girls.

Lutesinger got Manson on the phone, and he finally told her that Beausoleil had been arrested. Manson minimized it to her and said he'd be out of jail in a few days. He didn't tell her he was busted on a murder charge.

Kitty (her nickname), like a lot of the Manson Family, could not get along with her parents. On August 15th, 1969, she called Spahn's Movie Ranch and asked for a ride back to the Manson cult at Spahn's Movie Ranch. On August 16th, the police raided Spahn's Movie Ranch, and she was arrested with everybody else.

When the Manson Family moved to Myers Ranch in Death Valley, Lutesinger moved with them. Susan Atkins told Lutesinger that Beausoleil was in jail on a murder charge. Atkins joked about it. Lutesinger and Stephanie Schram, who were creeped out by the Manson Family murders, fled the last Manson hideout at Barker Ranch on the night of October 9th, 1969.

Lutesinger and Schram stopped a police car and asked for help. Lutesinger again told the police about Manson. Kitty told the cops that Susan Atkins had been involved in the Gary Hinman murder.

Lutesinger gave birth to a baby girl, named Jene, on February 11th, 1970. Kitty, a typical mixed-up Manson Family member, drifted in-and-out of the Manson Family from 1969 to the early 1970s.

Left to right: Margaret Qualley, Ruth Ann "Ouisch" Moorehouse, and Kathryn "Kitty" Lutesinger. Qualley portrayed Pussycat in *Once Upon a Time in Hollywood*. Her character was a composite of Moorehouse and Lutesinger. However, she looks more like Moorehouse.

She was still off-and-on with the Manson cult during the Tate/LaBianca murder trial. In November 1971, Kitty managed to get herself arrested for aiding and abetting the escape of Manson Family associate Kenneth Como. Luckily for Lutesinger, charges were dropped due to a lack of evidence.

Kitty Lutesinger was involved in sex or a romantic affair with Bobby Beausoleil like Leslie Van Houten was. She was the mother of Beausoleil's baby. Lutesinger was filmed sitting vigil on the corner of the courthouse during the Manson Family murder trial with other Manson girls (Nancy Pitman, Sandra Good, Catherine Gillies, Ruth Ann Moorehouse). They were singing Manson's songs.

Summary of Kathryn: Kathryn "Kitty" Lutesinger was one of those brainwashed Manson girls, mixed-up in their identity-crisis conflicts resulting from their dysfunctional families, led astray by bad company, and lost in the fog of the hippie-counterculture movement in the late 1960s.

Left: Kitty Lutesinger, Sandra Good, and Catherine Gillies. Right: Recent photo of Lutesinger.

She was in an approach-avoidance conflict with the Manson Family. At times she fled the Manson cult after Manson threatened her. Kathryn Lutesinger was brought into the family through her boyfriend Bobby Beausoleil. At the time, she was pregnant with Beausoleil's child. Charles Manson often threatened her, because he felt she was trying to lure Beausoleil away from the family.

Tired of Manson's death threats, Kathryn fled *Spahn's Ranch* on July 30th, 1969. She went directly to a nearby police station and reported her concerns about Manson, and then returned home to her parent's horse ranch. Then she continued to float in and out of the Manson Family orbit.

On February 11, 1970, she gave birth to a baby girl she named Jene. Bobby Beausoleil was the father. In 1973 Lutesinger was married, then divorced, and was living in Washington State with her daughter. Since the 1970s, Lutesinger has faded away.

Chapter 27

Dr. Dawson: You were convicted of ordering the murders and you participated in some violent murders. Another thing you worked on in prison was your music and songwriting. You even made some contacts in prison including Phil Kaufman who gave you a connection at Universal Studios in Hollywood. At Universal, in 1967 you recorded your songs.

Then through some strange connections, you hung out with Dennis Wilson of The Beach Boys and got an audition with Terry Melcher, a record producer. But when word got back to Melcher and others that you were murdering people, it kind of turned off people in the entertainment industry – you and your music got rejected.

Plus, from what I've heard and read you didn't have any talent beyond an amateur wannabe anyway. You're more infamous as a criminal mass murderer than you even would have been as an aspiring rock star. Do I have your story right?

Left: Charles Manson playing guitar in church. Right: Manson with a guitar.

Charles Manson: Jealous bastards in Hollywood stole my music.

Dr. Dawson: And that paranoid perception led you to murder a series of innocent people. Correct?

Charles Manson: Oh, goddamn it! You know prosecutors can indict a ham sandwich. The system needs to sell the public on criminals. It's all about corrupt mother fuckers!

Dr. Dawson: Okay, Charlie, let's take a look at your social deviance traits or symptoms of psychopathy. I think you jumped from a string of petty crimes to mass murder partly because of your social deviance characteristics including the fact that Charlie Manson is very impulsive and has poor behavioral controls.

Why should you get a legal job and earn money honestly when you can steal a car, steal credit cards and cash, and con your way through life? You need excitement and so you wanted to be a rock star. The problem is that you lack the responsibility to work for it as legit rock stars do.

You're in the habit of antisocial behavior which has been the case since your early behavioral problems as a child and teenager. You went down a criminal road which led to violent crimes and murder. Do I have your number? Or are you just a cool guy who is innocent and was wrongly convicted of murder?

Charles Manson: Right. I'm innocent. I got convicted because I was hanging out with bad company. Them fucked-up druggie hippie bastards roped me into their shit.

Chapter 28

Susan Bartell (1951-): Susan Bartell (aka Country Sue), 69 in 2020, born on June 21st, 1951, joined the Manson Family shortly after the Tate/LaBianca murders. As an introduction to the Manson criminal clowns, Bartell was arrested during a police raid on Barker Ranch in Death Valley.

A combined force of the California Highway Patrol, the National Park Rangers, and the Inyo County Sheriff's Office raided Barker Ranch and busted the Manson cult criminals and hangers-on.

In November 1969, Bartell again was involved with the Manson pseudo-hipster criminals and the cops. The Venice Police showed up to investigate the mysterious shooting of John "Zero" Haught.

The cops closed the case and accepted the story from the Manson criminal gang that Haught had shot himself playing Russian Roulette. The suspicious circumstances included: the gun was fully loaded, had no fingerprints, was wiped clean.

Susan Bartell (left) with Manson Family members, circa 1970. Center: Bartell, circa 1969, police mugshot. Right: Susan Bartell, 2014.

Summary of Susan Bartell: Bartell, who did not join the Manson Family cult until after the Tate/LaBianca murders, was one of those lost counterculture hippie wannabes who loved trouble.

At Canoga Park High School, she told her friends about a singing prophet named Charlie. She joined the Manson cult in time to get arrested at Barker Ranch during the police raids on October 10th and October 12th, 1969.

The spine-chilling Manson Family criminals at the Haught crime scene, including Bartell, convinced the police that Zero killed himself. However, it was a very suspicious killing.

Country Sue is alleged to have called members of the prosecutor's office during the Manson murder trials, making threats. She was later arrested with several Family members for abetting the escape of Kenneth Como. She served no time. Country Sue was reported to be living in Sonoma County, California.

Left: Sue Bartell in a high school photo. Center: Bartell in a police mugshot during her Manson cult days. Right: Bartell wrote "Helter Skelter" on this door at Spahn's Movie Ranch. Note how the Manson cult girls went from the happy-and-pretty-girl-next-door before they joined the Manson Family to depressed street criminals in police mugshots after hanging out with Charlie's criminal pseudo-hippies.

Bartell finally woke up, had enough of bad company, and left the Manson Family in the mid-1970s. Bartell may know the secret of who murdered John "Zero" Haught.

Chapter 29

Dr. Dawson: What led up to the Tate murders? You had been pitching your songs and music with the aim of a record deal. And along the road to fame and riches in Hollywood in the music business, you got involved with Dennis Wilson of The Beach Boys and Terry Melcher, a music producer.

Charles Manson: Bastards! Goddamn jealous snakes in my face. My songs got ripped off! I'm allied with the devil. In Hollywood, I gotta deal with a big incompetent jealous snake. No soul. You can buy 'em and sell 'em. See I was raised on the street and in prison. So when I was 20, I was about 50 in my mind. They put the poor people in prison and sell the public on more prisons – it's about the money.

Dr. Dawson: You felt taken advantage of. Okay. But in the spring of 1968 Dennis Wilson, one of The Beach Boys picked up two of your hitchhiking Manson cult women – Patricia Krenwinkel and Ella Jo Bailey. He drove them to his place in the Pacific Palisades and they hung out for a few hours.

9th August 1969

Charles Manson   Charles "Tex" Watson   Susan Atkins   Patricia Krenwinkel   Linda Kasabian

Steven Parent   Jay Sebring   Sharon Tate   Wojciech Frykowski   Abigail Folger

Top-row photos show the Tate killers who murdered on August 9th, 1969. In the bottom row, the Manson-gang-murder victims. Manson ordered Tex and the young women to kill. Tex Watson directed the murder crew at the Cielo Drive crime scene in Benedict Canyon.

The next morning, Wilson was returning home from a night recording session and when he pulled up in the driveway, you walked out of his house. You and a group of your hippie chicks were stalking him and squatting at his home uninvited. Was that how you expected to get a record deal?

Charles Manson: Wilson was a pussy. He asked me, "You gonna hurt me?" I told him, "No." I got down and kissed his feet. Record deal? Ya wanna be a star, ya gotta hang with stars.

Dr. Dawson: When Dennis Wilson went into his house, he found that about a dozen strangers were hanging out uninvited. Then over months, double that number of Manson Family members made themselves at home at Wilson's house. Most of them were young women. Don't you think stalking rock stars and squatting at their homes could spoil a record deal?

Sharon Tate (left, right) before and after Charles Manson's murder cult killed her.

Charles Manson: Dennis used my bitches as sex slaves and servants. Besides I could out-write The Beach Boys. I was comin' from life and death situations in the street and prison. What the hell could Dennis write about? His mamma bitchin' at him?

Dr. Dawson: You did some harm to Dennis. You and your nutty hippy cult cost him $100,000 – medical bills for STD treatment such as for gonorrhea, food, and you guys wrecked his uninsured car. The car bill was $21,000. You didn't make any amends and did not make that right. Did you?

Charles Manson: What the hell! I'd sing and tell Dennis stories. Did I get compensation for songs he stole from me? I met Wilson at a buddy's pad in San Francisco a year before in 1967. My old road buddy was Dennis's drug connection. He bought marijuana from him. Then Dennis invited me to stop by his place when I was in L.A. He gave me his Pacific Palisades address. Ain't no stalker or uninvited squatter.

Police sealed-off the Cielo Drive Tate-Polanski house crime scene after the August 9ᵗʰ, 1969 mass murders. Roman Polanski (right) looked over the bloody crime scene – "Pig" was written in blood on the front door.

Dr. Dawson: What songs did he record of yours and make money off?

Charles Manson: Don't fuckin' matter. According to egomaniacs in Hollywood, I've never done anything right. If I did something wrong, I'd regret it. But do you see me hitting my head with a hammer?

Dr. Dawson: I'm going down the road that led to you ordering the murders of a series of people such as Sharon Tate. From what I understand, Wilson was pretty good to you. He paid for studio time to record songs written and performed by you.

He introduced you to his contacts in the music business like Terry Melcher, Gregg Jakobson, and Rudi Altobelli. Rudy owned the home on Ciello Drive which he eventually rented to Sharon Tate and Roman Polanski. Terry Melcher had lived there before Tate and Polanski.

Charles Manson: Gregg Jakobson paid to record my music.

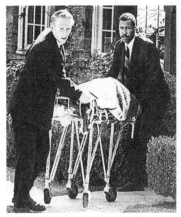

Homicide detectives removed Sharon Tate's body from the scene of her murder. Charles Manson (right) under arrest at Spahn's Movie Ranch in 1968.

Dr. Dawson: Jakobson was impressed with the Charlie Manson vibe – the whole package – artist, loose lifestyle, and philosophy. Do you remember another uninvited stalking incident over at Sharon Tate's place on March 23rd, 1969?

Charles Manson: I stopped by to see Terry Melcher. He was jerking me off – stringin' me along with signin' me for a record deal. But he'd moved out. Terry Melcher broke his contract with me and that's why those people were killed at the Tate house on Cielo Drive.

Dr. Dawson: It was Rudi Altobelli's property, Melcher was no longer the tenant. In February Sharon Tate and Roman Polanski had moved in. But a photographer, Shahrokh Hatami, met you and sent you to the guesthouse because you were asking for somebody he didn't know. He was there to photograph Tate before she left for Rome with Rudi.

Charles Manson: That bitch, Sharon Tate, stared at me through the front window. Hatami came out on the porch and asked me what was up. I asked him where Melcher was. He didn't know him.

He sent me to the back alley   out to the guest cottage. He followed me down the sidewalk while Tate stood in the doorway giving me the evil eye. Nobody was answering the guest cottage door and so I split.

Chapter 30

Catherine Share (1942-): Catherine Share (aka Gypsy, Manon Minette, Kathleen Diane Shore, Catherine Ann James, Jessica), 78 in 2020, born on December 10th, 1942, was born in Paris, France. Her Hungarian father and German mother were both members of the French underground and committed suicide during the war.

Catherine was put into an orphanage where she stayed until she was eight, then was adopted by an American couple (a blind psychologist and his wife), and moved to California.

When Catherine was still in high school, her adopted mother was afflicted by cancer, and took her own life. Catherine stayed and took care of her adopted father until he remarried. After graduating from Hollywood High School, she went to college, stayed there for three years, got married, and shortly after, divorced.

Like her father, Catherine was a violin virtuoso and had a beautiful singing voice. She spent the next few years drifting around California, occasionally scoring acting roles.

Pictured are Catherine Share, circa 1969-1970, with some Manson Family members.

On the set of soft porn entitled *Ramrodder*, Catherine ran into an old friend, a young musician named Bobby Beausoleil. *Ain't It?, Babe* was a folk-rock record released by Autumn Records in 1965, sung by Charity Shayne, Catherine "Gypsy" Share's stage name. Share got the record deal through her friend Bobby Beausoleil's connections.

She began living with him and his wife Gail, traveling with the couple for about eight months before deciding to go live with Manson, his criminals, and groupies (whom she met through Bobby) at Spahn's Movie Ranch.

Gypsy, as she became known in the family, was on of the oldest female members, and was very much in love with Charlie. She recruited new members, including girls like Linda Kasabian and Leslie Van Houten.

Gypsy was arrested on August 16th, 1969, at Spahn's Movie Ranch and on October 10th, 1969, at Barker Ranch in police raids. During police questioning, she didn't give any information about the murders and was eventually released. During the trials, Gypsy joined the other Manson Family girls in a vigil on the corner of Temple and Broadway.

She visited Linda Kasabian and encouraged her to lie about her whereabouts on the night of the Tate murders. She also helped convince Barbara Hoyt to go with Ruth Ann Morehouse to Hawaii as opposed to testifying against the family. On January 5th, 1971, Gypsy gave birth to a baby boy, which she named Phoenix.

Left: Catherine Share with Lynette "Squeaky" Fromme. Right: Share in a 2012 photo.

During the penalty phase of the Tate/LaBianca murder trial, Gypsy testified that the murders were Linda Kasabian's idea and that Linda, Sadie, and Leslie had committed the Hinman murder. The mass murders happened, according to her testimony, because Linda was in love with Bobby Beausoleil, and she wanted to commit copycat killings so the police would think Beausoleil was innocent.

On August 21st, 1971, Catherine was in a shootout with the Hawthorne Police. It started when Gypsy, Mary Brunner, Charles Lovett, Lawrence Bailey, Kenneth Como, and Dennis Rice were robbing a Western Surplus store in Hawthorne, California.

The group had stolen close to 150 guns when HPD responded to a silent alarm. Gypsy fired the first shot, and by the end of the shootout, had been wounded three times. The Manson Family members involved were planning to hijack a 747-jumbo jet, in which they would kill one passenger every hour until Charlie and the other convicted killers were released from prison. Fortunately, no one was severely wounded, but the stunt landed Gypsy in jail for 3.5 years.

Left: Catherine Share (recent photo). Right: Share circa 1970.

Gypsy went to the *California Institute for Women* in Frontera, where the other Manson girls were serving their sentences. While there, Gypsy and Mary Brunner, together with a group of *Aryan Brotherhood* members, conspired to break out of the prison using a pair of wire cutters but were caught at the last minute.

Gypsy had fallen in love with Kenneth Como (also imprisoned for the Hawthorne shootout) but stopped talking to him after Manson told her not to. Como was in love with Gypsy and angered with Manson, so he assaulted Charlie in the prison yard. Soon after, Como convinced Gypsy to forget about Charlie, and the two got married; Gypsy eventually divorced Como in 1981.

Catherine "Gypsy" Share was interviewed on Oxygen's *"Manson: The Women"* and asked what guilt or culpability do the Manson Family killers share for the 1969 murders of Gary Allen Hinman, Sharon Tate, Jay Sebring, Abigail Folger, Voytek Frykowski, Steven Parent and Leno and Rosemary LaBianca?

Left: Lena Dunham. Right: Catherine "Gypsy" Share. Dunham portrayed "Gypsy" based on Share in *Once Upon a Time in Hollywood*.

Share replied, "I felt very, very sad for the victims. I also feel very sad for the young people who were turned into murderers." She believed they committed murders because they were brainwashed by Manson.

Share did time in the same prison as Patricia Krenwinkel. "Patricia, at that time, she'd have all the pictures of Charlie up and then she'd tear them down. She was back and forth. Ultimately, my son helped me detach from Manson's ideology. I didn't want him to be an orphan. There was somebody besides me that I needed to take care of."

Summary of Catherine Share: While Share became a born-again Christian after her release from prison after 1975, she was an enthusiastic and devoted follower of Manson starting in the late-1960s.

Left: Recent photo of Catherine "Gypsy" Share. Right: Catherine Share, Ruth Ann Moorehouse, and Lynette "Squeaky" Fromme ca 1970.

She was one of Charlie's recruiters who located pretty young girls such as Leslie Van Houten and Linda Kasabian. Share pushed new members joining the Manson Family criminal cult to steal their parents' credit cards or money.

Catherine "Gypsy" Share was involved in various crimes such as the attempted murder of Barbara Hoyt – known as the "LSD-Laced Honolulu Hamburger" incident.

She joined the robbery of the California Western Surplus Store, stealing guns to hijack a Boeing 747 passenger jet and kill one hostage every hour until the Manson Family (Charles Manson, Watson, Krenwinkel, Van Houten, and Atkins) was released from prison.

Gypsy got into a shootout with the police and served 3.5 years in jail. Then Share got into a credit card scam, was arrested, jailed, and finally released in 1975.

Instead of following a life of crime, she should have gotten an honest job and worked on a career in music since she was a talented singer. She married Patrick Shannahan, a rat or prisoner turned informant. Share hid in the Witness Protection Program with him.

Gypsy was last said to have left her criminal ways, gotten religion, and was writing a book on her wild days living dangerously with Charles Manson, the Manson Family, and other criminals. She testified at Leslie Van Houten's 2017 parole hearing, said she regretted recruiting Van Houten into the Manson Family, but claimed Charlie threatened to kill them if they left his cult.

Chapter 31

Dr. Dawson: But that night, you went back to Tate's place and went to the guest cottage again. Rudi Altobelli was there. You asked for Melcher, but Rudi figured you wanted him since you knew Terry moved out.

Charles Manson: Rudi said Terry had moved to Malibu. He lied and told me he don't know his address. I had met Rudi at Dennis Wilson's the year before. Rudi had stroked me about my songs and music that Wilson had been playing. He complimented me in a back-assed way. He was brushing me off.

He said he was flying out of the country. I said I'd see him when he got back. He said he'd be gone for one year. Rudi was bugged because I came to his property. He told me not to bother his tenants. Sharon Tate got murdered because of *Rosemary's Baby* – the devil vibes from that. Polanski's evil movies.

Dr. Dawson: Altobelli flew off to Rome with Tate the next day. He said Tate asked, "Who was that creepy-looking guy who went back to the guest house?" I imagine you were very pissed off about getting blown off by Rudi, Sharon Tate, Terry Melcher, and Dennis Wilson.

Many of Charlie's supporters and demented fans pointed out that Star, 26, Charlie Manson's fiancee (left), had an uncanny similarity to original Manson cult member Susan Atkins (right). Maybe Star has the look the psycho-serial killer, 80, loves.

Charles Manson: In the world, I live in, I never look back and say I took a wrong turn here or there.

Dr. Dawson: Beausoleil was arrested on August 6th, 1969, after he had been caught driving Hinman's car. Police found the murder weapon in the tire well. Two days later, you announced to Manson Family members at Spahn Ranch, "Now is the time for Helter Skelter." What the hell is your definition of Helter Skelter?

Charles Manson: Helter Skelter was a prophecy of a race war – white against black. When it ended the Manson Family would rule. I rolled the dice and crapped out.

Dr. Dawson: It was August 8th, 1969, and you ordered Tex Watson to lead Susan Atkins, Linda Kasabian, and Patricia Krenwinkel into that house where Terry Melcher used to live.

Manson murder case figures – victims & murderers. Top row (left to right) Charles "Tex" Watson, Susan Denise Atkins, Abigail Folger, Sharon Tate. Bottom row (Left to right) Jay Sebring, Linda Kasabian, and Patricia Krenwinkel.

You directed your Manson-cult killers to destroy everyone in the house as gruesome as possible. You instructed the women to do exactly as Tex ordered. Why did you want to murder those strangers in the Cielo Drive home?

Charles Manson: I didn't order jack shit. I ain't got the power to order a pizza. Do you think those killer clowns gotta do what ole Charlie says? They ain't robots. So they had a bad drug trip that night. What the hell ya want from me?

Dr. Dawson: You got indicted for murder! And convicted!

Charles "Tex" Watson (left) and Susan Atkins (right) pictured in front of the western facade at Spahn Movie Ranch, a Manson "Family" hangout.

Charles Manson: Them goddamn morons could indict a ham sandwich. The fix was in. They targeted the demented guru of alienated hippy druggies. What am I, Hitler?

Dr. Dawson: Sharon Tate had seen you from the front door when you stopped by uninvited and claimed you were looking for Terry Melcher. But the people at 10050 Cielo Drive were strangers to you.

Eight and a half month pregnant Sharon Tate, a movie actress, wife of film director Roman Polanski, was socializing with some friends: 1) Jay Sebring, hairstylist, her friend, and former lover; 2) Wojciech Frykowski, a screenwriter friend of Polanski; and 3) Frykowski's lover Abigail Folger, Folger coffee fortune heiress. Roman Polanski was in London working on a film.

Charles Manson: They was Hollywood trash and Eurotrash. Sharon Tate couldn't act her way out of a paper bag. Sebring? What's one less perverted hairstylist?

Charles Manson in 1980. He didn't have enough talent to make it as a rock star. So he gave serial killing a shot. In his twisted, psychopathic mind he was getting revenge against those Hollywood- music moguls who rejected him by committing mass murder.

Folger was just a lazy, druggie, trust-fund bitch. Frykowski was a failed screenwriter – Eurotrash druggie. So Tex and the girls wrote 'em out of the Hollywood movie. Drop the fuckin' curtain.

Dr. Dawson: You don't feel any guilt or remorse? You've had about twenty years in prison to think about it.

Charles Manson: I ain't guilty because I'm innocent. Not guilty, dude.

Dr. Dawson: Your Manson murder crew showed up that night at the Cielo Drive property where Tate lived after midnight, August 9, 1969. Tex had been there with you before at least once and cased the place.

First, Tex climbed a telephone pole near the gate and cut the phone line. They parked their car down the hill and away from the gate. Next, they climbed up an embankment next to the gate – avoiding the gate in case it was electrified or alarmed – jumped down and walked onto the grounds.

Left: Abigail Folger, covered in blood, on the lawn of the Tate-Polanski property. Right: Patricia Krenwinkel stabbed Folger to death.

Charles Manson: Who the hell knows what those crazy kids were smokin' that night. I ain't responsible for their druggie nightmares.

Dr. Dawson: Yeah. And I'm Sigmund Freud. Your Manson murder crew proceeded onto the Tate-Polanski property and got startled by some car headlights coming their way. Tex confronted the driver and ordered him to stop while he pointed a handgun – a 22-caliber revolver – at him. Steven Parent, 18, was driving a Rambler.

Of course, you trained Tex to be ruthless and cold-blooded. So he slashed Parent's hand with a knife and shot him four times in the chest and stomach. This was after he had begged Tex not to hurt him. Tex commanded the women in his squad to push the car further up the driveway.

Charles Manson: Well, Doc. I was not there at that creepy-crawly murder party. That was just that crazy Tex and those dip-shit broads with him. I am not a murderer. That's what the judge and lawyers represent me to be.

Manson, 80, with Star, his fiancée, 26, an artist who was born in St Louis, Missouri, to a religious family. Her parents locked her in her room throughout her high school years after she refused to go to church and started taking drugs. In 2014 Charlie still attracted crazy-druggie-prison groupies. Star must be desperate, cracked, dazed, and confused to scrape the bottom of the barrel and hookup with a notorious-serial killer doing life in prison. They have "romantic" prison dates when she visits him in the penitentiary. Charlie had a happy ending, he fell in love with Star. He proved age was just a number.

Why ya think I'm in this crime factory? If anybody got killed at Terry Melcher's old place – Sharon Tate and all those goddamn idiots – it's because they asked for it. They wanna go see Jesus.

Chapter 32

Other Manson Family members & associates:

Sherry Ann Cooper:

Left to right: Sherry Ann Cooper, Donkey Danny DeCarlo, ca 1969. Sherry Cooper, recent photo.

Sherry Cooper (aka Simi Valley Sherri, Ruthie, Ruth Ann Heuvelhurst), born on May 17th, 1949, 71 in 2020, in Simi Valley, California, was a Manson Family member. She was a local girl in that her home was near Spahn's Movie Ranch. She was arrested in the police raid at Spahn's Movie Ranch.

idictments Returned In Tate Murder Case

Left to right: Ruth Ann Moorehouse, Danny "Donkey" DeCarlo; DeCarlo, Nancy Pitman. Manson cult members testified before a grand jury which returned indictments in the Tate/LaBianca murders.

She was romantically involved with Danny DeCarlo, and they had a daughter, Gina, who died in a car accident in 1991. Cooper moved on after living with DeCarlo in Canada and Oregon, got married, and has been living in California under her married name.

Sherry Cooper, like Barbara Hoyt, had some common sense and a little morality left. So, when they overheard Susan Atkins bragging about the Sharon Tate murder to Ruth Ann Moorehouse, both Sherry Cooper and Barbara Hoyt fled from the Manson Family.

Charles Manson, angry that the two girls had fled, went after them. He located them having breakfast in a restaurant in a small desert town. They insisted that they wanted to leave the cult, and Manson gave them $20.

There were rumors that Manson later sent some Manson Family followers to hunt them down, bring them back or murder them. In November 1969, an unidentified female body was found, and some said it could be Sherry Cooper. Later, police identified her as another woman and not Sherry Cooper.

Madeline Joan Cottage:

Madaline Joan Cottage, ca 1969.

Madaline Joan Cottage (aka Little Patty, Linda Baldwin), 74 in 2020, born on May 27, 1946, was a Manson Family member. Cottage was in bed with John "Zero" Haught when he allegedly committed suicide playing Russian Roulette on November 5th, 1969.

She was reported to tell the other Manson Family members, after the gunshot, that, "Zero shot himself, just like in the movies!" Madaline Joan Cottage seems to have split from the Manson Family shortly after the Haught shooting, which may have been a murder. The circumstances of John "Zero" Haught's death were suspicious.

Ella Jo Bailey:

Ella Jo Bailey

Ella Jo Bailey (aka Yellerstone), born January 15, 1947, in Omaha, Nebraska, was a Manson Family member. She died on September 14, 2015, in Florida. Bailey and Susan Atkins, in 1967, were living in a commune in San Francisco when they met Charles Manson. The two girls decided to exit the collective and join the Manson Family.

Manson then traveled up and down the West Coast with Ella Jo Bailey, Susan Atkins, Mary Brunner, Patricia Krenwinkel, and Lynette "Squeaky" Fromme. They picked up some others, mostly girls, and then moved to Spahn's Movie Ranch in 1968.

Ella Jo Bailey and Patricia Krenwinkel were hitchhiking in Malibu, California when they were picked up by Dennis Wilson of the Beach Boys. He took them to his mansion in Pacific Palisades, which led to the Manson Family using Dennis Wilson.

The Manson Family hung-out and stayed at Wilson's estate for months. Charles Manson tried to get Wilson to jumpstart his fantasy of becoming a rock star.

Dennis Wilson was interviewed about the Manson women and girls who moved into his mansion.

Bailey stuck around with the Manson parasites and criminals until the darker stages when Manson and his cult killers began murdering people. After Donald "Shorty" Shea was murdered, Bailey split from Manson's cult. She later testified for the prosecution during the Gary Hinman murder trial. Here are some excerpts from her testimony:

"Charles Manson stated that he had words with Mr. Hinman, and they had a heated argument, and then it became necessary for him to quiet Gary Hinman down, and he stated that he used a sword and cut Gary Hinman from his left ear down to his chin."

"He also said that he had quieted Gary down, and the girls put Gary in bed and that Mr. Hinman asked for his prayer beads, and after that, he said that he had left Bobby to finish up."

"He said that two or three shots had been fired at the house. He also said that Bobby was foolish to ever let Sadie (Susan Atkins) hold the gun on Mr. Hinman. He said that all they had gained from going to Gary's house were the two vehicles and around $27."

In an interview in 1968, Dennis Wilson revealed his connection with Charles Manson and the Manson Family girls. He estimated 17 girls were living at his mansion from the Manson cult. Wilson said:

"I told them about our involvement with the Maharishi, and they told me they too had a guru, a guy named Charlie who'd recently come out of jail after 12 years. His mother was a hooker. His father was a gangster, he'd drifted into crime."

"When I met him, I found he had great musical ideas. We're writing together now. He's dumb, in some ways, but I accept his approach and have learned from him. He taught me a dance. The Inhibition."

"You have to imagine you're a frozen man, and the ice is thawing out. Start with your fingertips, then all the rest of you, you extend it to a feeling that the whole universe is thawing out."

Chapter 33

Dr. Dawson: You say it was their fault your gang murdered them. Okay, let's continue the story. Your hit gang crosses the front lawn of Tate's home, Tex sent Kasabian to find an open window to enter. I guess you hadn't planned on crashing through the front door.

Frustrated, Tex cut a screen on a window. He sent Kasabian to watch the front gate. She stood guard by Steven's Rambler and waited – since he was the first to die. Watson climbed through the window and then let Susan Atkins and Patricia Krenwinkel in via the front door.

Charles Manson: Got nothin' to do with me – that shit is on another planet. It don't exist.

Dr. Dawson: Your charming killer crew then got into action. Tex kicked Frykowski, the aspiring screenwriter, in the head as he woke up on the couch. When he asked what the hell Tex was doing, Tex remarked, "I'm the devil, and I'm here to do the devil's business."

Charles Manson used an old bus (left) to transport his twisted-hippie, counterculture druggie dropouts who joined his cult – the Manson cult (right). The bus was abandoned in the desert at Spahn's Movie Ranch.

Watson told Susan to round up the others, and she and Krenwinkel herded Sharon Tate and Jay Sebring into the living room. Tex tied Sharon and Sebring together by their necks and hung the rope over a ceiling beam. When Sebring complained, Tex shot him. Folger was led back to her bedroom, and $70 was taken from her purse. Tex then stabbed Sebring seven times. Are you ashamed of yourself yet?

Charles Manson: Innocent man don't feel no guilt. No shame. San Quentin is where society hides people they throw away. Why should I feel shit?

Dr. Dawson: Since Frykowski's hands had been tied with a towel, he was able to free himself. He struggled with Susan who stabbed his legs. He fought her off and ran out the front door. Tex joined in after him, hit him on the head with the gun several times, stabbed him over and over, and shot him twice. He broke the gun grip in hitting Frykowski.

Manson's gun (left) was used by Tex Watson at the Tate murder scene. Manson (right) under arrest in 1969 at Spahn's Movie Ranch.

Charles Manson: Bunch of incompetent clowns. If I wanted to kill some loser, I'd do it like a man. Quick.

Dr. Dawson: If you were so manly, why'd you send your cult followers to do the dirty work? Why didn't you get revenge against Hollywood players yourself? It's easy to talk big while you're stuck in prison.

Charles Manson: Hey, goddamn it! I'm bigger than this prison. I live in the mountains, the desert, sail the ocean. But I ain't killed nobody. I am no criminal. I had no parents – was on the street. So they put me in prison.

Dr. Dawson: Blame it on no parents, huh? Okay, one of your killers went soft on the hit contract. Linda Kasabian went to the house after hearing "horrifying sounds." She was trying to stop the bloody slaughter and killing. She told Atkins that somebody was coming up the road. It was a lie.

Charles Manson: Them morons were just druggie fools.

Dr. Dawson: The occupants of the house were running for their lives – the ones who could escape. Folger, the coffee heiress, got away from Krenwinkel and ran out a bedroom door to the pool area.

In January 1971, Leslie Van Houten, Susan Atkins, aka Sadie Mae Glutz, 22, and Patricia Krenwinkel, 23, were transported from jail to court. They enjoyed goofing and performing for photographers.

Abigail was run down by Krenwinkel who stabbed her and tackled her. Tex joined in and they stabbed her at least 28 times. Frykowski still had some fight in him and as he crawled across the lawn, Tex stabbed him 51 times to be sure to kill him. They were following your gruesome orders to murder everybody, right?

Charles Manson: Hell, do I look like God? I ain't some gizmo switchin' on a bunch of robots. They got loaded on drugs and had a bloody party. No skin off my balls.

Chapter 34

Tate mass murders. Charles Manson, angry because Terry Melcher passed on getting Manson a record deal, sent his Manson Family cult killers to 10050 Cielo Drive in Los Angeles, the house formerly occupied by Terry Melcher, on the night of August 8th, 1969. Manson knew Melcher no longer lived at the Tate/Polanski house. I think Manson was just angry with rich and successful people and wanted to get revenge.

Revenge because he failed to get a big record deal from Terry Melcher. So, the Tate/Polanski couple and their friends represented the Hollywood or American establishment Manson blamed for his failures. It never crossed Charles Manson's mind that he needed to get an honest, legal job, and work to become successful. The murder victims, Sharon Tate, her guests, and the visitor were all strangers to the Manson Family killers.

Manson had coached his followers that the murders would trigger his apocalyptic prophecy of Helter Skelter, a race war between blacks and whites. Then Manson would rule the world. Insanity on psychopathic Manson's part.

Left: Sharon Tate, 26, dead, August 1969. Right: Sharon Tate, circa the mid-1960s.

In my opinion, Helter Skelter was just an excuse. Manson used to commit crimes of revenge. Manson even claimed that Helter Skelter, in his parole hearings, was just an after-hours nightclub at Spahn's Movie Ranch without a license. Helter Skelter was a hangout where the Manson Family and associates could sing, dance, drink, and do drugs.

But Manson's hippie-robot killers executed his mass murder plans. They created an infamous sensation because of the high profile of actress/model Sharon Tate, who was married to director Roman Polanski. Also murdered were Tate's guests: famous hairstylist Jay Sebring and coffee heiress Abigail Folger and her boyfriend, aspiring screenwriter Wojciech Frykowski. The first victim was Steven Parent, 18, a student who had been visiting the property's caretaker.

Charles Manson sent four of his followers to kill everybody in the Tate-Polanski house. He sent Charles "Tex" Watson to kill and run the killers, and followers Susan Atkins, Linda Kasabian, and Patricia Krenwinkel to kill everybody. Using a gun and knives, they slaughtered all five victims. Linda Kasabian was a lookout and did not shoot or stab anybody.

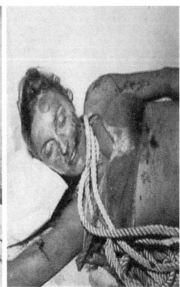

Left: Sharon Tate (center) in the *Valley of the Dolls* film. Right: Sharon Tate, dead, after the Manson Family killers murdered five at the Tate/Polanski home.

The most famous victim of the Tate mass murders was Sharon Tate, who was an aspiring starlet in Hollywood. Her career was advanced because of her successful movie director husband, Roman Polanski (*Rosemary's Baby*, *Chinatown*). Sharon Marie Tate, born January 24th, 1943, in Dallas, Texas, moved to Los Angeles in the early 1960s to seek acting work.

Sharon Tate's acting credits included parts in such films as *Eye of the Devil* (1966), *The Fearless Vampire Killers* (1967), *Valley of the Dolls* (1967), *The Wrecking Crew* (1969), and *The Thirteen Chairs* (1969). Polanski directed *The Fearless Vampire Killers*.

Left: Manson cult murder victims. Right: Tate/Polanski home, 1969.

Valley of the Dolls, based on pop culture, best-selling 1966 novel by Jacqueline Susann, sold 30 million books. Tate got a Golden Globe nomination. On a budget of under $5 million, *Valley of the Dolls* had a worldwide box-office gross of over $70 million, which was a big hit at the time. The theme song from the *Valley of the Dolls* movie by Dionne Warwick was an added haunting hit in the late 1960s.

The summer of 2019 marks the 50th anniversary of the Tate mass murders. Sharon Tate's profile is higher than a Hollywood starlet because she was one of the Manson Family's murder victims discovered on August 9th, 1969. The Tate house mass murders were particularly nasty, heinous, shocking, and evil because they were driven by Charles Manson's blood-thirsty aim of revenge.

Left: Susan Atkins, Patricia Krenwinkel, and Leslie Van Houten, who committed the Tate/LaBianca murders. Right: Charles "Tex" Watson, 1969 police mugshot. Watson led Patricia Krenwinkel and Susan Atkins into the Tate/Polanski home, aiming to murder all on the property.

The Tate mass murders were not as simple as if part of a robbery. They appeared to be devilish, cult murders with atrocious, monstrous, and wicked aspects. The papers reported that Sharon Tate, who was pregnant and almost ready to give birth, was wearing a bikini nightgown, had a cord around her neck, which was joined by the rope around Jay Sebring's neck and hung up.

The five Tate house victims were shot and stabbed many times, over-killed. It was a scary, terrorist-type homicide scene that created terror and fears among Hollywood actors, film/TV industry people, and the public in Los Angeles. Hollywood people hired extra bodyguards, bought guns, guard dogs, and additional security at their homes and offices as the Tate slaughter was publicized.

Left: Wojciech Frykowski, dead at the Tate/Polanski residence, 1969.
Right: Coffee heiress Abigail Folger, Frykowski's girlfriend, murdered.

The Manson Family's blood-thirsty massacre included a lot of bullet hits, repeated stabbing, and slashings, blood on the floors, and blood splatter on the walls. Sharon Tate suffered multiple-knife wounds. She was nine months pregnant, and her baby died with her.

Some of the press coverage was exaggerated and sensationalized. Some rumors were promoted that there were sex, drug, and witchcraft cult murderers on the loose. The caretaker, who survived in a separate little house on the property, was initially a suspect. Could the killers be connected to some drug gang or weird cult that could be part of the Hollywood subculture?

The next night, Manson ordered his killers into the LaBianca home to kill two more people. At first, these LaBianca murders were assumed to be the work of a copycat killer who created a "carbon copy" crime scene.

But because Susan Atkins and others had bragged or talked about the Tate/LaBianca murders, police eventually arrested Charles Manson, who ordered the mass murders, along with Susan Atkins, Patricia Krenwinkel, Linda Kasabian, a lookout who killed nobody, and Leslie Van Houten.

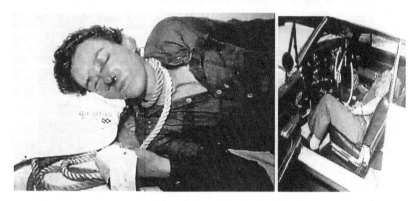

Left: Jay Sebring was discovered with a rope around his neck, thrown over a rafter, and connected to Sharon Tate's neck. Right: Steven Parent was killed in his car located on the Tate/Polanski driveway.

A problem for the police and the prosecutor was revealing the motive behind the Tate/LaBianca murders. Rumors, legends, and myths surrounded the Manson Family murders. What was the Manson commune? Some New Age from hell mystical, semi-religious hippie-and-drug-and-murder cult? Was it led by a short ex-con, the bearded-evil guru who ordered his zombie-like killers to murder upscale LA people and Hollywood stars?

The murders were made more gruesome and repugnant by the fact that words were scrawled on the walls and doors in the victims' blood. Usually, hippie communes were known for advocating peace, free love, and a mellow lifestyle.

But Charles Manson was a hardcore-career criminal who had spent half his life in prisons, jails, and reform schools. The Manson Family had been living a darker vision on the outer edge of Los Angeles at Spahn's Movie Ranch in a cult or semi-hippie commune known for loaded druggies, sex orgies, and mostly petty crime, credit-card fraud, burglary, drug dealing, and car theft.

Left: The Tate/Polanski home, 10050 Cielo Drive in Benedict Canyon, Los Angeles, where the Manson Family killers slaughtered Sharon Tate and four others. Right: Sharon Tate and Roman Polanski at their wedding.

Later, more murder cases resulted from the Manson cult followers and associates criminal activities. Hardcore members of the offbeat Manson Family crime group like Lynette "Squeaky" Fromme and Sandra Good objected to any adverse characterization of the Manson Family.

Fromme and Good claimed the Manson Family was just a New Age group devoted to Manson's music, dancing, singing, chanting, and concern about the environment (clean water, fresh air, protecting plants and animals).

In fact, in a recent interview, Lynette "Squeaky" Fromme still claims the Manson Family was just about Manson's music, dancing, singing, and protecting the environment. She was in complete denial about the sex orgies, crime, and murders committed by the Manson Family members.

Left: Charles Manson under arrest, circa 1970. Right: Victim Sharon Tate.

Fromme, in 2019, in YouTube interviews plugging her new book, claims the Manson Family was all about environmental issues, dancing, singing, and acting-out harmless stories. Squeaky said they didn't call themselves hippies, Manson Family, or anything. The Manson cult was just living Fromme said. Lynette answered softball questions focused on the positive.

After being released from prison after 34 years for attempting to murder President Ford, Fromme was amazed by smartphones. She said her relationships with the Manson Family members like Sandra Good were private, and she wouldn't discuss it. Squeaky favored releasing the Manson Family murderers from prison. Fromme said Sandra Good told her she thought Charles Manson preferred her. Fromme said Leslie Van Houten and Sandra Good were beautiful, and she was honored to be with them.

Aerial view of the Tate/Polanski house where the Manson Family killers murdered Sharon Tate, Steven Parent, Jay Sebring, Wojciech Frykowski, and Abigail Folger. The numbers mark the locations: 1) Abigail Folger; 2) Frykowski; 3) Tate and Sebring; 4) Parent; 5) Caretaker William Garretson was arrested here, later released uncharged.

Fromme said she was out with Charles Manson and Mary Brunner. Manson pointed out beautiful girls. But Fromme wasn't jealous, she just saw it as an expansion of love. Squeaky realized what was happening to the Earth, and Charles Manson was very sensitive to natural things. She said Charlie said when we were in the woods, animals like deer run from us because of what we've done to their habitat. Manson said we are animals' caretakers.

According to Lynette "Squeaky" Fromme, the Manson Family cult was like a combination of Boy Scout and Girl Scout troops, caring for the environment, doing good deeds, sharing love, singing, dancing, and living life spontaneously. Fromme said she is not allowed to contact Manson Family members. However, she got permission to call Catherine "Cappy" Gillies before she died.

Margot Robbie (left/right) played Sharon Tate (center) in a new film related to the Manson Family titled: *Once Upon a Time in Hollywood.*

Fromme said Charlie wanted to preserve the environment, the ocean, the sky, and the Earth. So, Charlie called his followers colors reflecting the environmental issues. She said the Redwoods were endangered by flooding and had shallow roots and might fall.

A large Redwood tree is a monument to history. She was critical of the lumber companies for clear-cutting the surroundings. Somehow the attempted murder of President Ford was related to Fromme's ecology concerns to raise awareness of the environment.

Left to right: Nancy Pitman, Lynette "Squeaky" Fromme, and Sandra Good. These Manson Family girls with guns all did prison time for murder, accessory to murder, or other dangerous felonies.

Squeaky said she started reading blogs about the Manson Family. But she dismissed them as projecting or talking about themselves. She says it short changes yourself to be critical of others and label them. So, the implication is that people should not be critical of the Manson Family crimes and murders. She talked about how she and Charlie and the Manson Family followers wanted a spiritual experience.

God is a cosmic consciousness inside us, including Charles Manson and Lynette "Squeaky" Fromme. Pain comes from not experiencing inner God-consciousness. Squeaky said people satirize the spiritual. She said it is important to use the word love like back in the 1960s. We need to get that garbage out of the ocean, Fromme said.

Left to right: Sharon Tate, Manson Family murder victim; Roman Polanski returned from Europe after his wife was murdered; Charles Manson police mugshot, circa 1969. According to Lynette "Squeaky" Fromme in a 2019 interview, the Manson Family was all about love and the environmental issue, which is the theme of the song *What About Me?* by Quicksilver Messenger Service. Does that comfort the friends, family, and loved ones of the Manson Family murder victims 50 years later?

Fromme said the song "What About Me?" (Quicksilver Messenger Service) from the old days relates to the environment issue and is a mournful song. She said it is up to you to figure out what you want. And if you don't find it, go someplace else. The song *What About Me?* is about comradery and protecting the environment Fromme said.

So maybe the friends, family, and loved ones of the Manson Family murder victims, according to Lynette "Squeaky" Fromme, should go to YouTube and listen to Quicksilver Messenger Service playing *What About Me?*

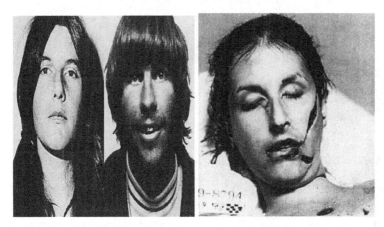

Left: Patricia Krenwinkel. Middle: Charles "Tex" Watson. Right: Abigail Folger, dead with lacerations to her face.

Because, from Fromme's viewpoint, the Manson Family was about protecting the environment and expressing love for the world. Squeaky's perspective sounds in line with Charles Manson's guru-psychobabble nonsense, such as life and death, which are the same thing. The Manson Family kills out of love. I recall Susan Atkins using these rationalizations while she was murdering to carry out Charles Manson's orders.

Patricia "Katie" Krenwinkel was one of three Manson cult killers who went into the Tate/Polanski home and committed murders. Krenwinkel, Susan Atkins, Leslie Van Houten, and Charles Manson were found guilty in the Tate/LaBianca murders. They were sentenced to death on March 29th, 1971, which was later commuted to life in prison.

Krenwinkel struggled with Abigail Folger, who ran out of the house and across the lawn. Krenwinkel chased down Folger and stabbed her many times. She said Folger implored her to stop by crying out, "I'm already dead." Manson picked Krenwinkel as one of the killers because he sensed she was his robot who blindly obeyed his orders and was capable of murdering innocent individuals.

Left: Patricia Krenwinkel, circa 1970. Middle: Krenwinkel after decades in prison. Right: Abigail Folger, dead, stabbed to death by Krenwinkel, 1969.

Paradoxically, Krenwinkel distanced herself from Manson quickly once she was in prison. After 23 years in prison, in 1994, Krenwinkel was interviewed and said, "I wake up every day knowing that I'm a destroyer of the most precious thing, which is life, and I do that because that's what I deserve, is to wake up every morning and know that." Although she has sounded remorseful, Krenwinkel has been repeatedly turned down for parole.

In January 1968, Tate and Polanski got married. But on the night of August 8th, 1969, Polanski was in Europe working on a film. Tate is expected to give birth in a week or two. Polanski had asked his friend Wojciech Frykowski to look out for his wife, Tate.

It was tragic that Sharon Tate's friends, keeping her company, were murdered along with her. Coffee heiress Abigail Folger, Frykowski's girlfriend, Tate's ex-boyfriend, celebrity hairstylist Jay Sebring, and Steven Parent, who was visiting the caretaker.

Left: Patricia Krenwinkel, in a photo taken after she had spent a few years in prison, seemed to be displaying a subtle hand gesture similar to those Manson Family members outside the courtroom used to indicate solidarity and honor to Charles Manson, their imprisoned guru. Right: Two Manson followers displayed the same finger gesture, circa the 1970s. So, it is unclear just when and if Krenwinkel honestly broke with Charles Manson and the Manson cult killers. The problem with antisocial or psychopathic killers, whose defense is drug abuse and brainwashing by Charles Manson in this case, is revealing and confirming the truth.

Because Terry Melcher, the record producer who rejected Manson for a record deal, and his girlfriend actress Candice Bergen, had occupied the Tate/Polanski home before Tate/Polanski, Manson picked the house as a revenge target. Manson was bent on punishing affluent Hollywood people or any successful establishment family. The Hollywood record industry had passed on making Manson a rock star, and so Charles Manson would teach them a deadly lesson.

Ironically, Manson probably became more infamous and well-known as a criminal icon after his murder conviction than he ever would have been as a musician. Some Hollywood artists said Manson had some talent as a songwriter of quirky or weird lyrics. Sort of an ex-con version of Bob Dylan.

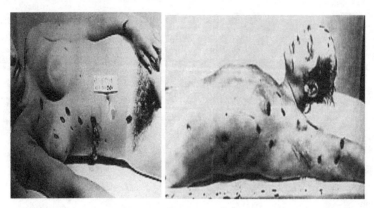

Left: Abigail Folger stabbed and slashed to death. Right: Wojciech Frykowski, dead after over 50 stabbing wounds. Both lovers murdered the same night.

But Manson was missing some ingredients such as a willingness to work at an honest, legit job, a cooperative personality, and the discipline needed to struggle to become a working musician and possibly a rock star. Manson has been the focus of many books, films, and documentaries. Vincent Bugliosi, the LA County Assistant District Attorney who prosecuted the Manson Family killers, co-wrote *Helter Skelter*, a 1974 best-selling, true-crime book.

Strangely enough, in 1977, Polanski pled guilty to drugging and engaging in unlawful sex with a 13-year-old girl while in a hot tub at Jack Nicholson's place. Absurdly, Polanski took a page from Charles Manson's book on underage sex with young girls. Although Manson was never severely punished for statutory rape or exploiting underage girls.

Charlie did some jail time for pimping and transporting girls across state lines for prostitution, however. But during the 1960s, the Summer of Love, and the hippie free love era, Manson was able to enjoy sex orgies with his followers who were often underage.

Left: Sharon Tate. Right: Roman Polanski inspected his home and noted "PIG" written in blood on the front door by Manson's killers.

Polanski's criminal sex charge happened decades before the Me-Too Movement against sex crimes, and so Hollywood didn't seem to mind. Polanski was awarded the Best Director Oscar for *The Pianist*. It had to be awarded in absentia because Polanski fled the USA to avoid a possible long prison sentence in 1977. Since Polanski does not want to get arrested again, he has remained in France since 1977.

The details of the Tate murders:

On the night of August 8th, 1969, Sharon Tate went out to dinner with three friends: her ex-lover and hairstylist Jay Sebring, coffee heiress Abigail Folger and her boyfriend, aspiring screenwriter Wojciech Frykowski. They left the El Coyote restaurant and returned to the Tate-Polanski home at 10050 Cielo Drive in Benedict Canyon, Los Angeles.

Left to right: Charles Manson, Patricia Krenwinkel, Charles "Tex" Watson, Krenwinkel, Leslie Van Houten, and Susan Atkins. The Manson Family girls, who were scripted and programmed by Charlie Manson, were singing, happy-go-lucky, and untroubled while they were on trial for mass murders. Their cold, cheerful attitude turned off the public.

Since Sharon Tate was 8.5 months pregnant and her husband, Roman Polanski, who was directing The Day of the Dolphin in London, asked his friends Frykowski and Folger to stay at his home with Tate. Polanski was expected back on August 12th.

Charles Manson had ordered four of his cult followers to kill everybody in the Tate/Polanski house, which Manson had associated with Terry Melcher, who turned him down on a record deal. Manson was angry the Hollywood players had passed on, making him a rock star.

So, to Charles Manson, if things don't seem to be going your way, you do a mass murder to fix it and get revenge. So, Manson told Watson and his crew to murder the occupants of the house in a disgusting, horrific, and "witchy" way.

Manson's killer crew arrived at 10050 Cielo Drive just after midnight, August 9th, 1969. Charles "Tex" Watson was the boss of the murderers, including Patricia Krenwinkel, Susan Atkins, and Linda Kasabian.

Left: Steven Parent's body was found in his car in the Tate/Polanski home driveway. Middle: William Garretson, property caretaker, who lived in the property's guest house was initially a suspect in the murders. Right: Steven Parent, who was visiting the caretaker Garretson, was about to drive out of the gate when Watson murdered him.

Kasabian was not hyped-up and capable of killing people, and she was left to be a lookout. Tex Watson later claimed he was driving off a lot of speedy drugs. And it seemed that, besides being loaded on drugs, Susan Atkins and Patricia Krenwinkel were brainwashed and loaded-gun robots who marched to Manson's orders.

The first killed was Steven Parent, who was exiting the Tate/Polanski property in his car after visiting the property caretaker. Watson cut and shot Parent to death. Next, Watson entered the Tate/Polanski house and spotted Frykowski sleeping on the couch. Tex kicked Frykowski in the head. Watson yelled, "I'm the devil, and I'm here to do the devil's business!" when Frykowski challenged him.

Left: Sharon Tate, up-and-coming name actress. Right: In the living room, Sharon Tate and Jay Sebring were murdered. The rope was tied around their necks and hung over a high ceiling beam.

At gunpoint, Watson had a .22 caliber revolver, Watson herded the others into the living room. Tate and Sebring were tied together with ropes around their necks. strung up over the ceiling beams. Watson shot Sebring after he complained about the rough treatment of Tate, who was visibly very pregnant. Watson and Krenwinkel admitted stabbing the victims multiple times.

Susan Atkins later claimed she stabbed Sharon Tate and then changed her story. Atkins, years later, stuck to the story that Tex Watson did the shooting and stabbing. Perhaps Atkins just held Tate down as Watson stabbed her. In the fury of the struggle, Frykowski and Folger managed to escape the house and run across the lawn.

Tate mass murder victims. Left to right: Wojciech Frykowski, Sharon Tate, Steven Parent, Jay Sebring, and Abigail Folger.

Both Krenwinkel and Watson chased them down and stabbed them many times to kill them. Folger, it was reported, was stabbed 28 times. Frykowski was stabbed 51 times and shot. Inside the house, Watson stabbed Sharon Tate at least 16 times while Atkins held her down. Tate begged for her life and offered herself as a hostage to protect her baby and was said to cry out, "Mother...mother..." as she was dying. Folger sobbed as Krenwinkel stabbed her and howled, "I'm already dead!"

Atkins was reported to use a towel and Tate's blood to write "PIG" on the front door. Manson had ordered them to "leave a sign...something witchy," and that was the motivation.

Manson's theory was that writing words in blood would trigger Helter Skelter because blacks would be blamed for mass murder. Then a race war would happen, the blacks would win, and then the Manson Family would take over the world.

Manson said blacks didn't have the experience to rule the world, so he would be the world's boss. But, on a deeper level below con-artist Manson's fake-apocalyptic vision, Manson just wanted revenge against the Hollywood entertainment industry people because he didn't get his rock star record deal.

William Garretson, the Tate/Polanski property caretaker, born August 24th, 1949, was a prosecution witness in the Manson Family murder trial.

The following morning, Winifred Chapman, the Tate/Polanski housekeeper, discovered the dead bodies. There were six deaths, including Tate's unborn baby boy caused by the Manson Family home invasion aimed at mass murder.

Let's circle back to the start of the Tate home invasion. Tex Watson had been to the Tate/Polanski residence at least once in the past. He knew the layout and had checked out the phone lines. Watson climbed a telephone pole at the entrance gate and cut the phone line to stop anybody calling for help. It was just after midnight when Watson, Krenwinkel, Atkins, and Kasabian arrived. So, it was August 9th, 1969.

Their car was then backed down the hill below the estate and parked. The four walked back to the residence. They climbed an embankment to the right of the gate to get to the grounds. This was to avoid either an electrified gate or a rigged alarm.

Left: Gated entrance. Right: Tate/Polanski residence grounds.

As Watson, Atkins, Krenwinkel, and Kasabian were entering the Tate/Polanski residence grounds, there were approaching headlights. Watson ordered the girls to hide in the nearby bushes. He flagged down Steven Parent, 18, and ordered him to stop. Parent was coming from the guest house where he had visited William Garretson, the property caretaker.

Watson held Parent at gunpoint. Parent, frightened, implored Watson not to hurt him and promised not to tell. Watson cut him with a knife and then shot him four times fatally in the chest and abdomen. He sent Kasabian to look for an open window at the house.

She couldn't find any open windows. Watson sent her back to the gate to be a lookout. Watson cut a screen off a window, took the screen off, and entered through the window. He let Atkins and Krenwinkel in through the front door. As I said, when Frykowski woke up on the couch, asked who they were and what they wanted, Watson kicked him in the head and told him, "I'm the devil, and I'm here to do the devil's business!"

Left: Tate murder scene. Open window Watson used to enter the Tate/Polanski house. Right: Living room showing Sebring roped to a ceiling beam.

Watson sent the two women, Atkins, and Krenwinkel, to search the house and bring everybody into the living room. They got Tate, Sebring, and Folger into the living room. After tying Tate and Sebring together by their necks, Watson shot and stabbed Sebring to death. Folger was taken back to get her purse, and they took her $70 in cash.

Frykowski, bound with a towel, broke loose, struggled with Atkins, who was stabbing his legs with her knife, fought his way out the front door, and ran across the lawn. Watson chased him down, shot, and stabbed him to death. In hitting him on the head with the gun butt several times, he broke the gun's right grip.

All the weird screams, shots, and fighting drew Kasabian up the driveway to the house. She told Atkins at the front door that somebody was coming in hopes that this false alarm would stop the mass murders.

'RITUALISTIC SLAYINGS'

Sharon Tate, Four Others Murdered

BY DIAL TORGERSON

Film star Sharon Tate, another woman and three men were found slain Saturday, their bodies scattered around a Benedict Canyon estate in what police said resembled a ritualistic mass murder.

The victims were shot, stabbed or throttled. On the front door of the home, written in blood, was one word: "Pig."

Police arrested the only one left alive on the property—a 19-year-old houseboy. He was booked on suspicion of murder.

Killed were:

—Miss Tate, 26, a star of "Valley of the Dolls" and wife of Roman Polanski, director of "Rosemary's Baby." She was eight months pregnant. He is in England.

—Abigail Folger, 26, heiress to the Folger's Coffee family.

—Jay Sebring, 35, once Miss Tate's fiance, a Hollywood hair stylist credited with launching the trend to hair styling for men.

— Voityck Frokowski, 37, who worked with Polanski in Polish films before they came to Hollywood.

—Steven Parent, 18, of El Monte, who left his home Friday morning after telling his family he was going to "go to Beverly Hills."

A maid, Mrs. Winifred Chapman, went to the sprawling home at the end of Cielo Drive at 8:30 a.m. to begin her day's work. What she found sent her running to a neighbor's home in a state of shock.

In a white two-door sedan in the driveway was the body of the young man, slumped back in the driver's seat, shot to death.

On the lawn in front of the ranch-style home was the body of Frokowski.

Twenty yards away, under a fir tree on the well-trimmed lawn, was the body of Miss Folger, clad in a nightgown.

In the living room, dressed in underwear—bikini panties and a brassiere—was Miss Tate. A bloodied nylon cord was around her neck. It ran over a beam in the open-beam ceiling and was tied around the neck of Sebring, whose body lay nearby. Over Sebring's head was a black

Sharon Tate

Related story, pictures on Page B.

Please Turn to Page 18, Col. 1

Left: Steve McQueen, a former lover of Sharon Tate, Tate, Polanski. Right: Panic swept Hollywood after news of the mass murders.

Inside, Folger had escaped out the bedroom door. She ran away from Krenwinkel, who charged after her with her knife. Krenwinkel caught up to her, tackled her, knocked her to the ground, and stabbed her multiple times to death.

Watson and Atkins then proceeded to hold Tate down and stab her to death. Atkins wrote the "witchy" word ("PIG") on the front door in Tate's blood with a towel, as Manson had instructed.

On the drive back to Spahn's Ranch, the Tate murder crew changed out of their bloody clothing and tossed the clothes and the gun and knives down a hillside.

As of January 2020, the Manson Family Tate killers have been punished. Patricia Krenwinkel and Charles "Tex" Watson are still in prison 50 years later, Charles Manson, and Susan Atkins both died in prison.

Left: The media reflected the shock over the Tate mass murders. Right: Linda Kasabian drove the killers to the Tate house. She later got immunity from prosecution for testifying against Manson and the cult killers.

The LAPD investigated the Tate mass murders. A memo was sent to Lt. R.J. Helder, Supervisor of Investigations, Robbery-Homicide Division. Police speculated on the cause of the Tate mass murders, August 9, 1969, with three theories.

1. The first theory was that just after midnight, about 12:30 a.m., the killers climbed a telephone pole by the front gate, cut the phone wires, and pressed a button inside to open the gate. Steven Parent, who was driving down the driveway, encountered them. The killers shot and cut him with a knife. Hired killers murdered Sharon Tate and her guests – Jay Sebring, Wojciech Frykowski, and Abigail Folger.
2. The second theory is that the killers were delivering or collecting money for various types of narcotics. An argument ensued over money or the possibility of bad drugs. As a result, Tate, Sebring, Frykowski, Folger, and Steven Parent were murdered.
3. The third theory is that the suspects went to the Polanski home to commit a residential robbery. Once at the location, a fight erupted between the suspects and the victims. The four victims were killed. As the suspects left the home, they observed Steven Parent, stopped him, and killed him to eliminate an eyewitness. The killers then cut the phone wires on the way out – to give them time to escape.

These were working theories LAPD followed until they got evidence connecting the Manson Family cult killers to the Tate mass murders. The LAPD officers repeatedly made mistakes in their investigation, mucking up the crime scene, and ignoring obvious clues. The LA law enforcement teams didn't cooperate, slowing down the investigation, and almost letting Charles Manson and his killer crew get away with murder.

Chapter 35

Dr. Dawson: Sharon Tate pled to be spared so she could give birth to her baby. She offered herself as a hostage. Sharon wanted to save her unborn child.

But your cold-blooded killers ignored her plea and stabbed her 16 or more times while she cried, "Mother, mother..." while she was being killed. I recall reading that Susan Atkins said something cold to Tate like she didn't give a damn about her baby.

Charles Manson: Sounds like Atkins. Susan's a cold cunt.

Dr. Dawson: As your killer crew left Spahn's Movie Ranch, you told the women to "leave a sign – something witchy." So Susan used a towel to write "Pig" on the front door in Tate's blood. After the killings, your cult followers got rid of their bloody clothing and weapons. Susan ended up at Sybil Brand Institute – a prison for women – and shocked her cellmates by confessing to the murders.

Charles Manson: That dumb bitch, Atkins. She never could keep her big mouth shut. Fuckin' snitch. I got no snitchin' on my jacket. Do my time clean.

Sharon Tate (in front) in *Valley of The Dolls*. Sharon and Roman Polanski at their wedding reception.

Dr. Dawson: Atkins told her cellmates she killed Tate. Like she was proud of it. But later she told a different story to her defense attorney, prosecutor Vincent Bugliosi, and before the grand jury. She claimed Tex did all the stabbing.

Even though later Tex said he alone did the stabbing of Tate, the prosecutor was convinced Susan also stabbed Tate. And you were convicted of masterminding all these murders. What do you have to say about that?

Charles Manson: The reason they locked me in a cage is because the justice system, judge, prosecutor – they're sellin' fear to the public. They gotta lock me in a cage and call me a criminal. It ain't real. Society raise them druggies to do some murders. Nothin' to do with me.

(At this point I move to a later interview.)

Sharon Tate and Roman Polanski (left). Sharon, pregnant (right).

Dr. Dawson: "Hey, Charlie. What's happening?"

Charles Manson: "Sorry, I'm late Dr. Dawson...I've been in 'the hole'...Still kind of dazed..." (He was smarmy, gave me a slimy smile.)

Dr. Dawson: "No problem. Smoke?"

I passed him a pack of cigarettes and lit a smoke for him. I also poured him a cup of coffee into a foam plastic cup from a thermos I'd brought and set some little packs of powdered cream and sugar in front of him.

He puffed on the cigarette and stirred several sugars into his coffee. I liked to make an effort to build rapport with inmates I interviewed by offering them smokes, coffee, and candy bars.

Because Manson was a psychopath, he was glib and superficial in his conversational style. He relaxed quickly and began chatting with me. Charles soon revealed himself to be egocentric, grandiose and displayed some wide mood swings. He stroked his chin at times, grinned, and winked at me.

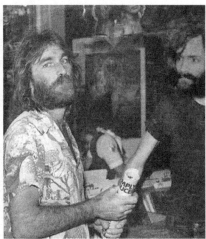

Dennis Wilson of The Beach Boys (left) and Wilson with Charles Manson (right) in 1968. Wilson played some of Manson's songs for music producers. But Manson never got a record deal. Charlie Manson and his "Family" of druggie girls sponged off Wilson and cost him over $100,000 for STD medical bills and a car Manson's girls crashed.

Dr. Dawson: "I heard you're being punished for contraband – guards found smuggled drugs in your cell? And you wouldn't explain how the marijuana got there?"

Charles Manson: "I am no snitch – I'm a brother in prisons all my life. No snitching on my jacket. I walk it like I talk it – no asking nobody for protection…"

Dr. Dawson: "Back in 1967, at age 32, you came up for parole. You'd been teaching yourself to play guitar, had written some songs, experimented with Scientology, and dabbled in Buddhism while you were in jail—"

Charles Manson: "I warned them. I told the warden not to release me. After all my life had been spent locked up, I couldn't adjust to the free world—"

Terry Melcher, 27, the music producer son of Doris Day whom Manson pitched record deals to. Terry Melcher and his girlfriend, Candice Bergen (right).

Dr. Dawson: "But you started with a bang. You went to San Francisco during the Summer of Love. You mastered the counterculture like a sharp con man. You picked-up the psychedelic gobbledygook, combined it with some jargon from Scientology, Buddhism, and New Age psychobabble."

"Soon you were a guru attracting a band of druggie dropouts – mostly naïve and emotionally insecure young women who adored, revered, and worshipped you."

Charles Manson: (He suddenly got antagonistic, his lips curled in disgust, his eyes blazed murderously at me.) "Doctor, society shaped me from a lump of clay into the mad-dog devil killer. The free world turned me into a crazy homicidal fiend."

Terry Melcher and his mother, Doris Day (left). Candice Bergen and Terry Melcher (right). Charlie Manson was angry when Melcher passed on doing a record deal with him. Terry rented the Tate-Polanski house before Sharon and Roman rented it.

Dr. Dawson: "Before I ask you about the murders, let's trace your journey from San Francisco in an old bus. You set up a dubious commune in shabby old Spahn Movie Ranch just outside of Los Angeles. Sex orgies and getting loaded on drugs was your main activity?

You were the messiah with an apocalyptic vision – you'd provoke Helter Skelter which would be African-Americans rioting, fighting whites. The Manson Family would hide in a cave under Death Valley and later come out and take over the world because you're superior. Isn't that a crazy plan?"

Charles Manson: (His eyes smoldered, he directed a cold stare at me.) "I live in hell - the underworld. I never told people what to do. They know what they are doing.

Sandra "Blue" Good und Lynette "Red" Fromme (left) – Manson cult girls. Charlie Manson pimped out his young women to stars like Dennis Wilson in hopes of getting a record deal and as payment for hanging out at Wilson's Pacific Palisades home. The Beach Boys – Dennis Wilson is at the right rear.

If they got their head up their asses, then don't hang with me because I'm very cruel, I'm very malicious. (He mixed English and Spanish next.) I'm very mal hombre, wicked. I'm a matador in a bullring. I run the bull – the nucleus of the world.

Don't play with me. I kill people. I'm too evil. I'm a corrupt guy. I'm the bandito. I'm crooked. I'm everything corrupt...You wanna make something out of it, Doc?"

Dr. Dawson: "How did you go from this sexually liberated, spiritual guru to multiple murderers? Didn't your music goal play a part in this? Some of the murders happened in a home where a music producer lived – Terry Melcher who passed on, rejected you for a record deal?"

Charles Manson (left) was escorted by officers while en route to court in 1971 after he was indicted as a serial murderer. Susan Atkins, convicted mass murderer and once a member of the Charles Manson "Family", stands behind a fenced-in women's prison on August 20th, 1981. Susan died of cancer on September 24th, 2009, at the Central California Women's Facility, Chowchilla, California.

Charles Manson: "You're getting ahead of the story. Go back to the Beach Boys. Pacific Coast Highway to Pacific Palisades."

Dr. Dawson: "Beach Boy Dennis Wilson picked up two of your Manson family girls who were hitchhiking on Pacific Coast Highway. I know the area. It's early in 1968. You turn up Sunset Boulevard, take a winding road into Pacific Palisades—"

Charles Manson: "The Manson family lived with Beach Boy Dennis Wilson for a time—"

Dr. Dawson: "But you threatened him with a bullet? My notes show Dennis Wilson moved out after the death threats. You made some business calls on Terry Melcher – Doris Day's son – who was a record producer. He lived in Benedict Canyon on Cielo Drive in a big, hillside mansion. Melcher moved out that summer of 1968."

Charles Manson (left) as a boy. Manson in 1969 (middle). Manson, age 80, Star, 26, his fiancee (right photo). Star was in love with a lunatic 54 years older than her.

Chapter 36

LaBianca murders. After the massacre at the Tate/Polanski home where Manson's killing crew murdered five people and one unborn baby, Manson ordered some of his followers to join him the next night of August 9th, 1969. Manson directed them from Spahn's Movie Ranch to 3301 Waverly Drive, Los Angeles, the residence of Leno and Rosemary LaBianca. The house was next door to a house where some of the Manson Family had visited in 1968.

Six Manson cult killers arrived at the LaBianca home. Including Charles Manson, Steve "Clem" Grogan, Leslie Van Houten, Susan Atkins, Patricia Krenwinkel, Charles "Tex" Watson, and Linda Kasabian. LaBiancas lived in the Los Feliz section of Los Angeles. Leno LaBianca was a supermarket manager, and his wife, Rosemary LaBianca, co-owned a dress shop.

Manson told his followers he would show them how to do it. He was not satisfied with the Tate murders because of the panic and chaos. Charles Manson and Charles "Tex" Watson went into the LaBianca's residence and tied up Leno and Rosemary LaBianca at gunpoint. Manson told them they would not be hurt. This was just a robbery. Their heads were covered with pillowcases.

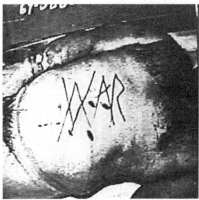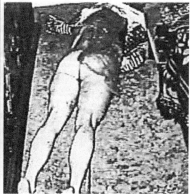

Left: Leno LaBianca's body had "WAR" carved into it. Right: Rosemary LaBianca, found in her bedroom, had a bloody pillowcase over her head, and a lamp cord was tied around her neck.

Charles Manson then left the LaBianca's house, returned to the car, and sent Patricia Krenwinkel and Leslie Van Houten into the home. His instructions to them were to kill the couple. Manson figured if he could get other people to kill for him and he was not actually at the scene while they were being killed, that he could avoid responsibility for the crimes.

Watson sent Krenwinkel and Van Houten into the bedroom, where Rosemary LaBianca had been left. Watson then returned to Leno LaBianca and began stabbing him with a bayonet, thrusting it into Leno's throat first. He heard some noises of a struggle in the bedroom and returned to help the girls murder Rosemary. Rosemary was swinging a lamp tied to her neck around to fend off Krenwinkel and Van Houten.

Watson stabbed her several times with the bayonet and returned to the living room to finish off Leno, who he stabbed at least 12 times with the blade. Watson then cut "WAR" into his exposed abdomen. Watson then returned to the bedroom, where Krenwinkel was stabbing Mrs. LaBianca with a kitchen knife.

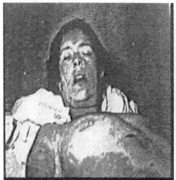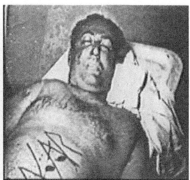

Pictured are post-mortem photos of Rosemary and Leno LaBianca.

He told Van Houten to join in the attack, and she used a knife to stab her about 16 times in her back and buttocks. Manson had left orders to make sure everybody was involved in the actual stabbing and killing. Many of Mrs. LaBianca's 41 stab wounds were delivered post-mortem.

Watson showered while Krenwinkel used the blood of the LaBiancas to write RISE and DEATH TO PIGS on the walls and HEALTER SKELTER (spelled Helter wrong) on the refrigerator door. Krenwinkel gave Leno LaBianca 14 puncture wounds with a fork, which she left stuck in his stomach. She also jammed a steak knife into his throat. Manson and the others (Kasabian, Atkins, and Grogan) drove off, leaving them to hitchhike back to Spahn's Ranch.

Manson, who was blood-thirsty and looking to retaliate at the Hollywood establishment and successful people because he was denied his rock-star record deal, instructed Kasabian to drive around looking for more people to kill. They drove to an actor's place in Venice, who was a friend of Kasabian. Manson was jabbering about killing another "piggy" to trigger the black-white Helter Skelter revolution.

Left to right: Rosemary and Leno LaBianca, murder victims. Convicted murderers: Charles "Tex" Watson, Patricia Krenwinkel, and Leslie Van Houten.

Manson dropped Kasabian, Atkins, and Grogan off at the actor's apartment building and drove back to Spahn's Ranch. His instructions were to kill the "piggy" actor and hitchhike back to Spahn's Ranch. Kasabian led them into the apartment building but purposely knocked on the wrong door to avoid another murder. A stranger came to the door, and they abandoned the mission and hitchhiked back to Spahn's Ranch.

The Tate/LaBianca murders reflect the dark side of the Hollywood-rock-star dream, which became Manson's nightmare of bloody payback to the music industry when Charles Manson's record deal didn't happen. When Manson's rock-star dream shattered in his mind, he got his followers to help him do mass murder.

Charles "Tex" Watson, Patricia Krenwinkel, and Leslie Van Houten delivered the fatal stabbings to Leno and Rosemary LaBianca following the directions Charles Manson gave them.

Left to right: Steve "Clem" Grogan, Susan Atkins, Patricia Krenwinkel, and Charles Manson. Kasabian, following Manson's instructions, drove with Grogan, Atkins, and Manson from the LaBiancas' residence to Venice, looking for more people to murder.

As of this time in 2019, Manson died in 2017, and the three others are still in prison about 50 years later. Watson, Krenwinkel, and Leslie Van Houten have been denied parole. Leslie Van Houten had been recommended for release on parole, but California's governor denied her release on parole in 2019.

Van Houten has received college degrees while incarcerated and been a model prisoner. Van Houten, who went into graphic detail about her role with Krenwinkel and Watson in the LaBianca murders, has told the parole panel: "I don't let myself off the hook. I don't find parts in any of this that makes me feel the slightest bit good about myself."

She also said Manson wanted the LaBianca killings to be more vicious, horrific, and dreadful than the Tate murders the night before. Van Houten also revealed, "Tex told Pat and me to go into the kitchen and get knives, and we took Mrs. LaBianca into the bedroom and put a pillowcase over her head. I wrapped the lamp cord around her head to hold the pillowcase on her head. I went to hold her down."

Left: "Healter Skelter" (spelled Helter wrong) and "Death To Pigs" was written on the wall and refrigerator using the LaBiancas' blood.

Van Houten said Mrs. LaBianca called out her husband's name, and at that point, she and Krenwinkel stabbed her in the torso. She received 14 to 16 stab wounds. Years ago, Van Houten was turned down for parole. Governor Brown who wrote:

"Both her role in these extraordinarily brutal crimes and her inability to explain her willing participation in such horrific violence cannot be overlooked and lead me to believe she remains an unacceptable risk to society if released."

Generally, the victims' surviving family members and loved ones have been against releasing the Manson Family killers on parole. For example, Cory LaBianca, Leno's daughter, and Rosemary's stepdaughter said, in a telephone interview with a journalist, that she very much disagreed with the parole board's decision to recommend Van Houten's release.

She said, "We all need to be held responsible for our behavior. The least we can do, for someone who commits a crime against another human being, is to keep them in jail. Maybe Leslie Van Houten has been a model prisoner. But you know what, we still suffer our loss."

Left: Door from Spahn's Movie Ranch with "Helter Skelter" written on it. Manson claimed, in a parole hearing, that Helter Skelter was an after-hours club at Spahn's Ranch where there was music, dancing, drinking, and drugging. Right: The LaBianca residence, circa August 1969.

Similarly, some of the Tate murder victims' family members have actively been against parole release for the Manson Family killers. The LA District Attorney and Sharon Tate's sister Debra Tate delivered 140,000 signatures of people opposing Van Houten's release to Governor Brown's office. Debra Tate also spoke at parole board hearings against the Manson Family killers' release.

While the Tate/Polanski house on Cielo Drive has been torn down and replaced with a new house and a new address, the LaBianca's home is still standing with a changed address. The Spahn's Ranch burned down in the 1970 wildfires. Some of the Manson Family members reflected on their experiences at Spahn's Movie Ranch with mixed feelings.

Left to right: Lynette "Squeaky" Fromme, Patricia Krenwinkel, Susan Atkins and Leslie Van Houten. These women had varied memories of the Manson Family experiences, such as at Spahn's Ranch and how Charles Manson conditioned them with sex orgies, drug abuse, and rock and roll.

Lynette "Squeaky" Fromme, who still is in denial, said the Manson Family cult was a wonderful group devoted to peace and love, dancing, singing, chanting, and protecting the environment. Her conviction for the attempted murder of President Ford and the 34 years she served in prison was just an ecology protest. To Squeaky, the Manson cult was like a Girl and Boy Scout troop.

Susan Atkins said, "We were just like wood nymphs and wood creatures. We would run through the woods with flowers in our hair, and Charlie would have a small flute." Atkin's memory is like Fromme's fantasy fairy tale of the Manson cult followers just doing harmless dancing, singing, chanting, and being in touch with nature.

Leslie Van Houten said life at the Spahn's Movie Ranch involved role-playing and exercises Manson directed. Manson's followers pretended to be pirates, cowboys, gypsies, and re-enacted the crucifixion with Manson playing Jesus Christ. Because Manson's Family was gullible and loaded on drugs, it worked.

Left to right: Catherine Gillies (left rear), Sandra Good, Lynette Fromme, Ruth Ann Moorehouse, circa 1970. These alienated, middle-class young women drop-outs were examples of Charles Manson's brainwashing. They had cut an X in their foreheads in solidarity with Manson. They were devoted to Manson because of hundreds of drug trips, sex orgies, and rock and roll. The Summer of Love's dark side was The Summer of Murder.

Patricia Krenwinkel said Manson programmed them by getting them loaded on drugs and telling them to forget what their parents, their mother, father had told them or conditioned in them. Lots of free sex, sex orgies with drugs sort of broke down their old moral hang-ups.

There was a significant impact on the Hollywood scene as a result of the Tate and LaBianca murders. Many movie stars, name actors, and Hollywood players in the music, TV/film industry were frightened or in a panic. They wondered if they would be the next murder victim.

Newspapers reflected the blood-thirsty cult's crimes of murder.

For instance, Frank Sinatra was reported to be in hiding, Mia Farrow was too scared to attend Sharon Tate's funeral, and Tony Bennett moved from a Beverly Hills Hotel bungalow and into an inside suite for greater security. Steve McQueen began carrying a gun in his sports car. It seemed like the decade of The Summer of Love had ended on a dark note.

One Los Angeles paper summed up the era: "Live freaky, die freaky... It was the dark side of paradise. People could shake their fingers and say, 'This is where your high-living, rich, hippie, movie-star lifestyle gets you. This is where the drug culture gets you.' It's the boomerang effect, the wages of sin."

While Patricia Krenwinkel, Leslie Van Houten, and Charles "Tex" Watson are still in prison 50 years later, as of January 2020, Charles Manson has died in prison. So the LaBianca family has received some justice. Ironically, LaBiancas' daughter supports parole for Watson.

Chapter 37

Charles Manson: "Goddamn owner of that house kicked me out. I stopped by looking for Melcher. He promised me a record deal."

Dr. Dawson: "From my research, Melcher and some other music business contact visited you at Spahn's Movie Ranch where the Manson Family lived? There was some interest in a record deal with you? You put together an album of your songs, a demo? Recorded at a studio?"

Charles Manson: "Sons of bitches stole my best music. I've written hundreds of songs. What else do I do in jail?"

Dr. Dawson: "Stolen? Sounds like Hollywood."

Charles Manson: "But I hated recording music. Down in the studio, they jam the mike in your face. Told me to come down to the studio to tape some of my songs. It's hard to sing into the microphone at just the right number of inches from it."

"The mike looks like a dick in my face. Phallic symbol. My unconscious mind is exploding. (He blows on his finger as if it's the mike. Laughs. He makes sucking sounds like oral sex.) Like music is subliminal – it streams and pours through me!"

Charlie Manson (left) at Spahn's Movie Ranch ca 1968. During the 1960s, Candice Bergen (middle) dated and lived with Terry Melcher, a music producer and the son of Doris Day. The couple lived at 10050 Cielo Drive in L.A. where Sharon Tate and others were murdered by Manson's murder crew. Terry and Candice had moved out to a place in Malibu. Doris Day and her son, Terry Melcher (right).

Dr. Dawson: "I'm not going to let you off the hook on those murders. Are you ready for some tough questions?"

Charles Manson: "Like I always say... From the world of darkness, I did loose demons and devils in the power of scorpions to torment...."

Dr. Dawson: "Charlie, how many people have you murdered or ordered your cult members to kill? Don't bullshit me! Do you feel remorse for those people you murdered?"

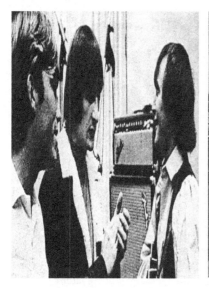 

Terry Melcher (left) and the Byrds in a recording studio in 1965. Candice Bergen and Terry Melcher (right).

Charles Manson: "Don't screw with me, Doc!" (Charles got up and paced the room. He raised his voice to a shrill, very angry level.) "Remorse? Goddamn, you establishment pricks have done everything in the world to me. Doesn't that give me equal rights to defend myself?"

(A guard yelled at Manson to sit down and calm down. Manson sat back down and leaned across the table and shot me a venomous look, his eyes narrowed with contempt, and he snarled as he continued speaking to me.)

"Who the hell are you to stick a finger in my eye? You people would convict a bacon-cheese burger of murder and the people wouldn't question it...Maybe I'll order my cult to cut your head off and mail it home to your old lady!"

Beach Boys record producer Terry Melcher, December 9, 1969. Melcher was indirectly involved in the Manson murder case. Charlie Manson originally planned to kill Terry because he rejected Charlie for a record deal. But Melcher had moved from the Cielo Drive home later rented to Sharon Tate and Roman Polanski. Dennis Wilson (front) and The Beach Boys.

Dr. Dawson: "You'll take the consequences. First, no more coffee or cigarettes for you." (I moved the pack of cigarettes and the thermos of coffee over next to me. Manson cracked up laughing at my little joke.)

Charles Manson: "You treat me right, I'll treat you right. You shit on me, then I gotta shit comin'."

Chapter 38

Gary Hinman murder. Gary Allen Hinman, born in
Colorado, on December 24th, 1934, was murdered by some
Manson Family followers on July 27th, 1969. Hinman was nice to
a fault. He was book smart in graduating from college with a
degree in chemistry.

But he was not streetwise. Hinman had a reputation as being kind,
gentle, and intellectual. He made the fatal mistake of opening up
his home to street people and assorted hippies, struggling
musicians or actors, druggies, and criminals like the Manson
Family. Did you need a place to crash? Well, overly nice guy Gary
Hinman will let you crash and hang-out in his Topanga Canyon
house.

Because Hinman was a musician and worked at a music shop. He
taught aspiring musicians how to play musical instruments such
as the bagpipes, piano, trombone, and drums. So, Hinman moved
in social circles involving musicians like Bobby Beausoleil and
Charles Manson.

 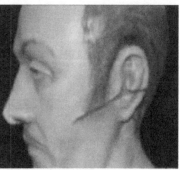

Left: Gary Hinman. Right: Illustration of where Manson cut Hinman.

Hinman was on a spiritual search. Like many hippies in Topanga Canyon. Gary was into Nichiren Shoshu Buddhism. He planned a religious pilgrimage to Japan. As the Manson Family cult killers were cutting, torturing, and stabbing Hinman to death, he chanted his Buddhist chant.

Hinman, who seemed to be a lost soul too open to dangerous criminals like Charles Manson and his crazy cult, set himself up for more trouble by dealing with drugs. Bobby Beausoleil, an aspiring musician, and actor who had stayed at Hinman's home claimed Hinman had sold him some second-rate mescaline, and he wanted his money back. Hinman said he didn't have any money to give him.

It seems the bad drug deal was an excuse to extort money out of Hinman. Bobby Beausoleil showed up on July 25, 1969, at Hinman's place with Susan Atkins and Mary Brunner, two of Manson's killer bitches. Manson had coached them to get money out of Hinman. Manson imagined that Hinman had a lot of money in stocks, bonds, owned an expensive house and two cars.

So, Manson told his followers to convince Hinman to join the Manson Family and donate all his assets to Charles Manson. Hinman refused. So Beausoleil called Manson, who showed up with Bruce Davis. Manson had a sword he used to cut Hinman's ear and face while Davis held a gun on him.

Left: Wall at Hinman's house – POLITICAL PIGGY written in blood. Right: Hinman murder knife used by Beausoleil.

Hinman tried his gentle, kind method with Manson's followers. He asked them why they were doing this and asked them to leave. Hinman asked to be taken to a doctor. But Beausoleil was afraid Hinman would tell the cops and get him arrested. Manson and Davis split in one of Hinman's cars.

Mary Brunner and Susan Atkins tried to stitch up his bleeding ear with dental floss. Hinman begged them to leave. Manson's people continued to torture and demand money from Hinman for three days. Finally, Beausoleil stabbed Hinman fatally in the chest. The three held a pillow over Hinman's face.

Beausoleil wrote POLITICAL PIGGY on a wall in Hinman's blood. This sick touch was Manson's idea to trigger Helter Skelter or race war and make it look like blacks such as the Black Panthers did the killing.

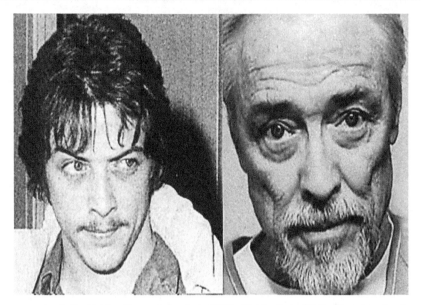

Left: Bobby Beausoleil, circa 1970. Right: Beausoleil after decades in prison in a more recent photo.

Hinman gripped his Buddhist prayer beads in his hand and chanted "Nam Myo Ho Renge Kyo Nam Myo Ho Renge Kyo" as he lay on the floor dying. The Hinman murder kicked off a series of murders directed by Charles Manson.

Hinman's murder was the start of a dark shadow that ended the Summer of Love consciousness and set the Manson Family on a course of Manson's revenge murders. Manson would never be a rock star. He failed to get his big record deal. When things don't go Charles Manson's way, go for mass murder. At least Manson could be the evil, pop-culture icon of serial murder.

While Manson and his followers may have committed murders before Hinman's, Gary Hinman is the first documented murder in the spree of killings in the summer of 1969. The Tate/LaBianca mass murders happened the following month.

Pictured is Gary Hinman's Topanga Canyon home.

Gary Hinman proves the adage, "No good deed goes unpunished." The thank-you Hinman got for being friendly to Manson's criminal cult was Manson's sense of entitlement to Hinman's money and assets. He said no to Charles Manson and Bobby Beausoleil, and it got him killed.

Beausoleil, who was an associate of the Manson Family but not a member, said he felt he had no way out, once Manson cut Hinman's ear and face. After Beausoleil was in prison, he said in an interview: "Gary was a friend. He didn't do anything to deserve what happened to him, and I am responsible for that."

Dianne Lake, a Manson Family member, recalled that Hinman had sold drugs to Beausoleil. Then Beausoleil sold the drugs to a third party who complained about the poor quality of the drugs. So, Beausoleil wanted his money back from Hinman.

Catherine "Gypsy" Share commented on the Hinman/Beausoleil conflict. Share said, "Bobby was driven over there to make it right with two girls that knew Gary very well. I think he had slept with both of them: Susan Atkins and Mary Brunner."

Left: Hinman's kitchen crime scene with arrows showing the path of a bullet. Right: Exterior of Hinman's Topanga Canyon house.

But Beausoleil couldn't rough up Hinman enough to get the money. So, he called Manson, who showed up with a sword and Bruce Davis. "Fear is not a rational emotion, and when it sets in. Things get out of control, as they certainly did with Charlie and me," Beausoleil said.

Hinman's ear and face were bleeding a lot after Manson cut him. Bruce Davis admitted holding a gun on Hinman. Hinman asked Manson why he assaulted him. Manson said, "To show you how to be a man." Beausoleil said, "I will never forget that..." Beausoleil tried to patch up Hinman's wound. And Atkins and Brunner tried to stitch the cut up with dental floss. Hinman demanded professional medical attention.

At that point, Beausoleil said, "I knew if I took him, I'd end up going to prison. Gary would tell on me, for sure, and he would tell on Charlie and everyone else. It was at that point I realized I had no way out."

Left: Bobby Beausoleil after many years in prison. Susan Atkins (middle) and Mary Brunner (right), circa 1970. Beausoleil, Atkins, and Brunner participated in murdering Gary Hinman.

Beausoleil said, "What I've wished a thousand times is that I had faced the music. Instead, I killed him." Beausoleil reflected on his crime after decades in prison. Beausoleil admitted to fatally stabbing Hinman twice in the chest.

Besides writing POLITICAL PIGGY in Hinman's blood on the wall, a panther paw was drawn in blood on the wall blame the murder on the Black Panthers. Manson's crazy theory was that this would trigger Helter Skelter, set off a race war, and blacks would win. Then Charles Manson would take over and rule the world.

After inciting race war, Manson said blacks were too inexperienced to run the world. So, Manson would then be king of the world. I doubt Manson believed this. But to his followers who were loaded on drugs and brainwashed, many of them seem to have swallowed Manson's crazy ranting and raving.

Left: Bruce Davis, circa 1970; Davis in a recent photo. Right: Manson was arrested during a Spahn's Movie Ranch police raid. Manson directed Hinman's murder. Bobby Beausoleil and Bruce Davis were convicted of Hinman's murder.

Beausoleil escaped in Hinman's car and was later pulled over by the cops and arrested for Hinman's murder. Bruce Davis also was detained for Hinman's murder. Dianne Lake commented, "This is when things start getting really dire, I mean really murderous."

Beausoleil and Davis, like the other Manson killers, were sentenced to death, which was commuted to life in prison. At age 71 in 2019, Beausoleil was recommended for parole release, but the governor of California denied his parole. Beausoleil said he regretted taking his friend's life.

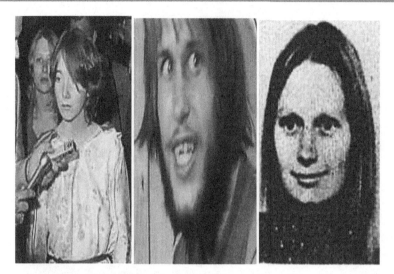

Left to right: Lynette "Squeaky" Fromme, Steve "Clem" Grogan, Mary Brunner. These Manson cult members have escaped punishment or done little prison time while involved in murders or attempted murders. Squeaky sugar-coated her attempted murder of President Ford as an ecology protest because of her environmental concern.

The Hinman murder was followed in a few weeks with the Tate murders of movie actress Sharon Tate, aspiring screenwriter Wojciech Frykowski, coffee heiress Abigail Folger, hairstylist to the stars Jay Sebring, and the caretaker's visitor Steven Parent. Manson was then on a very sick murderous road and continued killing the next night, directing his killers to slaughter Leno and Rosemary LaBianca.

Bobby Beausoleil (Robert Kenneth Beausoleil), an actor and a musician, born November 6th, 1947, has spent nearly 50 years in prison based on his first-degree murder conviction. Beausoleil had a lot of potential because he's not only a musician but also is a visual artist, instrument designer, and media technologist.

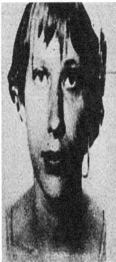

Left to right: Sue "Country Sue" Bartell, Catherine "Cappy" Gillies, and Nancy Pitman. These Manson cult members escaped punishment for the suspected Haught murder (Bartell, Gillies), and Pitman only did 18 months in prison for her involvement in the two Willett murders. Gillies is now dead. Punishments have been unfair if you consider Tex Watson, Bruce Davis, Bobby Beausoleil, Leslie Van Houten, and Patricia Krenwinkel are still in prison about 50 years later.

He has managed to record and release music from prison. The parole hearing Commissioner pointed out some positives in Beausoleil's favor: 1) he committed the crime at a young age, 21; 2) he has developed in prison in terms of creativity, personal growth, maturing, showing compassion and empathy.

I would agree that Beausoleil has developed, and it is nice to have empathy and compassion. But I think victims of the Manson Family related murders can argue with a parole release by asking where was Beausoleil's empathy and compassion for Gary Hinman when he was stabbing him to death. And, Mary Brunner, who walked away free based on her testimony against Beausoleil and Bruce Davis, helped murder Hinman along with Atkins.

Left to right: Madaline Joan Cottage, Ruth Ann Moorehouse, Bruce Davis. Bruce Davis has done nearly 50 years in prison for murdering Gary Hinman and Donald "Shorty" Shea. But Davis was never charged for the suspected murder of John "Zero" Haught. Madaline Joan Cottage was at the John "Zero" Haught alleged murder scene and was not charged. The Manson Family members claimed Zero died by suicide. Ruth Ann Moorehouse attempted to murder Barbara Hoyt with a drug overdose, and she skipped her sentencing hearing and never did one day in jail for the attempted murder. We can excuse Davis, who is still in prison 50 years later. How is this fair to Van Houten, Krenwinkel, and Beausoleil? Atkins and Manson died in prison years ago.

The fairness issue arises when comparing the punishment of almost 50 years for Beausoleil, Krenwinkel, Van Houten, Tex Watson, and Bruce Davis. Because if you compare other Manson Family members involved in murders or attempted murders, why release Steve "Clem" Grogan, Lynette "Squeaky" Fromme, Nancy Pitman, and let Mary Brunner off the hook.

Ruth Ann Moorehouse attempted to murder Barbara Hoyt, skipped her sentencing hearing, and did not serve any time. Other Manson cult criminals have gotten away with all kinds of crimes and never been punished. How about the Manson Family members who were likely accessories to murder when John "Zero" Haught was murdered and officially written off as a "suicide" from Russian Roulette.

Left to right: Bobby Beausoleil, Charles Manson, Bruce Davis, Mary Brunner, and Susan Atkins. These five Manson Family criminals killed Gary Hinman to extort money and possessions from him.

When police arrived at the suspected John "Zero" Haught murder scene, the Manson Family followers stuck to their story that Zero had committed suicide and left a fully loaded gun with no fingerprints. The Manson cult members at the Haught death scene included Bruce Davis, Sue Bartell, Madaline Joan Cottage, and Catherine Gillies. These Manson Family members should all have been charged with murder in the Haught case.

Chapter 39

Dr. Dawson: Dennis Wilson was interviewed for a newspaper article and discussed how he met and lived with 17 girls – your Manson cult young women.

He said, "It happened strangely. I went up into the mountains with my houseboy to take an LSD trip. We met two girls hitchhiking. One of them was pregnant. We gave them a lift, and a purse was left in the car. About a month later, near Malibu, I saw the pregnant girl again, only this time she'd had her baby. I was overjoyed for her and it was through her that I met all the other girls."

"I told them about our involvement with the Maharishi and Transcendental Meditation. And they told me they had a guru, a guy named Charlie who'd recently come out of jail after 12 years. His mother was a hooker, his father was a gangster. He'd drifted into crime but when I met him I found he had great musical ideas. We're writing together now."

"He's dumb, in some ways, but I accept his approach and I have learned from him. He taught me a dance, the Inhibition. You have to imagine you're a frozen man and the ice is thawing out. Start with your fingertips, then all the rest of you, you extend it to a feeling that the whole universe is thawing out..."

Sharon Tate, Manson murder victim, and her husband, Roman Polanski.

He was asked if he was supporting all these people. "No, if anything, they are supporting me. I had all the rich status symbols – Rolls Royce, Ferrari, home after home. Then I woke up, gave away 50 to 60 percent of my money. Now I live in one small room, with one candle, and I'm happy finding myself."

Charles Manson: See I went through what Dennis Wilson was going through when I was in prison – I rehabilitated myself by going inside myself. He's tryin' to find himself. It ain't a Rolls Royce, a Ferrari, or a mansion.

It's a spiritual journey. Transcendental Meditation, prison. Don't matter. Prison is like a monastery. But ya gotta go through hard knocks. How ya gonna feel good unless ya feel bad. Ya gotta go to hell to appreciate heaven. I'm from the 1930s generation, not the 1960s.

I didn't just come on the scene in 1969 like The Beach Boys. In the old days in prison, they used to beat me with leather straps. But prison was supposed to help you. But some sadistic ding dongs took over. I ain't trapped in no prison. I'm international – I go around the world.

Manson brainwashed members of his twisted hippie druggie commune known as "The Family" into butchering seven people, including film director Roman Polanski's pregnant wife Sharon Tate.

Dr. Dawson: Charlie, I'll run the Tate murder crime scene by you. The first cops on the scene found a young man murdered and slumped in a Rambler parked in the driveway. He was covered in blood from gunshots and knife wounds delivered by Tex Watson – your right-hand man you ordered to kill. Three LAPD Officers searched the cars around the house, the garage, and then entered Tate's house.

Charles Manson: The Manson Family felt sorry for me because Terry Melcher broke his promise to give me a record deal. Tex knew where Melcher lived on Cielo Drive in Benedict Canyon. What the hell ya want from me? Ya had druggie murderers out of control.

Dr. Dawson: The police found two dead bodies on the lawn. One was a white man in his 30s – Frykowski, the aspiring screenwriter. His head and face had been bludgeoned and he'd suffered dozens of knife wounds and some gunshot wounds.

There was a frustrated music motive – Charlie's record deal never happened - to the Manson murders. Charles Manson's relationship with Beach Boys' drummer Dennis Wilson (left) and record producer Terry Melcher led to his angry decision to murder everybody at Melcher's former home. Wilson revealed in a press interview (December 21, 1968) that Manson and his cult girls were camped out at his Pacific Palisades home.

The other body was a young woman in a nightgown who had multiple stab wounds – Abigail Folger, the coffee heiress. Since you ordered Tex and the three Manson cult girls to kill everybody at the Cielo Drive house, any comment?

Charles Manson: I seen that bitch Sharon Tate. Who the hell would miss her? She couldn't act. No talent.

Dr. Dawson: The three cops were anxious as they entered the house – not knowing what to expect next. First, they noticed the word "PIG" scrawled in blood on the front door. Near the couch, in the living room, they found a pregnant, young-blonde woman – Sharon Tate – covered in blood.

A rope was around her neck and over a rafter in the ceiling. The other end of the rope was around the neck of a man lying near her. He was also a bloody corpse. Are you proud of what Tex did in following your directions?

Charles Manson: Tex and those bitches were blood-thirsty demons!

Dr. Dawson: The LAPD Officers continued searching the estate and located the caretaker, William Garretson, who was in the guest cottage along with his dog.

He survived the night of bloody murder because he remained locked in the guesthouse the night before, listening to music, sleeping, and unaware of the gruesome murders.

Not knowing what his part was, the cops handcuffed and arrested him. It doesn't bother you that you ordered your murder squad to commit those five murders?

Charles Manson: Hey, dude. I can't get anybody to do anything. Don't put their shit on me.

Dr. Dawson: In 1969, on August 8, you told your cult members at Spahn's Movie Ranch, "now is the time for Helter Skelter." That evening the Manson killers, under your direction would commit the horrific murders of Sharon Tate, Sebring, Frykowski, Folger, and Parent. This led to other murders over the two-day period. What was your motivation to commit mass murder?

Charles Manson: Helter Skelter was some insane story I was workin' into my songs. How do I know what's in the heads of a bunch of hippie drug addicts?

Chapter 40

Donald "Shorty" Shea murder. Donald
Jerome Shea (aka Shorty), born on September 18th, 1933, in Massachusetts, a Hollywood stuntman and actor, was murdered by Charles Manson and his murder crew. Shea's wife was Magdalena Shea, and he had a daughter, Karen. Shea was 35 when he was murdered. He's buried in a community plot in Angeles Abbey Memorial Park in Los Angeles, California.

One of the killers, Steve "Clem" Grogan, in exchange for leniency, revealed to police where Donald "Shorty" Shea was buried, and the cops discovered his remains in 1977.

He was killed on August 26th, 1969, on the former Spahn's Movie Ranch grounds in the Chatsworth area, Los Angeles, California. Charles Manson, Bruce Davis, and Steve "Clem" Grogan were convicted of Shea's murder.

Pictured is Donald "Shorty" Shea, movie stuntman and actor.

Shorty Shea, an actor and movie stuntman, spent most of his time as a livestock wrangler, ranch hand, and handyman at Spahn's Movie Ranch. Charles Manson, his Manson cult of assorted hippies, drifters, petty criminals, and alienated young women and girls with an identity crisis were getting loaded on drugs, experiencing sex orgies, and programmed by Charles Manson. Both Shea and the Manson Family were at Spahn's Movie Ranch at the same time.

Why did Charles Manson order Shea's murder? Manson suspected that "Shorty" was informing the police about the Manson Family crimes. So, Manson organized a group of his Manson Family followers to kill Shea, including himself, Charles Manson, Bruce Davis, and Steve "Clem" Grogan. Other participants in the murder who were not charged included Charles "Tex" Watson, Bill Vance, and Larry Bailey (aka Larry Giddings).

Shea came to the L.A. area looking for acting work. George Spahn hired Shea to work with the horses and help around the ranch. When he got an acting or stuntman opportunity, he left the ranch and returned weeks later when the movie filming wrapped. Shorty was a big, stocky guy. He worked hard at Spahn's Movie Ranch and was loyal to George Spahn.

Police raid at Spahn's Movie Ranch, August 16, 1969. Danny DeCarlo and Charles Manson.

There was conflict and tension between Shea and Charles Manson. One issue, it was reported, was that Shea had married a black stripper who he had met in Las Vegas. Manson looked down on Shorty because Charlie hated black people.

Shea was aware that the Manson Family was both trashing Spahn's Movie Ranch and committing crimes such as credit card fraud, auto theft, and other crimes. On August 16th, 1969, police raided Spahn's Movie Ranch and arrested the Manson Family on auto theft charges. Manson suspected that Shorty had informed or snitched to the police, which led to the raid.

Pictured are Charles Manson and his Manson Family cult killers who murdered Donald "Shorty" Shea.

Twelve days later, on August 28, 1969, Charles Manson led his group of killers including Charles "Tex" Watson, Bruce Davis, Steve "Clem" Grogan, Bill Vance, and Larry Bailey to Donald "Shorty" Shea and took him for a ride. While Shea was in the backseat, Grogan hit Shea on the head with a pipe wrench. Tex Watson began stabbing Shea.

Manson's killer group dragged Shorty out of the car, took him down an incline behind Spahn's Movie Ranch, and continued stabbing him to death as Shea screamed. It was reported that Manson and his killers used machetes and chopped Shea's head off and dismembered him into nine pieces and buried him. Years later, after Grogan drew a map showing where Shea's remains were, police were able to locate his remains.

Police dug up the remains of Donald "Shorty" Shea on the Spahn's Movie Ranch grounds. In 1977, Steve "Clem" Grogan, in exchange for leniency, drew a map that helped the police find Shea's remains. Police authorities unearthed Donald "Shorty" Shea in 1977 included: Sgt. Bill Gleeson, LASO Homicide, Deputy Coroner John Mossberger and Deputy Sheriff Barry Jones, LASO Homicide.

Barbara Hoyt, a former Manson Family member, in grand jury testimony revealed that on the night of August 28, 1969, she heard Donald "Shorty" Shea's screams as Manson's murder gang was killing him. She responded that she was so scared she split from the Manson Family and ran away.

She said, "It was about 10:00 PM when I heard a long, loud, blood-curdling scream. Then it went quiet for a minute or so and the screams came, again and again, it seemed to go on forever. I do not doubt that Shorty was being murdered at that time." Grogan was given the task of burying Shorty Shea after he was cut into nine pieces.

Left to right: Gary Hinman, Donald "Shorty" Shea, and Ronald Hughes, who were all murdered by Manson cult criminals and associates because Charles Manson ordered it. The Ronald Hughes case remains unsolved. These three murder victims demonstrate the danger of associating with street criminals.

There is some conflicting testimony concerning the time, place, and Shea's expected reaction. Both Davis and Grogan, in parole hearings, disputed the time and date Hoyt cited. Also, a Windy Bucklee was interviewed and claimed that Donald "Shorty" Shea was not the type to scream and beg for his life. He would have gone down fighting, according to Bucklee.

Shea's 1962 Mercury was located on December 9th, 1969, with a footlocker in it of Shorty's items, including some bloody cowboy boots which belonged to him. Bruce Davis' palm print was found on the footlocker. Shea's skeletal remains were found on a hillside near Santa Susana Road next to the former Spahn's Movie Ranch in December 1977 based on a map Grogan drew for authorities. The autopsy report noted that Shea's body suffered many stabs and chopping wounds to the chest and blunt force trauma to the head.

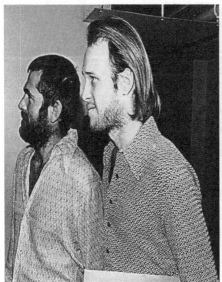

Left to right: Bruce Davis, Steve "Clem" Grogan, and Donald "Shorty" Shea. Davis, Grogan, and Charles Manson were convicted of murdering Shea. Davis is still in prison 50 years later. Grogan was released in 1985. And Charlie Manson died in prison in 2017 at age 83.

Police authorities at the site where Donald "Shorty" Shea was unearthed in 1977 included: Sgt. Bill Gleeson, LASO Homicide, Deputy Coroner John Mossberger and Deputy Sheriff Barry Jones, LASO Homicide. Gleason obtained the warrant to search Spahn's Movie Ranch for the police raid in 1969.

Charles Manson and his killer crew ended Donald "Shorty" Shea's dreams of becoming a full-time, working actor. The Spahn's Movie Ranch job was flexible for Shorty. He could go work on a film for a few weeks and come back later to his position at Spahn's Movie Ranch. Charles Manson and his band of crazies and street criminals murdered Shea. Shorty joined the list of those who were murdered or died tragically on the dark side of Hollywood.

Chapter 41

Dr. Dawson: Later on August 9th, 1969, Saturday night, you and your gang went to Leno and Rosemary LaBianca's home. Leno, Rosemary, and Susan Struthers, Rosemary's 21-year-old daughter, had driven back from a vacation. They drove Susan to her apartment and went home to their place at 3301 Waverly Drive in the Los Feliz area of Los Angeles.

They were last seen picking up a newspaper between 1:00 and 2:00 a.m. The next day, Frank Struthers, Rosemary's son, arrived home and noticed something was wrong. He noticed the speedboat was not garaged as usual. All the window shades were drawn down, which his parents never did.

He called his sister and she came with her boyfriend. They entered the house and found the dead bodies of the LaBianca couple. Leno was lying in the living room with a pillowcase over his head and a rope around his neck. Something was sticking out of his stomach. They called the police. How could you murder this couple you didn't even know?

Charles Manson: Anytime I had to use violence was in self-defense. You fuck with me, ya got some shit comin'.

Manson victims. Clockwise from top left: Gary Hinman, Abigail Folger, Jay Sebring, Leon LaBianca, Rosemary LaBianca, Wojciech (Voytek) Frykowski, Steven Parent, and Sharon Tate. Charles Manson led the Manson Family, a quasi-commune and murder cult that arose in California in the late 1960s. He was found guilty of conspiracy to commit the murders carried out by members of his Manson Family group at his instruction.

Dr. Dawson: The police and ambulance responders found Leno with a pillowcase over his head, and he had the cord from a lamp tied tightly around his neck. His hands had been tied behind him with a leather thong. A carving fork protruded from his stomach. The word "WAR" had been carved in his flesh. This was your Helter Skelter master plan, right?

Charles Manson: Can I help it if some wicked drifters misunderstand my song lyrics?

Dr. Dawson: In a bedroom, they found Rosemary lying on the floor with her nightgown up over her head. She also had a pillowcase over her head and had been strangled with a lamp cord. You used the victims' blood to write words on the walls: "DEATH TO PIGS," "RISE," and "HEALTHER SKELTER," Helter misspelled. Kicking off your Helter Skelter with a lot of blood on your hands, Charlie?

Terry Melcher – record producer, son of Doris Day. Manson sent his cult killers into the Cielo Drive home in Benedict Canyon previously occupied by Terry Melcher and Candice Bergen. Sharon Tate and others were butchered.

Charles Manson: All that grandiose shit was just words from my songs.

Dr. Dawson: Let's review who was slaughtered by your cult killers:

Eventually, all of the victims of the massacre at Sharon Tate's home were identified. The young man in the car was a teenager named Steven Parent who had come to visit Garretson, the caretaker. The two victims found outside the house were Abigail Folger and her lover, Voytek Frykowski. In the living room joined by a rope were Sharon Tate and Jay Sebring.

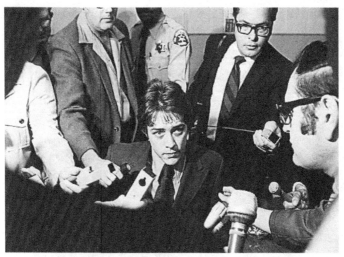

Robert Kenneth Beausoleil – Hinman killer.

Steve Parent, Jay Sebring, and Voytek Frykowski were shot by Watson with a .22 caliber handgun. Of the five victims, all but Steve Parent had been stabbed repeatedly. Sebring had been hit in the face and Frykowski had been repeatedly hit on the head with a blunt object.

The stab wounds suggested that only one knife had been used for the wounds. The nature of the wounds indicated that something like a bayonet was the weapon. A strange knife, a Buck brand clasp-type pocketknife that the housekeeper could not identify was found very close to Sharon Tate's body.

Sharon Tate had been a beauty all of her life. Even as a child she had won beauty contests. But her ambition was not to be a model but a movie actress. Finally, in 1963 at the age of 22, she found a sponsor in Producer Martin Ransohoff. With Ransohoff's help, she landed parts in the series *Beverly Hillbillies* and *Petticoat Junction*, and the movies *The Americanization of Emily* and *The Sandpiper*.

Chapter 42

Bernard "Lotsapoppa" Crowe shooting.

Manson used his followers to do various criminal scams. The Manson Family: 1) stole credit cards; 2) did credit card fraud; 3) took cars; 4) lifted anything of value; 5) got free food on garbage runs and dumpster diving behind supermarkets; 6) extorted money; 7) pulled drug deal rip-offs. Bernard "Lotsapoppa" Crowe was a drug dealer Manson ripped-off.

Tex Watson, one of Manson's most reliable enforcers, had the job of raising money. Manson was ranting and raving about a race war, Helter Skelter, which he claimed was coming and predicted by the Beatles' *White Album*. World doom was on the way, and the Manson Family needed money. The term Helter Skelter came from the *White Album*.

Manson sent Tex Watson to swindle money out of Bernard "Lotsapoppa" Crowe by cheating him in a drug deal. When Crowe realized he had been cheated, he threatened to kill all of Manson's Family. Manson met Crowe on July 1st, 1969, at an apartment in Hollywood and shot him with the same .22 handgun used in the Tate murders.

Left to right: Bernard "Lotsapoppa" Crowe, Charles Manson, Charles "Tex" Watson (Belladonna Police Mugshot). Manson sent Tex Watson to dupe Crowe in a drug deal.

Charles Manson did not realize that Crowe survived the shooting and did not report it to the police. There was a misunderstanding. Media reported that a Black Panther had been killed, and his body had been dumped near UCLA. Manson assumed it was Crowe who was the dead Black Panther and that his Helter Skelter fairy tale was coming true.

But let's get back to how the Crowe drug deception happened. First, you have to realize that Charles "Tex" Watson moved in and out of the Manson Family commune a couple of times. At times, Tex lived with a girl named Luella. With Luella, Tex had been making money selling marijuana and living with her in an apartment in Hollywood. Tex went into detail on this in his book *Will You Die for Me?* Which you can read if you're a fan of Tex Watson.

Manson's gun was used in the Bernard "Lotsapoppa" Crowe shooting and in the Tate murders.

Tex Watson got Luella pregnant, she got an abortion in Mexico, and their relationship went south. Tex moved back to Spahn's Movie Ranch with Manson's crazy commune in March of 1969. Tex tried to coax Luella to join the Manson cult, but she refused. She was smarter than Tex in some ways. But she was still a free spirit druggie.

In April 1969, Tex was arrested in Van Nuys, California, after overdosing on the drug Belladonna. Tex was on all fours like a crazy dog, crawling around and calling out "beep, beep, beep!" After the police arrested him, fingerprinted Tex, his prints later matched some at the Tate murder scene. His mugshot was then called the Belladonna Police Mugshot.

Los Angeles Times
Friday March 27, 1970
Page 2

Four persons, including two women, were arrested in a West Hollywood apartment in connection with a $250,000 forgery and burglary ring. According to sheriff's deputies, more than 100 stolen credit cards, a phony state seal stamp for drivers' licenses, a check writing machine and numerous bogus drivers' licenses and Social Security cards were confiscated in the apartment at 1211 N. Horn St. Booked on suspicion of burglary and forgery were: Bernard Crowe, 27; William Fuller, 29; Patricia H. Yellow, 29, and Jerry M. Perkins, a 21-year-old woman. All gave the West Hollywood address as their place of residence, deputies said.

Left: LA Times article disclosed Bernard "Lotsapoppa" Crowe's main criminal business. Right: Charles "Tex" Watson.

Tex told Manson about Luella. Manson's criminal mind began turning. Manson told Tex to get some money out of Luella to buy dune buggies. Luella refused to give money to Manson for his dune buggies. Tex then figured he could con Bernard "Lotsapoppa" Crowe out of cash in a drug-deal rip-off. Now keep in mind that Tex was brainwashed by Manson, loaded on drugs, and lost in a fog. Anyway, this is how Tex explained the Crowe drug swindle:

"I called Luella… on July 1st and said that the Family had $100 and wanted to buy a kilo of grass, but our Mafia vending-machine connection would only sell 25 kilos at a throw, for a cool $2,500…"

SO VENTURA CAL
47623
22 APR 1968

Left: Black Panther demonstration, February 1969. Right: Charles Manson. Manson imagined some Black Panthers coming to kill the Manson Family.

"She called back and told me that she knew somebody interested in buying the extra kilos, but she needed to make some money out of the deal as well."

Tex planned that he would pay the Manson Family's contact $2,500 for 25 kilos. Luella's client would pay $125 for each kilo. That would leave 3 kilos free. Luella would make a few hundred dollars. But only Tex could meet with the Manson Family's connection. Tex explained:

"TJ would drive me down to L.A. and drop me near Luella's apartment to make it look like I'd hitchhiked. He'd then go on to the dealer's place on the other side of town, parking in the back of the apartment house out of which the man worked."

Left: Luella, Tex Watson's girlfriend he betrayed in the Crowe drug deal rip-off. Middle: Tex Watson, circa 1970. Right: Bernard Crowe.

"Luella would drive me back there with the money, and I'd go in the front door and out the back with the bread, leaving her to explain things to her friend."

However, Crowe and his cronies were suspicious. Crowe was not comfortable giving Tex $2750 with no security. Because Tex's drug deal involved bogus kilos that did not exist. Tex revealed the drug deal intrigue:

"While he and one of his boys waited downstairs in their big black Caddy, another one of his men tried to talk Luella and me into letting them come with us. I tried everything I could think of, including walking out of the door, but finally, we ended up riding out to the connection's apartment in Crowe's big black car, with his men on either side of us, just like something out of a movie."

 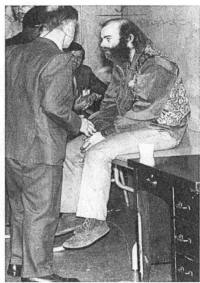

Thomas Walleman, aka TJ, TJ the Terrible, Thomas Jay Alden.

At the apartment, Tex was allowed to enter alone. However, Luella was held in the Caddy as collateral. The problem for Luella was that Tex didn't care what happened to her. It was like that scene in the movie *Go* when a girl was left for collateral.

"When Crowe threatened violence to her if I tried to cheat them, I gave him one of my Texas grins and drawled that they should know I'd be coming back when they had my girl. It didn't much matter to me what they did to Luella, as long as I got the money for Charlie. They gave me the cash, and I went straight into the front of the apartment and straight out the back, and T.J. and I were off to the ranch."

Left: Bernard Crowe. Right: Tex Watson and Susan Atkins. Manson sent Watson and Atkins into the hills with a sleeping bag to hide from Crowe and the Black Panthers.

When Bernard Crowe and Luella called the Spahn Ranch asking for Tex Watson, who had vanished with the money, Charles Manson took the call. Manson tried to bullshit them and said Tex had left Spahn's Movie Ranch weeks ago. But Crowe didn't buy Manson's lies. Crowe threatened to kill Manson and all his followers. Manson told Tex he'd handle Crowe. Susan Atkins (Sadie) and Tex Watson were sent to hide in the hills with a sleeping bag.

Manson went to an apartment in Hollywood with Thomas Walleman (aka TJ, TJ the Terrible, Thomas Jay Alden) who was packing the .22 Buntline Revolver, which was used in the Tate murders. TJ was too scared and did not pull the gun on Crowe at the meeting. Manson grabbed the gun from TJ and shot Crowe. The gun misfired and then Manson shot Crowe in the chest or stomach area. He then stole a buckskin jacket off one of Crowe's cronies. Manson and TJ split.

Manson assumed Crowe was dead and a Black Panther. Because when the news reported a dead Black Panther, he mixed that up with Crowe, who was not a Black Panther. Then Manson got more paranoid, bragged about how he "plugged the blackie" to all his followers. This incident was another step in the coming Helter Skelter revolution, Manson was feeding his gullible cult members. The Black Panthers were coming! The Black Panthers were not coming and were not aware of the Manson Family. Tex Watson wrote about it:

"Much later, I learned that Bernard Crowe, who never had anything to do with the Panthers, had not been killed, only wounded. His friends had taken him away and had lain low, fearful that if Charlie found out the Big Crow was still alive, he might have come after him again."

Bernard "Lotsapoppa" Crowe testified against Manson at his murder trial. When Crowe showed up, Manson said he thought he saw a ghost because he thought Crowe was dead. Crowe had the bullet in his body for the rest of his life.

Crowe was arrested for forgery and burglary. Not drugs. Crowe and his criminal buddies were forging driver's licenses and Social Security cards. Crowe and his cronies had made $250,000 from the forgery business.

Chapter 43

Charles Manson: "I'm a criminal! I'm a bandit! I'm a crook! I'm a gangster! (He paused, shook his fist at me.) I don't fire no warning shots! (Then suddenly he grinned devilishly at me and sat back down.)

Dr. Dawson: "If you are afraid to talk about the murders, let's talk about your sex life. How's your sex life? You've been charged with homosexual rape – sodomized other males while you've been doing time. Tell me about your sex life."

Charles Manson: "I don't gotta rape nobody. Do you think I'm too old to spank the monkey? Whack off? I don't need to fuck a pillow. I can get my roscoe up. I'm just as slick as in the old days."

Dr. Dawson: "I understand you've got some resentments against the prosecutor who got you convicted of murder – Vincent Bugliosi? You call him the Bug?"

Charles Manson: (He waved his arm around and shook his fist in the air.) "Bug's a liar. He knows I couldn't handle Helter Skelter – that's enormous. But that bastard won. He made money off me. Bug's a wizard. He took decades of my life. The Bug is a grimy little worm. He ain't got no honor. No conscience."

Steve Grogan, murderer, mugshot from Spahn's Movie Ranch raid (April 16, 1969).

Dr. Dawson: "Don't the Tate and LaBianca victims weigh down your conscience? Or do you lack remorse or guilt?"

Charles Manson: "Why should I cry for the Tate or LaBianca dead? F'chrissake, Sharon Tate was a sexy Hollywood starlet – she murdered people in the movies. She was beautiful on the outside and ugly inside – how many seedy Hollywood producers and directors did she screw? She used her body to get over. Sharon was in bed with a guy when the killings went down. That's some shit to jump off!"

Dr. Dawson: "When you were arrested, you put down Charles Manson, aka, Jesus Christ. Did you or do you have some deity complex? Do you think you're Christ? Because you've got some apocalyptic vision connected to Helter Skelter, don't you?"

Charles Manson: "I'm dying on the cross and now you're gonna interview, Christ? Ain't you got any idea of the magnitude of this situation? I am being crucified."

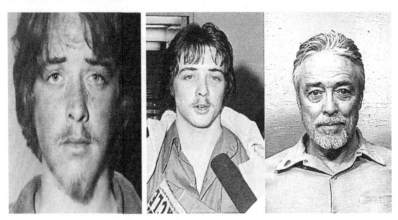

Left: Bobby Beausoleil mugshot after his arrest for the murder of Gary Hinman (August 6, 1969). Center: Beausoleil, ca 1970. Right: Beausoleil after nearly 50 years in prison.

Dr. Dawson: (I shook my head at him and shot him a skeptical look.) "I don't understand why you say you're Jesus Christ. Can you explain that?"

Charles Manson: (Growing frenzied, he jumped up and waved his arms around.) "Don't ask for proof they crucified Christ, ask for 'em to corroborate why they are crucifying me, Christ. When you square off with me, you're only one dude. I don't give a fuck who you are, Doctor Dawson. I'll smash you. Put you in the six feet underground. Wanna end up in a grave? What're you going to do about that, rock and roll? Who's got your back, Doc? Darling?"

Dr. Dawson: "If you're threatening me, maybe I'll file a complaint with the warden. Get your butt thrown in the hole for some solitary time. How'd you like that?"

Charles Manson: (He glared at me angrily, after some more scorching looks, his eyes narrowed with contempt. Then he smiled wickedly and chuckled.) "Okay, Doc. How about I talk about the murders and you forget filing a complaint?"

Left: Sandra Good mugshot (ca 1969) – she was in jail with Mary Brunner the night of the Tate murders. Right: Sandra Good, 2019, 50 years after the Tate murders. Good, a diehard Manson cult disciple, still supports Manson's twisted viewpoint in 2020.

Dr. Dawson: "I'm listening, Manson. But first I demand an apology from you."

Charles Manson: "Gotta kick a dog when he's down, huh? Sorry. Pretty please with sugar on it. Satisfied?

Dr. Dawson: "Don't begrudge me the truth. I'm confused about the narrative. I've researched what Bugliosi has said happened. What's your version of the story? There was a murder associated with a drug deal? And what else? I'd like to hear you put together the puzzle parts."

Chapter 44

John "Zero" Haught. John Philip Haught (aka Zero, Christopher Jesus) moved with his friend, Kenneth Richard Brown, from Ohio to the Los Angeles area. Haught made the mistake of moving in with the Manson Family at Spahn's Movie Ranch.

On October 12th, 1969, Haught was arrested with the Manson Family at the Barker Ranch in Death Valley. After Haught and the Manson Family members were released, Haught moved with some Manson Family members to a Venice Beach house, which was rented by Mark Ross.

Venice police got a call on Wednesday, November 5th, 1969, about a shooting and responded to the Venice Beach house at 28 Clubhouse Avenue. At the house, the Manson Family members (Bruce Davis, Madaline Joan Cottage, Sue Bartell, and Catherine "Cappy" Gillies) claimed that Zero had committed suicide playing Russian Roulette.

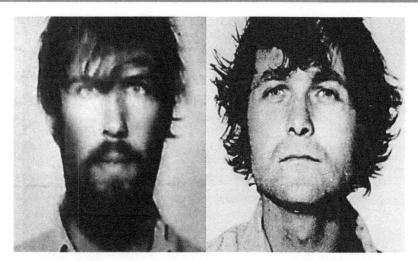

Left: John "Zero" Haught. Right: Bruce Davis. Some suspected Bruce Davis of murdering Haught and covering it up with a fake Russian Roulette "suicide" story.

John "Zero" Haught was lying dead on a mattress in a bedroom. He had a bullet wound in his right temple. A leather gun case and a revolver were lying next to his body.

Police questioned Bruce Davis, Madaline Joan Cottage, Sue Bartell, and Catherine Gillies. They all stuck to the same story. Zero had shot himself playing Russian Roulette. Cottage was in bed with Zero.

She said Zero said, "Oh, here's a gun." He picked up the case, took out the gun. Then Zero said, "It only has one bullet in it." Zero then held the gun in his right hand. Cottage said, "Zero spun the cylinder and placed the gun muzzle to his right temple and fired."

The Manson Family members said they were all in another room, heard the shot, and hurried into the bedroom. Cottage told them Zero had just shot himself. Cottage said, "Just like in the movies."

Left to right: Bruce Davis, Madaline Joan Cottage (aka: Little Patty), John "Zero" Haught. Cottage was in bed with Haught. Davis, one of Manson's enforcers and killers, may have murdered Haught.

They said they then called the police. Later, when police dusted the gun and gun case for prints, they found both were clean with no fingerprints. The gun was fully loaded with bullets. Since the Manson Family members had the same basic story, the police ruled it a suicide and closed the case.

At Sybil Brand women's prison, Leslie Van Houten was interviewed by Sgt. Make McGann on November 26th, 1969, and was informed that her friend Haught was dead. When she was told Haught had been playing Russian Roulette and that Bruce Davis was there, she got very suspicious. She asked McGann:

"Was Bruce playing it too?"
McGann advised her that he wasn't.
Leslie Van Houten: "Zero was playing Russian roulette all by himself?"
Mike McGann: "Kind of odd, isn't it?"
Leslie Van Houten: "Yeah, it's odd."

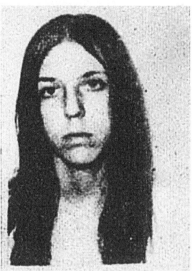

Left: Catherine "Cappy" Gillies. Right: Sue Bartell. These young women were at the scene where John "Zero" Haught died.

After the Barker Ranch police raid, when many of the Manson Family members were arrested on suspicion of grand theft auto, they began to snitch or inform the police of the Manson Family followers' crimes. They squealed on each other, which led to arrests for the Tate/LaBianca mass murders.

The legend is Charles Manson said Haught was a snitch and talked to authorities about the Manson cult crimes, including murder. Some Manson Family members said Haught knew too much and had been talking a lot to the cops. Haught, it seemed, was involved in several robberies.

It was a Manson Family mystery. An anonymous caller told a *Los Angeles Times* reporter that he was there when Zero died. And that it was one of the Manson Family girls who murdered Haught. But this could not be confirmed because the man vanished before the cops could question him.

Left: Barker Ranch, Death Valley. On October 12th, 1969, Haught was arrested with the Manson Family at the Barker Ranch in Death Valley on suspicion of grand theft auto. The Manson Family members began squealing on each other regarding the Manson cult crimes, including murder. Manson suspected Haught of snitching or informing the police of Manson Family crimes, which could have led to his death. Center: John "Zero" Haught dead, shot in the head. Right: Haught's gravestone – he was a US Navy veteran of the Vietnam War. The Manson Family killers like Bruce Davis and Charles Manson were more dangerous than the enemies in the Vietnam War.

Chapter 45

Charles Manson: "Tex Watson was having problems with a drug dealer named Bernard 'Lotsapoppa' Crowe, so he called me to come help him out, which I did... Lotsapoppa was layin' low in some cabin in the mountains... He was a shifty jitterbug...

I was packin' – had a handgun concealed under my jacket in my belt... We got into a yelling match. Lotsapoppa swung a machete at me when I demanded he pay me what he owed Tex. He gave me no choice. In self-defense, I shot that parasite. I found out later that I didn't kill him, but I thought I did at the time..."

Dr. Dawson: "How did Bobby Beausoleil fit into this brainteaser?"

Charles Manson: "Tex owed me one over the Lotsapoppa fight. A 'brother' musician buddy, Bobby Beausoleil – we called him Cupid... Cupid got into a clash with another fuckin' drug dealer - Gary Hinman. Beausoleil asked me to clean it up with Hinman... I went over Hinman's place to help out Cupid. Hinman was a hardass. We got into a nasty scene. He kicked me in the balls. Turnabout is fair play. So I took this sword I was carrying for protection and cut Hinman's face. I took off after that..."

Left: Paul Watkins mugshot (1969). He testified in the Tate-LaBianca murder trials. Center: Watkins, 1990, the year of his death from cancer. Right: Paul Watkins and Brooks Poston (ca 1969).

Dr. Dawson: "What happened to Hinman? He was murdered. You sure you didn't cut him enough to kill him?"

Charles Manson: (Manson threw his arms up as if he had no choice. He turned a cold eye on me.) "No good deed goes unpunished, sweetheart. I tried to help Beausoleil out. But then Beausoleil had a bigger problem than before. Because Hinman attacked me, I defended myself and injured him. Cupid had to figure out what to do with Hinman. He who was then hurt or wounded bad enough to snitch to the cops…"

Dr. Dawson: "What were you afraid would happen with the cops?"

Charles Manson: "The Family was hiding out at Spahn's Movie Ranch. Once Hinman snitched to the cops, the police would have come to Spahn's Movie Ranch lookin' for me and my groupies. Beausoleil wasn't going for that scenario. So Cupid killed Hinman. But somehow he got busted."

Dr. Dawson: "Beausoleil was arrested for killing Hinman? Then what happened?"

Left: Danny DeCarlo mugshot (1969). He testified at the Manson Family trials. Center: DeCarlo with the Straight Satans motorcycle gang (ca 1969). Right: DeCarlo (2014).

Charles Manson: (Charlie shook his head, sighed deeply and smiled wickedly.) "Then a rat at Spahn's Ranch got to brainstorming. The inspiration was to execute some more murders that had the same look, MO, or signature elements – whatever the cops call it - as the Hinman murder.

The notion was that, since Cupid – Beausoleil – was a murder suspect, he needed to get out of jail. The other killings would be his alibi. How could he be in two places at once?"

Dr. Dawson: "Sounds like a psychopath's solution which would make for even more criminal problems. What went down next? Who at the ranch brainstormed the multiple-murder alibi?"

Charles Manson: (His face was a dark mask of anger.) "I ain't no snitch! I'd saved Tex from his Hinman problem. Next, Cupid had a problem. I handed it off to Tex. Tex said, 'Let's get the Beausoleil out of the can. What do I do to get Cupid out of jail?' I said, 'How the hell do I know?

Left to right: A mugshot of Madaline Joan Cottage aka Little Patty (ca 1969). Sue Bartell, Catherine Gilles & Bruce Davis, John "Zero" Haught, Bruce Davis. Cottage was in the bed next to John Haught aka Zero, when he supposedly shot himself playing "Russian Roulette". One theory is that Bruce Davis murdered Haught because Manson suspected Haught had informed police about Manson Family crimes.

You figure it out and don't tell me. I'm walkin' on the cool side of the law. Do whatever the fuck you have to.' I figured what Tex's strategy was. But it was not my concern. He says, 'I'll kill everybody!' I say, 'Don't tell me that shit. I don't want to know!' They say, 'Well, we're going to go murder these people.' I say, 'Well, lots of luck.'"

Chapter 46

Ronald Hughes. Ronald W. Hughes, an attorney, had the misfortune to represent Charles Manson. He was born on March 16th, 1935, in Los Angeles. In November 1970, there was a ten-day recess in the Tate/LaBianca murder trial. Hughes went on a camping trip to escape the pressure of the trial. He vanished.

His dead body, his remains, were found four months later in March 1971 in Ventura County which is north of Los Angeles. The cause of Hughes' strange death could not be determined.

Charles Manson had resentment against Hughes, and the word was that the Manson Family murdered him. Some Manson Family members claimed Charles Manson wanted to retaliate against Hughes for not defending Manson the way he wanted. Nobody was charged with murder.

Left: Ronald W. Hughes, attorney for Charles Manson. Right: Hughes at a trial Halloween party one month before he disappeared.

One thing Hughes did make Charles Manson angry in particular. During the trial, Hughes drove Manson crazy because he questioned witnesses, including Linda Kasabian, in a way that showed Van Houten was brainwashed by Manson and under his control.

Manson wanted Van Houten to take the fall for him as a mass-murdering woman who had total free-will. Hughes would not let Van Houten testify to help Manson.

Ronald Hughes met with Charles Manson in December of 1969. But he was replaced by Irving Kanarek two weeks before the start of the trial. Hughes then represented Leslie Van Houten in the Tate/LaBianca murder trial.

Hughes was not a big-time criminal lawyer. He had failed the bar exam three times before he passed the exam, and Hughes had never tried a case in court. Hughes was sort of like the character in the movie *My Cousin Vinny*.

Left to right: Attorneys Ronald Hughes and Paul Fitzgerald, August 1970. Leslie Van Houten. Charles Manson. Sandra Good. Initially, Hughes represented Manson. Then he ended up representing Van Houten. It was rumored Hughes did drugs at Spahn's Movie Ranch with members of the Manson Family. Socializing and getting loaded on drugs with hardcore, murdering criminals led to his murder. Some Manson Family members bragged about killing Hughes. Sandra Good boasted about killing Hughes.

Bearded Hughes could pass for a hippie without the suit and tie. He was called "the hippie lawyer" because of his extensive experience in the hippie subculture. Thus, Hughes was able to raise questions about Linda Kasabian's credibility as a witness against the Tate/LaBianca murderers, including Van Houten. Hughes was said to get loaded on LSD at Spahn's Movie Ranch with the Manson Family.

For example, Hughes's knowledge of the hippie subculture helped Van Houten's defense at times. Hughes raised questions about Linda Kasabian's credibility as a witness for the state by asking her about the hallucinogenic drugs such as LSD she had taken hundreds of times.

Hughes questioned Kasabian about her ESP beliefs and her fantasies that she might be a witch. He also challenged her about vibrations. She said she got vibes from Charles Manson.

Pictured, the Manson Family attorneys: Fitzgerald, Kanarek, Shinn, and Hughes. The Manson Family clients resisted or refused to listen to their attorneys. Charles Manson's psychopathic, ego-maniac trait caused him to demand total control.

Hughes used a strategy in the Tate/LaBianca murder trial, which triggered Manson's anger. Manson wanted the other cult killers to implicate themselves in the murders and excuse Manson of any involvement. But Hughes aimed to separate the interests of Van Houten from those of Manson.

He worked to show that defendant Van Houten acted under Manson's control. Charles Manson wanted to exclude himself from any responsibility because he was not on the scene when the Tate/LaBianca victims were murdered. But since Manson ordered the murders, he was involved.

Manson organized outbursts and bizarre behavior such as crazy hand gestures, which he ordered his co-defendants to do in court. But after 22 weeks, the prosecution rested. The defense lawyers also rested. Manson wanted the girls to testify to help him get off. So, Susan Atkins, Patricia Krenwinkel, and Leslie Van Houten shouted out that they wanted to be a witness.

Left to right: Susan Atkins, Patricia Krenwinkel and Leslie Van Houten. These three co-defendants in the Tate/LaBianca murder trial disrupted the trial, at times, coordinating with Charles Manson's demands.

The three women (Susan Atkins, Patricia Krenwinkel, and Leslie Van Houten) yelled that they wanted to testify to committing the murders by themselves. They tried to clear Manson of any crimes. Van Houten's attorney, Hughes, objected to Manson's ploy. He said, "I refuse to take part in any proceeding where I am forced to push a client out the window." Manson made a statement to the court, and then he told the women they did not have to testify. Charlie pointed to Hughes and told him to never come back to court.

After that, Judge Charles Older ordered a ten-day recess to allow the attorneys to prepare for their final arguments. Hughes told the press that he expected to get an acquittal for Van Houten because she was a puppet controlled by Charles Manson.

Left: Ronald Hughes, Leslie Van Houten's attorney. Right: Irving A. Kanarek and Hughes leaving court after Judge Charles H. Older cited them for contempt of court.

Hughes then took a camping trip on November 27th, 1970. He went with two friends to the Sespe Hot Springs area in Ventura County, which is a remote location. James Forsher and Lauren Elder, Hughes's two friends, left him and hitchhiked out when their Volkswagen got stuck in the mud. There were flash floods near them in Ventura County.

Some campers saw Hughes on the morning of November 28th. They told the cops that Hughes was alone at the time. At that time, Hughes was unharmed and alone when he spoke with the campers. The rains continued, and the area was evacuated. But apparently, Hughes was located away from the floodwaters and mudslides.

The court reconvened on November 30th, and Hughes failed to appear. The Ventura County sheriff launched a search for Hughes. Judge Older, on December 2nd, ordered the trial to proceed and appointed a new attorney, Maxwell Keith, for Van Houten.

Left: Kanarek and Hughes, Manson Family attorneys during the Tate/LaBianca murder trial. Right: Hughes' client, beautiful, brainwashed Manson cult member and druggie-burnout Leslie Van Houten.

Naturally, this was an excuse for the three women who were on trial for murder, to demand the firing of their attorneys and they wanted to reopen their defense. Their request was denied by Judge Older. After Hughes had been missing for two weeks, Manson started a noisy demonstration in court and accused Judge Older of doing away with Ronald Hughes. They were removed from the courtroom.

Police made more than a dozen searches for attorney Hughes. All the Tate/LaBianca Manson Family defendants were convicted on March 29th, 1971, and received the death penalty, later commuted to life in prison. On the same day, March 29th, 1971, two fishermen in Ventura County stumbled across Hughes's body, wedged between two boulders in a gorge.

Hughes remains were so decomposed that the cause of death was undetermined. Manson Family followers may have murdered perhaps 35 to 40 people. However, Hughes's death could have been an accident, or maybe he was another Manson cult victim. Sandra Good bragged that they killed Hughes.

Left: Leslie Van Houten, 1978, out of jail on bond. Right: Van Houten retried, headed for court in 1978.

The aftermath of the trial included a new trial for Leslie Van Houten in 1976 because she was denied a proper legal representation because Hughes vanished before he could make the closing arguments. But her retrial in 1977 ended in a hung jury.

Van Houten was released. She was out of jail on a bond. Van Houten, retried in 1978 in a third trial, was convicted of first-degree murder of Leno and Rosemary LaBianca and conspiracy concerning the Tate mass murders. Van Houten got life in prison.

Chapter 47

Dr. Dawson: "But Bugliosi and the cops didn't buy your innocent story. But you're trying to sell it to me now? How naïve do you think I am? You ran the Family. You ordered the murders, right?"

Charles Manson: (He stuck his chin out defiantly at me.) "Wrong. I couldn't get anybody in the so-called Family to go get me a hamburger if I paid 'em ten bucks..."

Dr. Dawson: "Okay, so off Tex and the young women went to murder people to give Cupid – Beausoleil – an alibi. Was it an accident that they went to the house where Terry Melcher lived – the guy who rejected your record deal? Sounds like you wanted to get revenge and sent them to murder people. Or was this just part of the insane Helter Skelter blueprint for taking over the world? I'm lost while I've been trying to follow the logic of your story."

Charles Manson: (Charlie's face turned red, then purple – his face flushed with indignation.) "I told you I ain't no killing machine. I ain't murdered nobody..."

Left: A mugshot of Catherine Share, aka Gypsy (ca 1969). Center: Share, as Charity Shayne, her stage name, sang "Ain't It?, Babe" released by Autumn Records in 1965. Right: Recent photo of Catherine "Gypsy" Share.

Dr. Dawson: "Back to the murder story. Tex, Leslie Van Houten, Susan Atkins, and Patricia Krenwinkel took off to do some alibi murders for Beausoleil which was Tex's scheme to spring Cupid – Beausoleil – out of the slam. Is that your story?"

Charles Manson: (His eyes raked the room nervously and he nodded.) "Hey, Tex was crazier than a shithouse rat. And them broads were bloodthirsty, drug-addled bitches."

Dr. Dawson: "Okay, let me summarize where we are. This Family kill squad went to the house on Cielo Drive in Benedict Canyon. It was rented to record producer Terry Melcher, Doris Day's son. But he didn't live there at that time.

Melcher had come out to the Spahn's Movie Ranch a couple of times because some promoter had dragged him out there. Melcher heard your music and passed on signing you to a record deal. No record deal. You didn't have the talent he was looking for. But you bragged to everybody that Melcher was offering you a record contract."

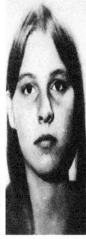

Left to right: A mugshot of Claudia Leigh Smith, a lesser-known Manson Family member. She was arrested with the Family at the Barker Ranch in October 1969. Sherry Cooper, ca 1969. Sherry Cooper, aka Simi Valley Sherry, and Danny DeCarlo, who had a romantic relationship and led a life of crime for many years.

Charles Manson: (His mouth contorted grotesquely.) "Goddamn it. I got talent, man. I coulda been a big rock star—"

Dr. Dawson: "You could have been a contender anyway, huh? Like the Marlon Brando line?"

Charles Manson: (His lips curled in disgust.) "Whatever, Doc... Yeah, it was Terry Melcher's house. He'd moved though. Now after the auditions at Spahn's Movie Ranch, Melcher started bullshitting everybody about my music."

Dr. Dawson: "Oh my god! I guess the only solution was to kill some people. Right, Charlie?"

Charles Manson: (His veins in his neck stood out in livid ridges. He showed me angry facial expressions.) "I wasn't even at the fuckin' murder scene, idiot—"

Dr. Dawson: "Don't call me names, Charlie. What happened? Tell it straight."

Charles Manson: (He smiled maliciously at me.) "Melcher perjured his ass off. He fibbed to everybody at the ranch. He broke his promises. What the hell – he got the Family's dreams and aspirations on top of a mountain. You follow, Doc?"

Dr. Dawson: "A record producer passed on giving you a recording contract. So a lot of people had to die. Charlie, did it occur to you that millions of artists, actors, musicians in Hollywood get rejected or have their projects blown off every day?"

Chapter 48

Hawthorne Shootout. The Hawthorne Shootout on August 21st, 1971, was another insane Manson Family triggered crime. A silent alarm was set off at the Western Surplus store in Hawthorne, California. Hawthorne police responded. Cops arrested six Manson Family members after a shootout. The Manson cult followers arrested included: 1) Mary Brunner; 2) Catherine "Gypsy" Share; 3) Charles Lovett; 4) Lawrence Bailey; 5) Kenneth Como; 6) Dennis Rice.

Like all the Manson Family crimes and antisocial activities, the Hawthorne shootout and gun-store robbery had a stupid and crazy motivation. They stole about 150 guns, which they aimed to use to hijack a 747-jumbo jet. Then these geniuses would kill one passenger every hour until the authorities released Charles Manson and associates from prison.

In an interview, Mary Brunner summed up why most of these losers joined the Manson Family and continued in criminal activity. Brunner had graduated college, had a librarian job, and was bored in her dull routine: work, go home, shopping, sleep, work, go to a movie, and more boring routine.

So, when Brunner was picked up and exploited by Manson, like the other Manson cult followers, Brunner got off on the sex orgies, drugs, rock & roll, and brainwashing.

Left to right: Lawrence Edward Bailey, Kenneth Como, and Dennis Rice. Bailey, Como, and Rice.

The dangers of petty crime and murder further put an edge on the Manson Family experience. Brunner testified against the Hinman killers and escaped responsibility for her part in killing Hinman.

A clerk at the Western Surplus store had set off the silent 211 robbery alarm. Four men and a woman had entered the store with a sawed-off shotgun. They ordered two customers and three employees to lie down on the floor. They smashed glass cases and took guns to a 1966 Ford van, which was parked in the alley where another woman was waiting.

Police officers Jim McInerny, Kenny Cox, arrived in front of the Western Surplus store and were spotted by the Manson Family robbers. When Lieutenant James Kobus came, he was asked to cover the back alley. The robbers ran out the back door, and the cops then covered the back alley. The cops and a police vehicle came under shotgun fire.

Police fired shotguns and .38 bullets at the van and occupants. Some of the suspects attempted to flee on foot, and one got away temporarily. More shotgun blasts by the police resulted in a woman, wounded, falling out of the van when the door was opened, and she was handcuffed.

Left: Catherine "Gypsy" Share, Mary Brunner, circa 1973. Right: Kenneth Como. Share and Como were a romantic item, got married, and divorced.

The cops were in a firefight with four suspects as one ran away. Then they surrendered and were arrested. About 30 officers from several police departments, including Hawthorne, El Segundo, Redondo Beach, and the Lennox Sheriff's Station responded to Kobus's shots-fired radio call. A helicopter from the LASO arrived and helped search for the sixth suspect who escaped on foot.

Under arrest were Mary Brunner (aka Jerry Sherwin), Lawrence Edward Bailey (aka Joseph Jones), Dennis Rice, and Kenneth Como. Charles Lovett was the sixth suspect who was arrested later. None of the police were wounded. But Brunner, Share, and Jones were injured. Catherine Share, the van driver, was hit in the shoulder. Brunner was wounded in the hand. Bailey had a shattered knee cap.

Police revealed a motive for the crime – to steal weapons so the Manson Family group could raid the Gary Hinman and Donald "Shorty" Shea murder trial and free Charles Manson. Trials for the six Hawthorne shootout suspects happened in 1972 and 1973. Charles Lovett was convicted and sentenced to 10 years-to-life for participating in the robbery.

The others were convicted as follows: Dennis Rice was sent to San Quentin for six months to 20 years, was released two years later. In 1973 Catherine Share, Lawrence Bailey, Mary Brunner, and Kenneth Como went on trial. They claimed they were not guilty because of insanity. But they were found sane.

What was the punishment? 1) Catherine "Gypsy" Share, ten-years-to-life; 2) Kenneth Como, 15-years-to-life sentence; 3) Mary Brunner and Lawrence Bailey, 20-years-to-life sentences. Share and Brunner went to the California Institute for Women at Frontera. Share and Brunner got in more trouble in attempting to break out of prison with a pair of wire cutters. But prison authorities caught them before they escaped.

To add a romantic comedy touch to this bizarre Manson Family intrigue, Share fell in love with Kenneth Como. But Manson sent word to Share to stop talking to Como. Como then assaulted Manson in the prison yard. Como and Share got married and divorced in 1981.

Catherine "Gypsy" Share was on a crime spree and continued her criminal activity in the late 1970s and early 1980s. Gypsy, busted on federal charges in a credit card scam, served several years in the slam, did the usual in becoming a born-again Christian, and married Patrick Shannahan, who was a convict.

Mary Brunner, released after six-and-a-half years, joined her son fathered by Charlie Manson, Michael (aka Pooh Bear), who was living with her parents. Brunner was last reported living with an assumed name in the Midwest. Kenneth Como was finally released from prison in 2003 and died a year later.

Chapter 49

Dr. Dawson: "If they all went out and murdered seven or more people to get even, nobody would be left alive in Los Angeles. Did it occur to you, Manson, that you overplayed the incident? It's over the top to commit mass murder because some Hollywood record producer bullshits you."

"Or am I missing something? Because I was surprised Melcher took the time to come to audition you at Spahn's Movie Ranch twice. And I understand he gave you money, right? It seemed like some of his music crowd – the Beach Boy and the promoter thought you had commercial potential."

Charles Manson: (He smiled in defiance.) "Fuckin' rights I have potential. I got talent. But Melcher let us all down. Get it? Melcher was Doris Day's spoiled Hollywood brat. He was fuckin' Candace Bergin f'chrissakes. Terry had seven cars, exotic sports cars. He didn't have a goddamn thing to worry about. I beat Melcher in a card game and won a house."

Dr. Dawson: "Come on, Charlie. How dumb do you think I am? How the hell did you win a house in a card game?"

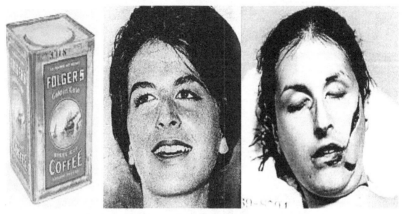

Center: Abigail Folger, coffee heiress, Manson Family victim. Right: Folger morgue photo.

Charles Manson: (Manson's eyes sparkled and danced.) "Okay, Doctor. I had cheated Melcher in that card game. It was part of a con game. Devilish. (Charlie giggled.) But I won a house. Melcher owed me big time."

"From Tex's angle, Terry Melcher was part of the game of war. Terry did a lot of things that ain't kosher. But, hell, I wasn't mad at Terry Melcher. No way Jose. Melcher was just in Tex's mind I guess, and when they went by Bel-Air or Benedict Canyon or what-the-fuck, it rang bells in Tex's muddled brain, and the gang ran to a familiar place."

"Sharon Tate and her rich prick pals – they were in the wrong place at the wrong time. Tex is a crazy mother fucker. Him and those dizzy bitches did the creepy crawlin' witchy number. Tex thought he was a righteous soldier. They all did the duty for Beausoleil. Should have given him a medal of honor. Goddamn standup groupies."

Dr. Dawson: "You got convicted of ordering the murders. So the jury didn't buy your story. You were the boss of the Manson Family who committed the murders. Some of your Family testified against you or accused you of directing the murder scene."

Pictured, Abigail Folger and her lover, Wojciech Frykowski, a lesser-known victim of the Manson Family.

Charles Manson: (His brows furrowed deeply and he shrugged.) "Life's a crapshoot. Ya win some. Lose some."

Dr. Dawson: "There is some confusion or conflict in various accounts. There have been reports that you went over to clean up after your bumbling Manson Family killers. What's the truth? Were you at the Tate scene of the crime?"

Charles Manson: (Manson regarded me critically.) "Doc, I always tie up my elephant. When my gang scratches my back, I scratch their ass. Maybe I did go to the Tate crib and maybe I didn't... Some of this fairytale is stayin' in the shadows..."

Dr. Dawson: "How about the LaBiancas?"

Charles Manson: (He was squirming in his chair. Then he threw his arms around.) "Let me set the stage. Next door to the LaBiancas was a party house we used to hang at – Harold True's pad. We'd go over to LaBiancas to crash after the parties or to nail chicks because they were never home."

"Imagine my shock when I went in there and some old dude was in the living room. I told LaBianca, 'Dude, sorry to bother you. Last time I was here nobody was here. I'm splittin'...' I left LaBiancas'. But Tex was tagging along like a puppy. The ball was in Tex's court. What shots Tex called was up to that dimwit—"

Dr. Dawson: "Charlie, you were the boss of the Manson Family gang. Tex played the game as you told him. Right or wrong?"

Charles Manson: (Manson slumped back like he was recoiling in pain. He got out of his chair, shook his fist and waved his arms around. His face was twisted in pain. He spoke in a sniveling sing-song.) "Tex shot his pool balls. The balls roll like the balls roll. You see, Doc, Tex was a football player in high school. Old Tex had a dozen too many head injuries, concussions."

Chapter 50

James and Lauren Willett murders. Some
of the Manson Family members and associates continued their
lives of crime after the Tate/LaBianca murder convictions. Charles
Manson was taken off the street, locked up, but his influence on
some of his cult followers continued. When some people crossed
paths with Manson's former members and associates, they
sometimes became victims of murder or other crimes.

James Willett was a Marine who served in Vietnam. He was living
in Los Angeles with his wife, Lauren, and their daughter, who was
8-months old. The Willetts ran into several of Manson's cult
members and associates in 1972 and were murdered within a few
months.

The Manson gang included Nancy Pitman (aka Brenda McCann),
Priscilla Cooper, Lynette "Squeaky" Fromme, Michael Lee Monfort,
and James T. Craig. The guys were members of the Aryan
Brotherhood and prison buddies.

Left: Lauren Willett holding baby Heidi, James Willet. Right: Michael "Red Eye" Monfort, James Craig. Montfort, Craig, and some other Manson Family crime cult members murdered the Willetts. Red Eye is Nancy Pitman's ex-husband.

Arrested in connection with the murder of the Willetts: Michael Monfort, James Craig, William Goucher, Nancy Pitman, Priscilla Cooper, and Lynette "Squeaky" Fromme. James Willett was found dead in Guerneville, California. Then Lauren Willett was found buried in a house on West Flora Street in Stockton, California.

I am not particularly surprised that Nancy Pitman and Lynette "Squeaky" Fromme got into trouble and were linked to these murders. I watched Pitman and Fromme in an interview as they carried on like two psycho witches chattering and revealing their self-righteous attitude about Manson Family crime.

On November 8th, 1972, a hiker found the remains of James Willett in the Guerneville, California area. Willett's hand was sticking up from his grave. The killers forced Willett to dig his own grave and then shot him. His head and one hand were missing, which was the result of scavenging animals or cut off by the murderers.

Left to right: Lynette "Squeaky" Fromme, Nancy Pitman, and Priscilla Cooper. Right: News article on the Willett murders.

Police located Willett's station wagon outside a house in Stockton. In the home, police arrested Manson crime cult members who were living there, including Nancy Pitman, Lynette "Squeaky" Fromme, and Priscilla Cooper. Police found the dead body of Lauren "Reni" Willett, James Willett's wife, buried in the basement. A gunshot to her head killed her.

At first, the Manson cult criminals told the police that her murder was an accident. They tried the fake Russian Roulette "suicide" angle that worked with John "Zero" Haught. But the Stockton police did not buy that lie. It seemed that the killers were worried that Lauren Willett might reveal who murdered her husband since his body was discovered and was all over the news. Heidi Willett, the Willett's infant daughter, was alive in the house and orphaned.

Michael Monfort pled guilty to murdering Lauren Willett. Priscilla Cooper, James Craig, and Nancy Pitman pleaded guilty as murder accessories after the fact. Monfort and William Goucher later pled guilty to the murder of James Willett. James Craig pled guilty as a murder accessory in the James Willett killing. The Manson Family crime group had been living in the house while committing robberies.

ARRAIGNED ON MURDER CHARGE — Two men and three "Manson Family" women were arraigned in Stockton Municipal court late yesterday on murder charges. They are left to right: Michael Monfort, 24; James Craig, 33; Lynette Fromme, 24; Nancy Pit- man, 24; and Priscilla Cooper, 21. They were charged with the murder of James Willett, 26, and his wife Lauren, 19. The hearing was continued until November 27 and all were held without bail. (UPI)

Three women from Manson family, three men held in murder probe

STOCKTON, Calif. (UPI) — Three young women scarred with the "Manson family" insignia and three ex-cons with "Aryan Brotherhood" tattoos on their chests were charged Monday with killing an ex-Marine and his teen-age wife to keep them from talking about a crime spree.

The three women and two of the men were taken into custody at a two bedroom house in this central California farming center when police found the body of Lauren Willett, 19, in the basement.

The headless body of her husband, James T. Willett, 26, a recently discharged Marine from Los Angeles, was found last week in a shallow grave about 100 miles away, outside the resort town of Guerneville. He was killed a month ago.

Authorities were led to the woman's body by an escaped convict who used Willett's name and papers to get free on bail after he and a partner were arrested for a Stockton liquor store holdup two weeks ago.

Joseph Baker said Mrs. Willett, who had traveled with her husband's accused killers for a month "apparently of her own free will," was shot in the head with a .38 bullet last weekend to prevent her from talking to authorities about Willett's death.

When the three female suspects appeared in court, the scars of crosses cut into their foreheads as a tribute to mass murderer Charles Manson were barely visible. The "A.B." tattoos of a white racist "inmate hoodlum" group known as the Aryan Brotherhood were covered by the coveralls worn by the two men.

Lynette "Squeaky" Fromme, 24, Nancy Pitman, 24, and Priscilla Cooper, 21, were neatly attired in blouses and slacks as they appeared before Municipal Court Judge Lawrence Drivon after being led into court in handcuffs and chains.

Miss Fromme and Miss Pitman spent months in a vigil outside a Los Angeles courthouse during the trial of Manson and

trying to smuggle him LSD in his jail cell. Miss Cooper's only known connection with the "Manson family" was the scar on her forehead.

Michael Monfort, 24, stocky, unshaven escaped convict with a moustache, and James T. Craig, 33, a bearded parolee who had been sought for return to prison, wore blue jail coveralls during their court appearance.

"Yeah," they answered when Drivon asked if they understood the charges. The judge ordered the five suspects held without bail and continued the arraignment until Nov. 27.

Momfort, Craig and William M. Goucher, 23, an ex-convict being held in Stockton for an Oct. 30 liquor store robbery, were charged later Monday with the murder of Willett.

Sonoma County District Attorney John Hawks accused them of shooting Willett with a pistol and two shotguns "on or about Oct. 10" in order to keep him from

Six Charged With Murder . . .

Bardstown Man Says Body Is That Of Son

BARDSTOWN, Ky. (AP) — The president of a well-known distillery here said he assumes a decapitated body found last week in California is that of his son.

Six persons have been charged with murder in connection with the case, two of the disciples of Charles Manson.

"If you were told beforehand this was going to happen, you wouldn't think you could go through it," said A. Thompson Willett, "but you can, with the help of God."

Willett, president of the Willett Distilling Co., said he learned of his son's death several days ago from a Stockton, Calif., bailbondsman.

"He thought the man who committed the robbery was our boy," Willett said. "He was carrying his papers."

California authorities believe that Willett's son, James T. Willett, 26, was killed to prevent him from telling police about robberies in the Los Angeles area.

"He was killed because the others were afraid he'd tell about robberies the three men committed in the Los Angeles area," said Sonoma County Dist. Atty. John Hawkes.

"Apparently Willett was not involved in the robberies and his relationship with the men is unclear."

Willett's wife, Lauren, 19, was also slain. Both bodies were found buried near the town of Guerneville, where authorities said the Willetts and the three men arrested in the case had shared a resort cabin.

An infant girl was found inside the house who police believe is the Willetts' child. The victim's father said they had an 8-month-old daughter.

"We've never been notified officially," Willett said, "but on the basis of what we've been told, we assume that it's our son."

"We're still hoping, but it's fading fast."

Willett said he feels there's no question that his son and wife were held captive by the three men.

"He had no part in their illegal activities," Willett said. "When they discovered he was going to make a break, they shot him."

His father said young Willet had "no fear at all."

"He was the kind of fellow who would take them on."

Willett also said his daughter-in-law had written her parents that she and Willett were afraid of Manson.

Willett said his son was concerned about conditions in Los Angeles, and was teaching the underprivileged.

Willett said he saw his son

See BARDSTOWN on Page 7.

Tiny Girl Orphaned

STOCKTON (UPI) – A tiny eight-month-old girl, orphaned by the gunshot slayings of her parents and cared for by three "Manson girls" until their arrests for murder, waited today for someone to claim her.

Heidi Willett, who was found by police in a house where her mother's body had been dumped in the basement, was described as a "healthy, well-developed child" at the county dependent children's home.

Her father, James T. Willett, 26, a former Marine from Los Angeles, was gunned down Oct. 10 and buried in a shallow grave outside the resort town of Guerneville, Calif.

Her mother, Lauren, 19, was shot in the head last weekend in a Stockton home where she and the child had been living with three young women and three ex-convicts charged with the two killings.

The women, who had the scars of "Manson family" crosses on their foreheads, and two of the men were apprehended at the house Sunday.

The suspects in the two murders were Lynette "Squeaky" Fromme and Nancy Pitman, two 24-year-old followers of mass murderer Charles Manson who held vigils outside his first trial, Priscilla Cooper, 21; Michael Monfort, 24; James T. Craig, 33, and William M. Goucher, 23.

Left: News on Heidi, orphaned infant Willett's daughter. Right: Nancy Pitman, Manson Family cult member who served time for the Willett murders. Pitman, her lover, Red-Eye (Michael Monfort), James Craig, Lynette "Squeaky" Fromme, and Patricia Cooper were responsible for the Willetts' eight-month-old girl being orphaned.

Monfort had used Willett's ID after being arrested for the armed robbery of a liquor store. James Willett wanted to move away from the Manson criminals. But the Manson gang feared Willett would snitch to the police and so they killed him and his wife. Willett was a Marine veteran who served in Vietnam and had been an ESL teacher for immigrant children.

In keeping with the dark romantic comedy of the Manson cult followers, Nancy Pitman fell in love with murderer Michael "Red-Eye" Monfort, a convicted double-murderer and former Manson Family associate. Monfort was released from prison after 12 years for killing the Willetts.

  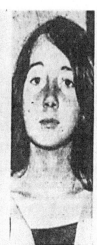

NANCY LAURA PITMAN   LYNETTE ALICE FROMME

Left: Willett's house in Stockton. Right: Nancy Pitman, Lynette "Squeaky" Fromme. Pitman and Fromme were arrested linked to the murders of the Willett couple, leaving Heidi Willett an orphan.

It was true love for Nancy Pitman and Monfort because Pitman married him while he was serving time at the California Training Facility prison at Soledad. She moved to Napa, California, and Monfort joined her there. Nancy Pitman only served 18 months in jail as an accessory to the Willett murders.

When Stockton police observed Willett's station wagon parked in front of a house at 720 West Flora Street on Saturday, November 11th, 1972, they were refused entry to the house. Police broke in, arrested two men and two women. They found pistols and shotguns.

The females were Priscilla Cooper, 21, and Nancy Pitman, 20, both Manson Family members with X's on their foreheads showing they identified with Charles Manson. Then Lynette "Squeaky" Fromme, 24, ex-officio leader of the Manson Family since Charles Manson was in prison, called up and asked for a ride to the house. Police then arrested her.

Left to right: Michael "Red-Eye" Monfort, James Craig, Nancy Pitman, and Priscilla Cooper. These four did prison time for the Willett murders.

The two male killers were Michael Monfort, 24, and James Craig, 33, both state prison escapees. These guys were wanted for a string of armed robberies in California. Both were Aryan Brotherhood members and had AB tattooed on their chests. The Aryan Brotherhood consists of a cult of white prison inmates involved in various crimes, including murder contracts.

Police obtained a search warrant, having noticed freshly turned earth in the basement, they dug and exhumed the remains of Lauren Willett, 19. She had been shot in the head. When interrogated, Priscilla Cooper claimed Lauren Willett had committed suicide playing Russian Roulette. Stockton police did not accept the Russian Roulette defense. The two men and three women were charged with the Willett murders.

Chapter 51

Charles Manson: "He was a dizzy cowboy from Texas. Now, toss some drugs into his system – psychedelics, reefer, snortin' heroin, you name it. Tex was a druggie garbage head. I was lookin' for a crash pad. God knows what Tex was fixin' to pull off." (Charlie laughed and sat back down.)

Dr. Dawson: "I don't understand how conflicting chronicles keep coming out? Tex reported that you – Charles Manson – tied up the LaBiancas before you split. Then you told Tex and your groupie girls to kill both of them."

Charles Manson: (He spit out his words with contempt.) "I did not do diddly squat to the LaBiancas. No, I did not tie 'em up. Hell no. Goddamn! Tex was dizzy from his football injuries acting up on his drug-fried brain."

Dr. Dawson: "Charlie, with all that violence and death? You were at the scene, you were in charge of your scatter-brained, dazed, and dippy Manson groupies. You barked and your cult members jumped. But you're innocent of the murders?"

Pictured are Sharon Tate, Jay Sebring – Manson-cult victims.

Charles Manson: (He spoke with bitter resentment, raised his voice as he spoke. Charlie shook his fist in the air.) "Murder? Violence? You're jumpin' from spot A – murder and violence and Charlie's guilty to spot B. Spot B is where you find my butt cuz I didn't kill shit. And where the hell is your forgiveness for what you are judging me for? Ain't no evidence but Manson's guilty? Bullcrap."

Dr. Dawson: "You're innocent of any violence or murder?"

Charles Manson: (He started screaming in exasperation.) "Tell me, Doc. You think you're so goddamn brilliant. What's so violent about stroking the trigger of a gun with my finger? It's a magic act – I bend my finger and whoosh. The bastard vanishes. Where's the murder? Where's the violence? Up in the sky? On Tex's druggie flight to Mars? Don't be such a woozy-brained bimbo!"

Dr. Dawson: "Charlie, you were the chief of the tribe of your mentally volatile cohorts and devotees. The guru of murder and you've just jammed the puzzle parts together in a new pattern. I don't follow that?"

Jay Sebring & Sharon Tate, Manson Family murder victims. Sebring was Sharon Tate's former lover.

Charlie Manson: (His voice rose hysterically.) "You sound like that nutty detective on TV – Colombo. He was always too dumb to add two plus two. Facts are facts even after 18 years. Repaint the little puzzle pieces and jam 'em together like the cops and snitches."

"Helter Skelter is under the goddamn puzzle pieces. Pull it out of Bugliosi's butt. Dozens of cops, prosecutors, and psycho-hippie assassins all got opinions like assholes. Ya wanna jump on the Bug's perspective – grab the cops' memory. Don't shove Bug's viewpoint down my throat."

"Crazy things surrounded the puzzle parts. Rumors. Drug trips. Psychosis. Shit went down. Add up Tex's-psycho psyche plus some ditzy-druggie babes, toss in every hanger-on's own motives – you got a twisted, jumbled, scrambled murder flare-up. But it don't collate to me. Guilt's in the eye of the beholder."

Dr. Dawson: "How come you always come out clean? No guilt attaches to Charlie?"

Charles Manson: (He took a self-righteous tone of voice. Charlie's voice carried an edge of indignation.) "See a dynamic force spun out from Tex's drug deal gone bad. I popped Lotsapoppa as a favor to a brother."

"But I didn't kill Lotsapoppa. Dangerous explosions spiraled from that. Millions of insane things exploded that summer of 1969. Beausoleil was stuck in jail. Mix in a band of drug-addled dropouts. Pop some LSD. Acid-heads rule. Drug deals gone wrong. Guns and swords. Cheap fucks held out on the money."

"Black Panthers were backing' up the drug dealers. Manson groupies got busted for stolen cars. Who was gonna snitch on me about Lotsapoppa? Tex was building Beausoleil's alibi with a murder nightmare. What's your formula for finding me guilty in all that shit?"

Dr. Dawson: "You want to blame it all on Tex zigzagging, careening and twisting off a drug deal gone bad? There was no Helter Skelter – the insane mission to kill some upscale white people, blame black revolutionaries, and kick-off a race war? You're innocent? Why were you convicted of murder?"

Charlie Manson: (Then his voice was cool, icy.) "Sadie – Susan Atkins – came back to the ranch with a bloody knife. I knew that was the start of the end for me. I figured they'd blame all that crap on the ex-con – Charlie Manson. I was on my way back to the slammer."

"I warned the warden – I was not ready for the crazy free world. But they released me anyway. I couldn't handle all that freedom. Them acidhead bitches, Tex, and his football-injured dippy scatter-brain. I saw a prison homecoming."

Chapter 52

Attempted murder of Barbara Hoyt.

Barbara Hoyt, born December 27th, 1951, died December 3rd, 2017, at age 65 due to kidney failure. Hoyt, a former member of the Manson Family commune, was a witness for the prosecution in the murder trials against the Manson crime cult killers.

When Hoyt first joined the Manson Family in early 1969, as many of Manson's recruits to his cult, she was looking for love and acceptance in all the wrong places.

Some of the Manson Family girls said the Manson cult or semi-hippie commune was kind of innocent in the beginning. I don't believe that in that Manson was a career, hardcore criminal who was always hustling and committing various crimes before he got his crime organization to commit mass murder.

Left: Bugliosi, Assistant District Attorney, Barbara Hoyt, circa 1970. Middle: Recent Hoyt photo. Right: Hoyt in a police mugshot, circa 1969.

But anyway, the myth is that the Manson Family was one big happy hippie family or commune. It was in keeping with the Summer of Love. In a prison interview, Leslie Van Houten told about how the Manson Family, during the first stage from her viewpoint, was relatively innocent. It was about druggie trips, free sex, sex orgies, and love.

If you talk to Lynette "Squeaky" Fromme, she'll still tell you today in 2020, that the Manson Family commune was just about love, dancing, singing, listening to Charles Manson's music, play-acting at Spahn's Movie Ranch, and caring for the environment. Just a happy Boy Scout and Girl Scout troop on a camping trip.

But by 1967, Manson's parole officer said you'd need more than a flower in your hair to go to San Francisco's hippie activities. You needed a .45 handgun. By 1967, hardcore druggie element criminals had infiltrated the innocent, peace, and love hippie movement. Charles Manson was a prime example.

Left: Charles Manson, circa 1970. Middle/right: Barbara Hoyt in her young and innocent days, circa the late 1960s.

Besides Manson sending his hippie robots out to get free food by dumpster diving on garbage runs, Manson ordered criminal activity. Creepy Crawly missions involved burglary, home invasions; credit card theft meant credit card fraud. Manson had his crime cult doing every crime he could think of, which led to a series of murders.

Barbara Hoyt intended to testify against the Manson Family killers. To get her out of town and bribe her not to testify, the hardcore Manson Family members, who didn't want the killer prosecuted, offered Hoyt a free trip to Hawaii to get her out of town.

While she was in Hawaii with Ruth Ann Moorehouse, Moorehouse spiked Hoyt's hamburger with psychedelic drugs, which was a big overdose of LSD. Moorehouse then took off and flew back to Los Angeles. Hoyt freaked out and was taken to a hospital emergency room. The plan was to murder Hoyt in a drug OD via the psychedelic hamburger crime.

Left: Susan Atkins, circa 1969. Right: Barbara Hoyt, circa 1970. Hoyt had heard Atkins talking to fellow Manson Family followers about Atkins's involvement in the Tate mass murders.

The Manson Family plan to eliminate Hoyt as a threat backfired because Hoyt then contacted ADA Bugliosi and said she'd testify. She returned to Los Angeles and was a witness against the Manson cult killers. Hoyt had come to get the real Manson Family agenda, which was not just sex, drugs, and rock and roll. It was a crime operation run by Charles Manson, who used his control of the cult to exploit young people for sex, money and used them to commit various crimes, including murder.

I don't buy that a con artist like Charles Manson believed in Helter Skelter as some apocalyptic doomsday revolution between blacks and whites, which would enable Manson to rule the world. Some of his followers might have been loaded on drugs and brainwashed enough to believe that. Manson's visions of anarchy, his threats, self-destructive lifestyle, and serial murders caught up to him and his criminal gang. And Hoyt was a witness to it.

Left: Paul Watkins (center), Brooks Poston (right) at Barker Ranch. Middle: Police raid at Spahn's Movie Ranch, 1969. Watkins and Poston escaped from the Manson Family, as Hoyt did. Right: Barker Ranch. As the heat and police raids increased on the Manson crime group, they stayed off-and-on at Barker Ranch and Myers Ranch in remote Death Valley.

After the Tate/LaBianca murders, Hoyt was hearing a lot of disturbing things indicating that some of the Manson cult members committed homicides. She was friendly with Donald "Shorty" Shea, and he went missing. The last night she saw him, later that night, Hoyt heard blood-curdling screams and assumed Shea was being murdered.

At the Barker Ranch, Death Valley hideout, Hoyt heard Susan Atkins confessing to the shocking Sharon Tate murder. Hoyt ran away from the Manson cult a couple of times. But like many in Manson's hippie sect, Hoyt had mixed feelings about entirely breaking off from the commune. The murder charges and arrests scared her and turned her off.

Several Manson Family members plotted to kill Barbara Hoyt to stop her from testifying in the Tate/LaBianca murder trial. Ruth Ann Moorehouse, who accompanied her to Hawaii, at the airport (right) bought her a psychedelic hamburger laced with a massive OD of acid or LSD. Hoyt freaked out in Hawaii, collapsed, and almost died. She recovered in the hospital emergency room. The plot backfired when Hoyt testified.

She accepted the offer of the free trip to Hawaii as payment for not testifying. But after Moorehouse and Manson's cult criminals tried to kill her with a drug OD, she freaked out, ran through the streets, and collapsed. Fortunately, she was taken to a hospital, and her life was saved. This assault became a motivation for her to testify against the Manson faction killers.

Hoyt was Bugliosi's star witness for the prosecution at the Tate/LaBianca murder trials and other Manson Family trials. After the trials, Hoyt went to school and became a critical-care nurse. She remained below the radar for years. However, she emerged from anonymity to help Debra Tate, Sharon Tate's sister, and other victims' families to testify at parole hearings for the Manson Family members and associates.

Left to right: Ruth Ann "Ouisch" Moorehouse, Steve "Clem" Grogan, Moorehouse, Lynette "Squeaky" Fromme, Fromme, Catherine "Gypsy" Share. Moorehouse, Grogan, Fromme, Share, and Dennis Rice plotted to kill Barbara Hoyt to stop her from testifying in the Tate/LaBianca trial.

Because Hoyt was an eye witness to the criminal horrors Charles Manson and his illegal followers were causing, she was significant in helping to convict the murderers and other criminals following Manson. Behind the façade of the Summer of Love, peace and love, enlightenment, New Age psychobabble, and other propaganda Charles Manson was pitching was his actual criminal agenda. Manson was a hardcore criminal and serial murderer.

The plot to convince Hoyt not to testify or to kill her was hatched and carried out by five demons of the Manson cult, including Catherine "Gypsy" Share, Lynette "Squeaky" Fromme, Dennis Rice, Steve "Clem" Grogan, and Ruth Ann "Ouisch" Moorehouse. The plan was for Ruth Ann "Ouisch" Moorehouse to accompany Hoyt to Hawaii. If luring her to Hawaii did not result in Hoyt's refusal to testify, Moorehouse was to kill her with a drug OD.

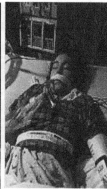

Police found Barbara Hoyt collapsed on the street in Honolulu, an ambulance rushed her to a hospital ER, she survived the attempted murder and testified against the Manson Family killers.

On September 9th, 1971, Hoyt was about to board a flight back to Los Angeles. Moorehouse bought Hoyt a hamburger and spiked it with a massive dose of LSD, expecting that Hoyt would OD and die. Because Hoyt could not be convinced not to testify, her death would prevent Hoyt from testifying against Manson and the other killers: Susan Atkins, Leslie Van Houten, Patricia Krenwinkel, and others later.

Barbara Hoyt survived the attempted murder by the psychedelic hamburger laced with an OD. And the culprits were initially charged with attempted murder. The charge was reduced to conspiracy to dissuade a witness from testifying. A 90-day jail sentence was served at the Los Angeles County Jail by Catherine "Gypsy" Share, Lynette "Squeaky" Fromme, Steve "Clem" Grogan, and Dennis Rice. Ruth Ann "Ouisch" Moorehouse failed to show up for the sentencing hearing and never served her sentence.

It was not long before Barbara Hoyt began getting contrary, conflicting messages while she was living with the Manson commune at Spahn's Movie Ranch. She moved to Spahn's Movie Ranch in April 1969.

It was only four months later that Susan Atkins told Hoyt to get three sets of dark clothing from the Manson cult's clothing collection. When she came back with the garments, Manson told her his crew had already left. Susan Atkins leaned out of the car as they left and told a ranch hand, "We're gonna go kill some mother fucking pigs!"

The next day Hoyt was disturbed when some cult members were laughing and happy about the Tate murder reports on the TV news. The magical mystery tour of the Manson Family turned dark. Charles "Tex" Watson began giving lessons on how to stab and cut people with knives.

The next shoe to drop was the police raid on August 16th, 1969, at Spahn's Movie Ranch when the Manson Family, including Barbara Hoyt, was arrested on a grand theft auto charge. Then a week later, she heard the desperate, blood-curdling screams of Donald "Shorty" Shea as some of the Manson Family criminals were murdering him behind the Spahn Ranch with blunt force weapons, knives, and machetes.

At the Barker Ranch in Death Valley, Hoyt got even more creeped out when she overheard Susan Atkins bragging to Ruth Ann Moorehouse that she murdered Sharon Tate. Hoyt ran away from the Manson Family with another girl, Sherry Cooper.

Manson found them at a café in a small desert town. He gave them $20 to get back to Los Angeles. Manson then sent three Manson cult followers to get the girls and bring them back or kill them.

At first, Hoyt did not want to testify against the cult murderers in the Tate/LaBianca murder trial. So, she flew with Ruth Ann Moorehouse to Hawaii on a little all-expense paid vacation. The assumption some cult members made was that Hoyt was bought off.

Moorehouse sensed that Hoyt could not be trusted to keep her mouth shut. Moorehouse took a cab to the airport with Hoyt and told her she could stay in Hawaii. But Ruth Ann said she had to get back to L.A.

Moorehouse bought Hoyt a psychedelic hamburger, laced the hamburger she gave Hoyt with at least 10 tabs of LSD or acid. Moorehouse dashed aboard a jet to Los Angeles. The OD kicked in and Hoyt freaked out, ran for blocks, and collapsed.

Luckily, she recovered in a hospital emergency room. She notified Bugliosi she wanted to testify. Her mother flew to Hawaii the next day, brought Barbara back to L.A. and Hoyt was very motivated to testify against the Manson Family, who almost killed her.

Hoyt was a good witness for the prosecution and helped convict the Manson killers. She went back to school, became a nurse, was married, divorced, lived with her daughter in Washington State, and died in December of 2017.

Chapter 53

Charles Manson: (He started screaming in exasperation.) "Tell me, Doc. You think you're so goddamn brilliant. What's so violent about stroking the trigger of a gun with my finger? It's a magic act – I bend my finger and whoosh... The bastard vanishes. Where's the murder? Where's the violence? Up in the sky? On Tex's druggie flight to Mars? Don't be such a woozy-brained bimbo!"

"Black Panthers were backing' up the drug dealers. Manson groupies got busted for stolen cars. Who was gonna snitch on me about Lotsapoppa? Tex was building Beausoleil's alibi with a murder nightmare. What's your formula for finding me guilty in all that shit?"

"Helter Skelter is under the goddamn puzzle pieces. Pull it out of Bugliosi's butt. Dozens of cops, prosecutors, and psycho-hippie assassins all got opinions like assholes. Ya wanna jump on the Bug's perspective – grab the cops' memory. Don't shove Bug's viewpoint down my throat."

Sharon Tate

"Crazy things surrounded the puzzle parts. Rumors. Drug trips. Psychosis. Shit went down. Add up Tex's-psycho psyche plus some ditzy-druggie babes, toss in every hanger-on's motives – you got a twisted, jumbled, scrambled murder flare-up. But it don't collate to me. Guilt's in the eye of the beholder."

Dr. Dawson: "An inmate who shared a dorm room with Susan Atkins at the Sybil Brand Institute for Women in the fall of 1969 reported that Susan told her about the killings in a gleeful tone."

"After killing Tate, prosecutors said Atkins tasted the actress' blood and used it to scrawl 'PIG' on her front door. On that shocking, ghastly night, the Manson Family also killed Abigail Ann Folger, Voytek Frykowski, Steven R. Parent, and Jay Sebring..."

"This inmate, Virginia Graham, revealed that Atkins said you had preached of an apocalyptic race war which was predicted in the Beatles song 'Helter Skelter.' Your followers including Atkins believed they would control the United States, if they performed heinous crimes for you. Is this all true?"

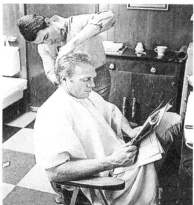

Left: Jay Sebring, a hairstylist with Paul Newman. Right: Sebring with Steve McQueen.

Charles Manson: (He presented a devil-may-care attitude, rolled his eyes, and shook his head.) "Sadie – Susan Atkins – was a wacky-job. She was a madcap druggie who did too many acid trips for her own good. What can I say – some parole-violating snitch wanted to get out of jail for ratting on us?"

Dr. Dawson: "This inmate recalled Atkins said she murdered in cold blood a woman who was going to have a baby. Susan was full of joy and glee when she was telling her how it was done. By the way, Susan was arrested for the murder of music teacher Gary Hinman. You told me you just cut Hinman and Tex finished him off? Was Atkins your right-hand murderer?"

Charles Manson: (Manson shot out his arms, did some macho posturing, and then stared at me coldly.) "I'm not to blame for Atkin's zany, bloodthirsty antics. Who knows what these girls were smokin'? Snortin' cocaine. Inhaling pot laced with PCP? She was just off the wall."

Chapter 54

Lynette "Squeaky" Fromme attempted to kill President Ford. Lynette "Squeaky" Fromme was busted for trying to assassinate President Ford on September 5th, 1975, with a .45 handgun (Colt M1911). She was convicted and served 34 years from 1975 until her release on parole in 2009.

President Ford was scheduled to be in Sacramento, and Lynette "Squeaky" Fromme showed up at Sacramento's Capitol Park looking for President Ford. Squeaky was full of hate, anger, and self-righteousness, which she was pumped up on from her hardcore brainwashing in the Manson Family.

Squeaky never renounced Charles Manson. Her excuse to threaten President Ford was that she was doing an ecology protest. She claimed she was protesting the plight of the California Redwood trees.

Left: Pictured: .45-caliber handgun. Fromme threatened President Ford with a .45-caliber handgun. Right: Fromme showing off with a gun.

Fromme was dressed in a red robe and was packing a .45-caliber semiautomatic pistol, loaded with four rounds. There was no round in the chamber, and fortunately, she did not shoot Ford.

Squeaky refused to cooperate with her defense during the trial. She was convicted of the attempted assassination of President Ford and received a life sentence. Fromme said she could have shot the president because he was two feet away from her. Secret Service agents arrested her at the scene.

Prosecutor Dwayne Keyes asked for severe punishment for Fromme because she was full of hate and violence. Squeaky showed her hostility by throwing an apple at Keyes, hitting him in the face, and knocking his glasses off. Squeaky's statement to the press was: "I came to get a life. Not just my life but clean air, healthy water, and respect for creatures and creation."

Left: Fromme seemed to enjoy being infamous. Right: Fromme under arrest after her 1975 attempt on President Ford's life, which she portrayed as an ecology protest about the California Redwood trees.

As of 2019, in interviews, Fromme is still claiming the Manson Family was innocently about love and concern for the environment, air, water, the Redwoods, the land, and animals. She's in total denial about the rabid hatred, violence, and murder she and the Manson Family was involved in.

Fromme was up to her old tricks and attacked another inmate with a hammer in 1979 while she was incarcerated at the Federal Correctional Institution, Dublin. Fromme then escaped on December 23rd, 1987, from the Federal Prison Camp, Alderson, West Virginia. She tried to meet Manson. Two days later, she was caught and then locked up at the Federal Medical Center, Carswell, Fort Worth, Texas.

Left: Fromme in 1975 and a recent photo. Right: President Ford at the time Fromme attempted to assassinate him, 1975.

Sandra Good and Lynette "Squeaky" Fromme have continued to be mesmerized and hypnotized by Charles Manson. Fromme told the press, "The curtain is going to come down on all of us, and if we don't turn everything over to Charlie immediately, it will be too late."

Fromme was granted parole in July 2008. Time was added to her sentence because of the 1987 prison escape. Finally, she was released on parole from the Federal Medical Center, Carswell, on August 14th, 2009. She moved to Marcy, New York. Skulls decorate her house. She lives with her boyfriend, Robert Valdner, who pleaded guilty to a manslaughter charge in 1988.

Chapter 55

Dr. Dawson: "Graham said Atkins was doing cartwheels up and down the aisle. She was in a total state of happiness. 'Truthfully I thought she was in for a drug bust,' Graham said. She asked Atkins what she was in for and expected her to say cops caught her with marijuana."

"But Susan said murder. 'The next day or day after that is when she plopped herself down on the cot and started talking about murders up in Benedict Canyon. She said, 'Well, you know who did it don't you?' I said no. She said, 'you are looking at her.' I didn't believe her. But I was nosy enough to question her.' Atkins obliged."

"'She was somewhat proud,' added Graham. 'She believed by killing these people that she was sending them to another world and that you had to love them to kill them.' Then in prison, years later Atkins became a model prisoner and became a born-again Christian at the California Institution for Women."

"Years later Graham was asked if Atkins should get parole. 'I know she was young,' said Graham about Atkins. 'But this born again stuff. They all find Jesus when they go to jail. I am not a cold lady...but this was so terrible.'"

Left: Leslie Van Houten, Patricia Krenwinkel, and Susan Atkins. Right: Krenwinkel, Atkins, and Van Houten. These young women turned off the public with their silly, carefree, and smirking attitude during their trials. Years later, they revealed Charles Manson was coaching their antisocial behavior.

"'Why in the world should she be given any compassion? What goes around in life comes around. I wonder what Sharon Tate must have gone through. I have no empathy for this one at all. Hasta la vista baby.' How does that grab you?"

Charles Manson: (Laughed) "That little jitterbug bitch got what was coming to her."

Dr. Dawson: "Do you ever feel remorse or guilt for all those young lives you either ended or ruined? You got convicted of the murders and apparently, you psyched-out those drugged-out groupies to murder by counterintuitive con artist tricks – like telling them they had to love Sharon Tate to kill her? Wasn't your Svengali-like charisma behind all these murders?"

In 1971, Charles Manson was convicted of first-degree murder and conspiracy to murder seven people.

Charles Manson: (He waved his hand blithely.) "Man, I gotta live for today. What happened back in my sex-drugs-rock-and-roll days on the outside? It's history. Done. Fairy story. Make-believe."

Dr. Dawson: "The murders at Tate's home were make-believe?"

Charles Manson: "Make believe to the weird crew that went in to kill Tate and the others, yeah."

Dr. Dawson: "Tex Watson testified in court that you told them to go to Terry Melcher's former place and kill everybody in a very gruesome way for Helter Skelter."

Charles Manson: (He shot me a quirky, wild-eyed look.) "Goddamn it, you got any idea what shit Tex was smoking in them days? Hash, heroin, PCP, acid – you name it, he dropped it."

Dr. Dawson: "Tex was lying? You didn't send him and the young women to murder that night?"

Charles Manson: (He let out a long sigh. His eyes darted back and forth.) "Do you know Tex lost his mind? On the witness stand, he couldn't tell his mother from himself from Charlie Manson. Clean your windshield, Doc. Tex's mind was playing a different game. Unknown to anybody was the Hells Angels under all this. So motivations spun out of control."

Dr. Dawson: "How do you feel about all the pain and suffering you caused the victims, their families, and loved ones?"

Charles Manson: (His mouth dropped open.) "Pain and suffering? I'll tell you about it. I've had my butt beat down in every jail and reform school for decades. Tell me about pain!"

Dr. Dawson: "But it sounds like you didn't learn from the pain. You have spent most of your life in jail. Why don't you learn to stop the bullshit – stop breaking laws?"

Charles Manson: (He slumped in his chair with a pained expression.) "I was raised up in the joint. The older cons brought me up. Told me what to do. Where to sit. What to say. That's what I got from pain."

Dr. Dawson: "You know the difference between right and wrong, Manson. You were not found innocent of the murders."

Charles Manson: (He gave me some furtive, evasive looks.) "I didn't know shit when I got released from prison in 1967. These goddamn hippie kids were protesting the Viet Nam war. I was like a little kid in Alice and Wonderland's nightmare. And just because I was found guilty in court don't mean I ain't innocent. The judge knew I was innocent but the people wanted a guilty conviction."

Chapter 56

Chapter 12: Other suspected murders and various crimes linked to the Manson Family? Cold-case murders.

Reet Jurvetso. Reet Jurvetso (aka Sherry Doe, Jane Doe 59) was a 19-year-old Canadian woman who was stabbed to death in November 1969. Her body was found in dense bushes off Mulholland Drive in Los Angeles. The Manson Family was suspected along with possibly a guy named John or Jean she had traveled from Canada to meet in L.A.

Using DNA, recently, L.A. Police have identified Reet Jurvetso of Montreal, Canada. It was a cold case for decades. Her sister, Anne, had recognized a photo of Reet's body online. Reet had moved to L.A., the same year 150 stab wounds killed her.

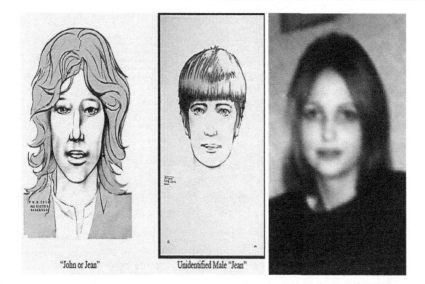

"John or Jean"   Unidentified Male "Jean"

Left: These sketches released by the Los Angeles Police Department show two men police are looking for in connection with the death of a 19-year-old Canadian woman found stabbed to death in Los Angeles in 1969. Right: Reet Jurvetso, 19, murder victim.

She had no ID on her. The location of her body on Mulholland Drive in L.A. was near the Tate murders in Benedict Canyon and during the time of the Manson Family serial murders. Police questioned Charles Manson in prison about Reet Jurvetson. But, as usual, police found interviewing Manson like talking to a wall.

A witness in Montreal had seen Reet Jurvetso at a café with a friend named John or Jean. Also, there was a shorter male associate with a Beatles-type haircut, possibly named Jean.

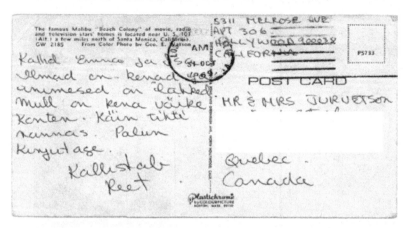

(rear of postcard)

A postcard Reet Jurvetson sent to her family shortly before her death. Dated Oct. 31st, 1969, it read: "Dear Mother and Father, The weather is nice, and the people are kind. I have a nice little apartment. I go frequently to the beach. Please write to me. Hugs, Reet."

Laurence Merrick. Laurence Merrick was shot and killed on January 26th, 1977, outside a Hollywood studio. The killer was a young, heavyset man who ran off and was never caught. Merrick, who was Sharon Tate's old acting coach, was a co-director of *Manson*, a documentary.

The documentary included interviews with Manson Family members. It was released in 1972 and was nominated for an Academy Award for Best Documentary.

Because no suspect has been arrested, the killer's connection to the Manson Family can't be presently verified.

Police artist's sketch of suspect in killing of film producer Laurence Merrick was released yesterday. Suspect has stocky build, around 5-10, 180-190 pounds with dark complexion.

Left to right: Pictured are Laurence Merrick, co-director of the documentary Manson, with Paul Watkins, the former Manson Family member. *Manson* documentary poster. Police sketch of the murder suspect.

Nancy Warren & Clida Delaney. The dead

bodies of Nancy Warren and Clida Delaney were found in the Ukiah, California area on October 13th, 1968. Nancy, eight-months pregnant, like Sharon Tate, was the wife of a California Highway Patrol officer. Clida Delaney was her grandmother and neighbor. They had been beaten and strangled to death.

Warren and Delaney were strangled with leather thongs. Manson had used leather thongs to tie up Leno LaBianca. Guess who was in Ukiah, California, at the time of the murders? Some of the members of the Manson Family.

But nobody in the Manson Family was charged in the murders and no arrests were made. The connection to the Manson Family seems like a wild guess or a fragile link.

Mark Walts.

Mark Walts, 16, hung-out, at times, at the Spahn Ranch during the time the Manson Family was living at the ranch. On July 18th, 1969, Walts' dead body was found near Mulholland Drive. His face had been viciously beaten, and he'd been shot three times in the chest.

Walts' brother called Charles Manson and threatened to get revenge against him after the murder. He was sure the Manson Family had killed his brother. A few months later, the Manson Family killers were arrested for a series of murders.

An investigation of Mark Walt's murder by the Los Angeles Sheriff's detectives included Spahn Ranch. However, no concrete evidence could be developed, and the murder was not solved.

Marina Habe.

Marina Habe's dead body was found dumped in the same area on Mulholland Drive, LA, as Reet Jurvetso was. Similarly, Habe had been stabbed ferociously like Jurvetson. Habe was the daughter of writer Hans Habe and actress Eloise Hardt.

Habe, 17, was home from college and out on a date on December 27th, 1968. She was kidnapped in the early morning hours of December 28th from her home driveway. Two people in a black sedan took her. Her remains were located in the brush off Mulholland Drive.

The autopsy revealed more than one person stabbed her. She had been beaten and stabbed many times in the back and chest. After the Manson Family arrests, the Manson cult followers were suspected. She knew some Manson sect members. Her murder is still unsolved.

Darwin Scott.
Darwin Scott was found stabbed to death on May 27th, 1969, in his Ashland, Kentucky apartment. Charles Manson's father was Darwin's brother, Walker Scott, a colonel in the army. At the time of Darwin's murder, a band of hippies was in town dealing LSD. After townspeople burned the hippies' house down, they left. Charles Manson was out of prison at the time and out of touch with his parole officers. The murder was not solved, and Manson and his cult followers might be suspects.

James Sharp & Doreen Gaul.
Both James Sharp, 15, and Doreen Gaul, 19, were found stabbed to death in a Los Angeles alley. They were stuck 50 to 60 times. There were similarities to the Tate/LaBianca murders: no motive, vicious stabbings, and they were found close to where the LaBiancas lived.

Another strange connection was that both Sharp and Gaul were part of a splinter group of Scientologists called The Process or The Process Church of the Final Judgment. Charles Manson had a connection to The Process. Manson had studied Scientology in prison and used their ideas in his guru pitch to his followers.

Also, Bruce Davis, a Manson Family member, was sent to London by Manson and visited The Process headquarters. The Process followers visited Manson in prison, and he gave them an interview for their publication. It is not known if the Manson Family killed Gaul and Sharp. However, stranger deaths were committed by the Manson cult.

Joel Pugh.
Joel Pugh was a Manson Family member who was involved romantically or married to Sandra Good (aka Blue). When Good had a baby, she gave it the last name Pugh. Police found Pugh's body on December 1st, 1969, in the Talgarth Hotel in London.

Left: Sandra Good and lover Joel Pugh. Right: Bruce Davis, circa 1970, and a recent prison photo. One theory is that Bruce Davis murdered Joel Pugh and made it look like a suicide.

His death was ruled by a drug-induced suicide. His wrists had been cut, and his throat was slit twice. No suicide note was found, there was some writing on the mirror, and the hotel manager recalled seeing "Jack and Jill" written on the mirror. Was it murder in the form of a fake suicide?

The suicide or murder happened when the Manson Family cult killers were being arrested for various mass murders, including the Tate/LaBianca killings. Some theories have emerged about Pugh's death. Was Pugh so guilty he committed suicide? Or was he killed at Charles Manson's direction because he knew too much?

Who in the Manson Family could have murdered Pugh? Bruce Davis, who murdered and was convicted of killing Donald "Shorty" Shea and Gary Hinman, had the opportunity to kill Pugh. Bruce Davis had been in London earlier in 1969 and could have been in London at the time of Pugh's death. Sandra Good denied Pugh was her husband and seemed to want to distance herself from him.

Chapter 57

Dr. Dawson: "Let's talk about your mother. Didn't she teach you right from wrong?"

Charles Manson: (He showed some facial tics, then stuttered at first.) "My mom was living in the Blue Moon Café. She got in a fight with some guy and hit him with a whiskey bottle. She then took me and we moved away to Indiana."

"My mom did a damn good job of raising me. My grandma helped. Grandma was from the mountains of Kentucky. She cooked for the Salvation Army. They both took care of me. Then I learned a lot in reform schools."

Dr. Dawson: "From what was testified to in court, you tied up the LaBiancas and told them they would not be hurt. Then you went outside and sent Tex, Susan Atkins, Kasabian, and Krenwinkle into the house with orders to kill both the LaBiancas."

Charles Manson: "Mmmhmmm… Who told you that?"

Dr. Dawson: "It's a court record. Newspaper accounts. Did you order those murders on August 10th?"

Left: Steve "Clem" Grogan, killer who was convicted of murder, released from prison in 1985. Center: Grogan singing and playing with his band. Right: Grogan having fun playing croquet. Most of the Manson Family murderers either died in prison or are still in prison 50 years later. Grogan has been free for over 35 years as of 2020!

Charles Manson: "That's like askin' Jesse James if he's gonna get in a gunfight..."

Dr. Dawson: "Why are you avoiding the question? The news media calls you a monster, a cult guru. A lot of hanky panky went down at the ranch – sex and drugs with the girls."

Charles Manson: (He gave me a look of wide-eyed innocence, got up and danced around, then sat back down.) "I went to San Francisco, Haight-Ashbury. Some little 12-year-old kid comes up to me and asks me if I want LSD – acid pills. Then we smoked some marijuana."

Dr. Dawson: "What drugs have you done? Did they hurt you?"

Left: Steve Grogan, murderer. Right: Grogan with his band having a blast. Grogan is shown on the left with the white hat on.

Charles Manson: (Chuckled) "No hard drugs – narcotics that would hurt me. I smoked grass, acid, mescaline... Psilocybin, peyote, mushroom... No, they didn't hurt me."

Dr. Dawson: "I did some research. It seems you hit your mother and your ex-wife. You had a son with her?"

Charles Manson: (He shook his head.) "I hit her once. My ex-wife took off with some truck driver. I don't know where she and the kid are."

Dr. Dawson: "Do you like women?"

Charles Manson: (Laughs) "Sure I like 'em. They're soft and spongy. As long as they keep their mouths shut and do what they're told."

Dr. Dawson: "Are you afraid of dying?"

Charles Manson: "I'm not afraid of dying. I'm afraid of living. Living is what scares me. Dying is easy. But I've been an outlaw ever since I was borned."

Chapter 58

CHARLES MANSON (1934-2017): Manson, a 5'2" songwriter, musician, cult leader, and convicted murderer, was born on November 12th, 1934, in Cincinnati, Ohio. His parents were W.H. Scott Sr. and Kathleen Maddox. He was listed: No Name Maddox on his birth certificate. Manson is also known as Charles Milles Manson, Charles Maddox, The Wizard, Jesus Christ, JC, The Gardener, and the Devil.

His mother, Kathleen Maddox, was a 16-year-old runaway and part-time hooker. His stepfather was William Manson, who his mother was briefly married to, and from him, Manson got his last name. Charles Manson's criminal mother, at age 22 in 1940, was convicted of strong-armed robbery and did five years in Moundsville State Prison.

Left: Manson, 1970.   Right: Manson at age 80.

As a child, Manson ping-ponged among various dysfunctional relatives, including grandparents, aunts, and uncles. His grandparents were uptight, strict, fundamentalist-religious fanatics. He stayed with a crazy uncle who labeled him a sissy, dressed him in girls' clothing, and sent him to school. Another uncle killed himself in a moonshine still because the law was taking his property.

He was married twice to Rosalie Willis (m. 1955, div. 1958) and Leona Stevens (m. 1959, div. 1963). His partners included various members of the Manson Family, including Mary Brunner and Susan Atkins. Manson had two or three children. But because he was a sex addict and had many female sex partners, he may have had other children.

Manson was sort of a chameleon, mercurial, and often looked different from one time to another.

Charlie briefly lived with his mother after she was released from jail, but was given up to the state after his mother's boyfriend said he didn't like having Charlie around. Manson was sent to the Gibault Home for Boys in Terre Haute, Indiana. Manson repeated a pattern of escaping from institutions.

Manson was sent to Father Flanagan's Boys Town after he got arrested for stealing a bike. After a few days, he split and took a car. He then committed armed robberies. After his subsequent arrest, Manson ended up in the Indiana School for Boys in Plainfield, Indiana, where he claimed he was raped. Years later, in prison interviews, he denied being raped.

Manson, who did not believe in getting an honest job and staying out of trouble, followed his impulses, escaped from the Indiana School for Boys, stole a car, and was busted in Utah. He then did time in several different reform schools or prisons for teenagers, including:

Left: Charles Manson and Rosalie Jean Willis at their wedding in 1954. Right: Charles Milles Manson Jr with mother, Rosalie Jean Willis. Manson's son committed suicide, haunted by his mass-murdering father.

- National Training School for Boys in Washington, D.C.
- Natural Bridge Honor Camp
- Federal Reformatory at Chillicothe, Ohio

At age 21, in 1955, Manson married Rosalie Jean Willis, 17. Charlie did his SOP (standard operating procedure) and stole a car while traveling to California. Rosalie became pregnant, and so a judge gave Manson, family man, probation after his next arrest for stealing a car. Next, Charlie broke his probation rules. He went away to Terminal Island Prison for three years. Rosalie met a truck driver, fell in love, and left town with their kid and the truck driver.

Manson's son he had with Rosalie Jean Willis, Charles Milles Manson Jr., changed his name to Jay White to distance himself from his father, Charlie, the notorious Manson Family cult leader. Jay White was so haunted and filled with self-hatred that he eventually committed suicide because his mass-murdering father's reputation haunted him.

Charles Manson turned disaffected, alienated would-be hippies in the late 1960s into zombie-like robots following his orders.

On June 29th, 1993, he killed himself. His death certificate stated his death was from a self-inflicted gunshot wound to the head at Exit 438 on Interstate 70 at 10:15 AM in Burlington, Colorado.

Released from Terminal Island Prison in 1958, would Charlie look for a legit job at age 24? Of course not. Manson pimped hookers in Los Angeles. Manson stole a check for $37.50, which he tried to cash. Busted, he got a 10-year-suspended sentence. In 1959 Manson got married again to Leona Stevens.

Manson drifted around working as a pimp earning money from prostitutes. He was arrested in Laredo, Texas, for pimping and violating the Mann Act, which bans crossing state lines for prostitution. He then had to serve the 10-year sentence for the stolen check in McNeil Island Penitentiary in Washington State.

Left: Manson Family appeared to be a happy-hippie group. At left is Lynette "Squeaky" Fromme (later did 34 years in prison for the attempted assassination of President Ford). In the rear is Bruce Davis and Steve "Clem" Grogan. Right: Davis (still in jail as of 2019) and Grogan (released from prison in 1985) during their murder trial.

His wife, Leona, gave birth to his son Charles Luther Manson, served him with divorce papers, and Charles was single again while in prison. He took up playing guitar in prison and also learned some Scientology buzz words and doctrine. He transferred to Terminal Island Prison in 1956.

On March 21st, 1967, Manson was finally paroled in time for the Summer of Love in the summer of 1967. Manson asked the warden to let him stay in Terminal Island Prison. Institutionalized, Manson was at home in prison. But the warden told Manson he had to leave prison.

Manson traveled to San Francisco, checked out the Haight-Ashbury district, and got into the counterculture hippie movement. The hippie lifestyle appealed to Manson because he hated working at legal jobs and preferred to live free by scams, petty crime, and exploiting young women.

The Manson Family is pictured at Spahn's Movie Ranch during a police raid.

He met Mary Brunner on the Berkeley campus, where she was a librarian. She was the first girl in his Manson Family. He sponged off Mary, got her sexually and emotionally attached, and then drifted around the West Coast with Mary, recruiting more Manson Family, hippie-cult members.

His third child was born on April 1st, 1968, when Mary Brunner gave birth to Valentine Michael "Pooh Bear" Manson. Manson named him after the main character in Robert Heinlein's *Stranger in a Strange Land*.

Because Manson had some prison contacts in the music business, he took his followers to Los Angeles. Manson got in touch with some people at Universal Studios and was looking to record his music and get a record deal. Manson and his cult Family tried to network at Hollywood parties where they met productive, famous Hollywood players, movie stars, rock stars, and talent scouts.

The question was, did Manson have any talent? Were his songs worth a record deal? Some seemed to think his songs and singing and playing had potential. But over time, Terry Melcher, a record producer, passed on Charlie's songs. And as Hollywood players heard about his crimes, he was rejected.

Left: George Spahn, owner of Spahn's Movie Ranch. Right: Some of the Manson Family members at Spahn's Movie Ranch. From left to right: Mary Brunner, Sandra Good, Jennifer, Catherine "Gypsy" Share, Chuck, Cathy "Cappy" Gillies, Ruth Ann "Ouisch" Moorehouse, Danny, and Lynette "Squeaky" Fromme.

Manson Family members Ella Jo Bailey and Patricia Krenwinkel were hitchhiking and were picked up by Dennis Wilson, drummer of The Beach Boys. Manson took advantage of this connection and temporarily moved his Manson Family into Wilson's mansion in Pacific Palisades. Wilson nicknamed Manson The Wizard and was impressed with him for a time.

The Manson Family cost Wilson a small fortune because the hippie-cult members were parasites. They cost him over $100,000 for 1) food; 2) clothing; 3) dental bills to fix their teeth; 4) crashing his expensive cars like an uninsured Ferrari; 5) medical bills such as for sexually transmitted disease treatments and medicine; 6) damage to his house and property; 7) stolen items; 8) other costs. Finally, The Beach Boy's manager kicked them out.

Charles Manson under arrest and headed for jail.

Wilson introduced Manson to Gregg Jakobson, a talent scout, and Terry Melcher, The Beach Boys record producer. Wilson tried to help Manson get a record deal. Melcher, son of actress Doris Day, was a successful record producer of rock bands, and Jacobson worked for Melcher.

Melcher even went out to Spahn's Movie Ranch and heard Manson and his girls do some of his songs. Melcher passed on his weird songs. The irony was that after Manson became infamous and was locked in prison convicted of mass murder, some rock groups recorded some of Charlie's songs.

Manson enjoys attention in court, 1970.

By the summer of 1969, Manson had not become a big rock star. So, Manson continued to escalate his criminal activities such as stealing cars, stealing credit cards, and stealing anything he could. Tex Watson, a key Manson Family enforcer and murderer, had taken $2,000 from Bernard "Lotsapoppa" Crowe, a black drug dealer. Crowe was threatening the Manson Family.

Manson met with him, got into a confrontation, and shot Crowe in the stomach. Manson fled and later heard on the news about a dead Black Panther. Manson assumed it was Crowe. He got paranoid that the Black Panther militants were going to come after the Manson Family and kill them. Crowe lived and did not go to the police. Anyway, Manson began collecting more weapons, expecting a war with the Black Panthers.

Spahn's Movie Ranch.

Gary Hinman, a Manson Family associate, and small-time drug dealer was a target Manson wanted to rob. Manson figured he could get thousands of dollars from Hinman. Manson, in late July 1969, sent Bobby Beausoleil, Mary Brunner, and Susan Atkins to demand money from Hinman. Hinman refused and claimed he had no money. They called Manson, who arrived with Bruce Davis. Davis held a gun on Hinman as Manson threatened to cut him.

Charlie got into a yelling match with Hinman over the money, took a sword, and cut Hinman's ear. Manson and Davis left in one of Hinman's cars. Manson ordered them to get the cash from Hinman. So, they tortured him, and Bobby Beausoleil fatally stabbed Hinman. Beausoleil stole Hinman's other car and was later arrested and charged with murdering Hinman.

Members of the Manson Family are shown at Spahn's Movie Ranch including Steve Grogan (left), Lynette "Squeaky" Fromme and Sandra Good.

Manson continued his serial-murder spree that summer. He ordered a murder crew consisting of his Manson Family hippie killers to go to 10050 Cielo Drive and kill everybody in the house. Revenge murders seemed to be his big blow against the Hollywood establishment because while he knew Melcher and his girlfriend Candace Bergin had moved out, he wanted to send a message to the rich and famous in Hollywood who had failed to make him a rock star.

Susan Atkins, Patricia Krenwinkel, and Linda Kasabian were told to go with Tex Watson and to do what he told them. Manson told Watson to slaughter all the people in the house rented to Polanski and Tate. They drove to the mansion on Cielo Drive on August 9th, 1969, and arrived about 12:30 a.m. Watson began by killing Steven Parent, who was visiting the caretaker, and who was in his car in the driveway when Watson shot and cut him. The killers entered the Polanski-Tate home and killed Jay Sebring, Wojciech Frykowski, Abigail Folger, and Sharon Tate in a brutal bloodbath.

Some of the Manson Family cult pictured at Spahn's Movie Ranch.

Manson continued the mass-murder spree the following night. Manson led the killers the next night and was with Tex Watson, Susan Atkins, Patricia Krenwinkel, Steve Grogan, Leslie Van Houten, and Linda Kasabian. They went to 3301 Waverly Drive, home of Leno and Rosemary LaBianca. Manson and Watson entered the house first and told the couple they were being robbed and would not be hurt. Watson tied the couple up.

Leslie Van Houten and Patricia Krenwinkel entered the house after Manson left. He ordered them to kill the LaBiancas. They were told to hitchhike back to Spahn's Movie Ranch. Manson drove off with Susan Atkins, Steve Grogan, and Linda Kasabian, and they wandered around that night looking for possible victims they could kill to help start his Helter Skelter race war.

Shown are Charles Manson and his associates under arrest after a police raid at Spahn's Movie Ranch.

On August 16th, 1969, a whole group of the Manson Family was arrested after a police raid at Spahn's Movie Ranch. Auto theft was the charge. But they were soon released over a technical error – a misdated warrant. Because Manson assumed Donald "Shorty" Shea, a ranch hand and movie stuntman, had informed the cops about stolen cars, Manson ordered his murder.

A Manson Family crew murdered Donald "Shorty" Shea. The killers included Charles Manson, Bruce Davis, and Steve Grogan. Some others, not charged, were suspected of helping to murder Shea: Tex Watson, Bill Vance, and Larry Bailey (aka Larry Giddings). They killed him, dismembered him into nine pieces, and buried him behind Spahn's Movie Ranch.

As Manson's paranoia grew, he decided to move the Manson Family commune to Barker Ranch near Death Valley. The Manson Family members were arrested again at Barker Ranch in October 1969. By that time, police had gotten enough information on some of the Manson cult murders that they could make arrests that stuck.

Manson crossed paths with many celebrities, including Terry Melcher (left), son of Doris Day, a record producer who rejected Manson and passed on giving him a record deal. Angela Lansbury's daughter, Deidre Shaw (middle right), was a Manson follower at one time. She introduced Nancy Pitman (right) to the Manson Family.

Manson, a hardcore criminal, and psychopath, was released from prison in 1967. He was on the street during the "Summer of Love" and used his streetwise skills to recruit a group of mostly-female followers. Charlie exploited the "Summer of Love" spirit, which permeated the hippie movement, which resulted in an estimated 100,000 young people converging on San Francisco's Haight-Ashbury area.

They wore hippie fashions, promoted free love, were anti-war, pro-environment, free-spirited, anti-establishment, and counter-cultural rebels. In the radical-leftist-hippie crusade, Manson's ex-convict status was a plus. Charlie, who led a criminal lifestyle, had no intention of getting an honest job and working for a living. His work was as an illegal con artist.

Left: Pictured are Manson Family members Steve "Clem" Grogan and Paul Watkins. Right: Photo from the 1967 Summer of Love in San Francisco's Golden Gate Park.

Under the façade of the Summer of Love hippie subculture, Manson hustled young women and girls to join his Manson Family pseudo-hippie harem. They then explored free sex, drug trips and got brainwashed by Charlie's psychobabble he picked up from street-corner gurus, pimps, criminals, and New-Age books. His cult was about 5-to-1 female-to-male, and Manson could attract a few useful idiot young men by offering them sex with his girls. He called his prettiest girls, his Front-Street Girls, and pimped them to guys he used.

Groups such as the radical-left, anti-capitalist Diggers organized free food at soup kitchens, set up open stores where homeless hippies could get clothing or other items without charge, complimentary crash pads, and a free-medical-care clinic. There were parties at no cost with free or cheap drugs like LSD and marijuana and free music provided by the Grateful Dead, Janis Joplin, Jefferson Airplane, and other rock bands in San Francisco parks or other places. Charlie's growing cult took advantage of all the freebie activities.

Susan Atkins was confused, stunned, and hypnotized by Charlie. She threw her life away by joining the Manson Family. She got convicted of murder and died in prison.

Manson's Family would just be written off as a weird cult or group of homeless-street bums and criminals in the 1950s. But in the late-60s, the Manson Family became an attractive-pseudo-hippie commune. Charlie played guitar and sang strange lyrics, which gave him a mystical, mysterious vibe. By the time the Manson Family had moved from San Francisco to Spahn's Movie Ranch in the LA area and then to Barker Ranch in Death Valley, about 100 young hippie drifters and criminals had floated in and out of the Manson Family.

Charlie failed to impress most of his Hollywood contacts with his songwriting, singing, and guitar playing. Manson was unable to get a record deal or become a rock star. Instead of taking the hint and trying a different line of honest work, Manson got revenge by sending his murder crew out to kill successful Hollywood players and establishment people. Manson and his killers robbed and murdered Gary Hinman. They also slaughtered Donald "Shorty" Shea and others suspected of being police informants.

Charles Manson, shown angry and in prison.

Charles Manson and some of his followers were convicted of murder, got the death penalty, and then the sentence was overturned to life in prison. Manson died of a heart attack, respiratory failure, and colon cancer at age 83 on November 19th, 2017, in the California State Prison in Corcoran. He was cremated on March 20th, 2018.

Manson, a career criminal, through mass murder in the summer of 1969, helped bring an end to the utopian fantasies of the 1960s. Manson had developed a sick skill from a childhood of using mostly girls to attack people to get revenge. He continued using females to get payback for his rock star disappointments by ordering his Manson Family assassins to kill.

Manson Family police mugshots.

Charlie's crazy-apocalyptic nightmare, Helter Skelter, that the Beatles' White Album track predicted a black-white race war, which he brainwashed the Manson Family cult to believe and take action on it, was an indication of his paranoid insanity and psychopathy. Charlie lied that the Tate/LaBianca and Hinman murders would trigger Helter Skelter. But in reality, the mass murders were reprisals over Manson's failure to be a rock star.

Then in his grandiose, ego-maniac vision, the Manson Family led by Charles Manson would rule the world. The Manson Family had to be stupid, gullible, and loaded on drugs to be brainwashed to believe Manson's fake agenda. Charlie was a con artist who did not believe in Helter Skelter.

After Charles Manson nailed down his core Manson Family harem cult consisting of Brunner and Lynette Fromme, nicknamed Squeaky, he continued to collect followers from San Francisco to Los Angeles from 1967 to 1969. Manson controlled a group of 20 to 30 passionate-cult followers by 1969, and they moved onto Spahn's Movie Ranch as a commune.

9th August 1969

Charles Manson Charles "Tex" Watson Susan Atkins Patricia Krenwinkel Linda Kasabian

Steven Parent Jay Sebring Sharon Tate Wojciech Frykowski Abigail Folger

Murderers (top row) and murder victims (bottom row) involved in the mass murders at the Tate/Polanski home on August 9th, 1969.

Besides recruiting Manson Family members along the California coast, Manson traveled with some of his key followers like Brunner, Fromme, and Susan Atkins to other Western states like Washington, Oregon, and Nevada.

By sexually servicing George Spahn, owner of Spahn's Movie Ranch, with his girls and ordering his followers to do chores around the ranch, Manson was able to live rent-free at Spahn's Movie Ranch with his eager-hippie-druggie followers.

Manson Family girls pictured dumpster diving for food behind a supermarket. Manson got the idea for dumpster diving from the Diggers in San Francisco. If Manson told them to live like dogs and get free-stale food from garbage cans, it was hip and slick. Manson's pseudo-hippies were so cool, huh? The Manson girls were a cheap date. Lunch? Take her to a garbage dumpster behind a supermarket.

So, between 20 and 30 fervid cult members stuck around Spahn's Movie Ranch. Up to 100 young hippies, aimless drifters, and criminals, passed in and out of the Manson Family from 1967 to the early 1970s. Manson preached the 1960s doctrine of peace, free love, wild sex orgies, and freedom.

But his actual aim was that Charles Manson was the boss and dictated orders to all his Manson Family cohorts. For those needing more persuasion, Manson kept enforcers like Tex Watson, Steve "Clem" Grogan, and Bruce Davis around armed with illegal firearms, knives, and swords. A few beefy motorcycle gang members sometimes hung-out for sex with the girls and enforced Manson's orders.

Some Manson Family members pictured during the murder trials. From left to right: Charles "Tex" Watson, Patricia Krenwinkel, and Bobby Beausoleil.

Spahn's Movie Ranch, in Los Angeles County, was near the Los Angeles suburb of Chatsworth. Manson sent his mostly female gang into the local towns and L.A. to do dumpster diving to get stale, discarded food from the garbage containers behind supermarkets. Manson Family members committed various petty crimes such as shoplifting, stealing credit cards and IDs, stealing cars, and anything of use to the commune. Thus, at times, his hangers-on got arrested for petty crimes, car theft, credit card fraud, drug charges, and finally, murder.

To better understand Manson as a street-corner guru who entertained and hypnotized his Manson Family disciples, who were 5-to-1 female-to-male, consider some of his sayings, quotes he used to rationalize his crimes and crazy behavior and control his hippie cultists:

Manson under arrest and at his murder trial.

"You know, a long time ago being crazy meant something.
Nowadays, everybody's crazy."
— **Charles Manson**

"Look down at me, and you see a fool,
Look up at me, and you see a god,
Look straight at me, and you see yourself."
— **Charles Manson**

"I can't judge any of you. I have no malice against you and no
ribbons for you. But I think that it is high time that you all start
looking at yourselves and judging the lie that you live in."
— **Charles Manson**

With a combination of New-Age maxims, prison-con-artist
sayings, platitudes, and axioms, Manson could shape his young
fans into obedient robots ready to kill or at least do some petty
crimes. Because, f'chrissakes, we would not want Charles Manson
to have to do an honest day's work. Right?

Manson under arrest and during his murder trial.

How about these Manson quotes for keeping his followers in line? Manson could justify his dictatorial paranoia by saying:

"Total paranoia is just total awareness."
— **Charles Manson**

"I'm nobody
I'm a tramp, a bum, a hobo
I'm a boxcar and a jug of wine
And a straight razor if you get too close to me."
— **Charles Manson**

Notice how Manson can chatter nonsense and include a violent threat to scare his kids and keep them jumping to Manson's orders. Let's say somebody wants to make a logical argument against Manson's way of doing things. He can say the following nonsense to confuse his hippie-cult followers, loaded on drugs and only semi-awake to reality:

"We`re not in Wonderland anymore, Alice."
— **Charles Manson**

Manson, during his murder trial.

"I don't wanna take my time going to work. I got a motorcycle and a sleeping bag and ten or fifteen girls. What the hell I wanna go off and go to work for? Work for what? Money? I got all the money in the world. I'm the king, man. I run the underworld, guy. I decide who does what and where they do it at. What am I gonna run around like some teeny bopper somewhere for someone else's money? I make the money, man, I roll the nickels. The game is mine. I deal the cards."
--Charles Manson

"The real strong have no need to prove it to the phonies."
— **Charles Manson**

"In my mind's eye, my thoughts light fires in your cities."
— **Charles Manson**

If the Manson Family flower children were not convinced and anxious to please Charlie, he could spout more mottos, adages, dictums, and proverbs to get his gang to stop thinking for themselves. Because some Manson Family members still had a little common sense and morality left, here are some slogans to get them to comply with Manson's authority. How about the following to justify mass murder?

Manson, during his murder trial.

"Sanity is a small box; insanity is everything."
— **Charles Manson**

"Death is the greatest form of love."
— **Charles Manson**

"The mind is endless. You put me in a dark solitary cell, and to you, that's the end, to me it's the beginning, it's the universe in there, there's a world in there, and I'm free."
— **Charles Manson**

Are you confused enough to blindly follow Charles Manson's criminal lifestyle yet? How about some more quotes from the ultimate guru, Manson:

"It seems a shame to have to sneak to get to the truth. To make the truth such a dirty-old-nasty thing. You gotta sneak to get to the truth, the truth is condemned. The truth is in the gas chamber. The truth has been in your stockyards. Your slaughterhouses. The truth has been in your reservations, building your railroads, emptying your garbage."

Three Manson girls were shown during their murder trial, left to right: Susan Atkins, Patricia Krenwinkel, and Leslie Van Houten. These young women, brainwashed and acting like they were from another planet, detached from reality, giggling, singing Manson's songs, and chanting on the way to court.

"The truth is in your ghettos. In your jails. In your young love, not in your courts or congress, where the old set judgment on the young. What the hell do the old know about the young? They put a picture of old George on the dollar and tell you that he's your father, worship him. Look at the madness that goes on; you can't prove anything that happened yesterday."

"Now is the only thing that's real. Every day, every reality is a new reality. Every new reality is a new horizon, a brand-new experience of living. I got a note last night from a friend of mine. He writes in this note that he's afraid of what he might have to do to save his reality, as I save mine. You can't prove anything."

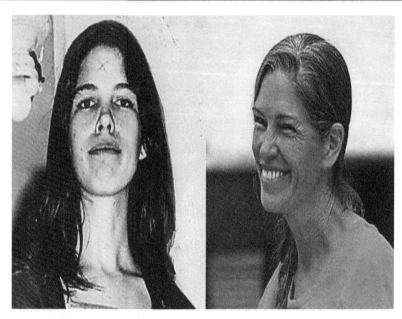

Left: Leslie Van Houten, 1970. Right: Leslie Van Houten, convicted of murder, after decades in prison.

"There's nothing to prove. Every man judges himself. He knows what he is. You know what you are, as I know what I am, we all know what we are. Nobody can stand in judgment; they can play like they're standing in judgment. They can play like they stand in judgment and take you off and control the masses, with your human body."

"They can lock you up in penitentiaries and cages and put you on crosses like they did in the past, but it doesn't amount to anything. What they're doing is, they're only persecuting a reflection of themselves. They're persecuting what they can't stand to look at in themselves, the truth."

— **Charles Manson**

Pictured is director Roman Polanski and actress Sharon Tate, Manson Family murder victim, at their wedding in January 1968.

Are you convinced that the only truth is Charlie Manson's truth? Therefore, you must do as he says. If you're a pretty young girl, you must service Manson sexually. If Charlie tells you to have sex with some guy so he can manipulate the guy, you must do it. Why? Well, here's some more of Manson's psychobabble, guru slogans to impress you with his genius:

"No sense makes sense."
— **Charles Manson**

How can Manson rationalize murder? Here's Manson's excuse:

"These children that come at you with knives--they are your children. You taught them. I didn't teach them. I just tried to help them stand up."
— **Charles Manson**

Left to right: Patricia Krenwinkel, Leslie Van Houten, and Susan Atkins watching photographers as they are on the way to their murder trial.

And when Manson sent his killers out to do mass murder, he advised them:

"If you're going to do something, do it well. And leave something witchy."
— **Charles Manson**

Manson meant you should torture and kill and write slogans in blood at the scene of the crime like: "Political Piggy" or "Helter Skelter".

To discredit authorities at his murder trial, Manson said:

"You people would convict a grilled cheese sandwich of murder, and the people wouldn't question it."
— **Charles Manson**

Charles "Tex" Watson: police mugshots, Watson at Spahn's Movie Ranch. Watson under arrest.

And if you asked Manson if he felt guilty about ordering murders, had any remorse, he'd snap at you with gibberish and nonsense because Manson knew he could take advantage of naïve people by confusing them:

"Do you feel blame? Are you mad? Uh, do you feel like wolf kabob Roth vantage? Gefrannis booj pooch boo jujube; bear-ramage. Jigiji geeji geeja geeble Google. Begep flagaggle vaggle veditch-waggle bagga?"

— **Charles Manson**

"Remorse for what? You people have done everything in the world to me. Doesn't that give me equal right?"
— **Charles Manson**

If Manson were angry, he'd justify beating up a girl in his Manson Family by saying:

"Pain's not bad, it's good. It teaches you things. I understand that."
— **Charles Manson**

Charles "Tex" Watson

"I know and understand you are much more than what I think you are, but first, I must deal with you the way I think you even if that's only my own thinking and not you."

— **Charles Manson**

"You got to realize; you're the Devil as much as you're God."
— **Charles Manson**

"Fear of Vikings build castles."
— **Charles Manson**

It's always trendy to pretend to care about the environment. Lynette "Squeaky" Fromme is big on protecting the environment. Manson could get agreement and praise from his followers for talking about cleaning up the ecosystem while ordering them to do mass murder in the next moment:

"Animals shouldn't be hunted, and nature shouldn't be disturbed, even destroyed, to benefit the whims of mankind."
— **Charles Manson**

Charles "Tex" Watson pictured during his murder trial.

Okay, do you still have some doubts about doing things, Charles Manson's way? Well, here are a variety of Manson's "expert" or guru slogans to help you get your mind right and become a Manson Family robot:

"Now, I am too beautiful to be set free."
— **Charles Manson**

"The way out of a room is not through the door. Just don't want out. And you're free..."
— **Charles Manson**

"From the world of darkness, I did loose demons and devils in the power of scorpions to torment."
— **Charles Manson**

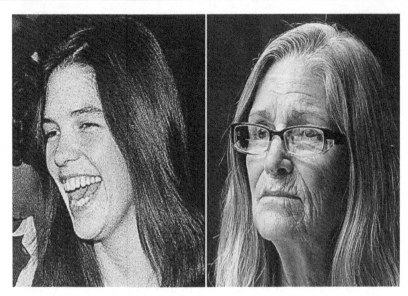

Left: Leslie Van Houten in 1970. Right: Van Houten, after nearly 50 years in prison.

"I have ate out of your garbage cans to stay out of jail. I have wore your second-hand clothes. I have done my best to get along in your world, and now you want to kill me, and I look at you, and then I say to myself, 'You want to kill me? Ha! I'm already dead, have been all my life'. I've spent twenty-three years in tombs that you built."

— **Charles Manson**

"I'm Jesus Christ; whether you want to accept it or not, I don't care."
— **Charles Manson**

"There is no way that you can know the taste of water unless you drink it or unless it has rained on you or unless you jump in the river."
— **Charles Manson**

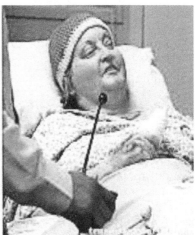

Left: Susan Atkins, 1970. Right: Susan Atkins, 2009, dying of cancer in prison.

Manson wanted to represent himself at his murder trial which is typical of ego-maniac psychopaths. The judge ruled against it because his case was much too complicated. Manson claimed he was innocent and did not order any murders. But he was convicted of seven counts of first-degree murder and one count of conspiracy to commit murder.

Charlies got the death penalty, but the following year California abolished the death penalty. So he got life in prison as did the other Manson Family killers. Subsequently, convicted of two more counts of first-degree murder for the murders of Gary Hinman and Donald "Shorty" Shea. He also got a life sentence for those murders. He was eligible for parole in 1978 but was always turned down by the parole board. Over the nearly 50 years in prison until Manson died in 2017, he was moved around among several prisons in California in the following order:

- San Quentin Prison
- Folsom State Prison
- California Medical Facility at Vacaville
- Folsom State Prison
- San Quentin Prison

- California Medical Facility at Vacaville
- San Quentin Prison
- California State Prison at Corcoran
- Pelican Bay State Prison
- California State Prison at Corcoran

Manson's record in prison was not that of a model prisoner. He was attacked at least twice in prison, once by a member of the Aryan Brotherhood. Second, by a Hare Krishna who was arguing religion with Manson. The Hare Krishna inmate splashed paint thinner on Manson's head and lit him on fire. He suffered mostly 2nd, and 3rd degree burns to his face and scalp.

As a result of Manson's infamous reputation, he was last held in protective custody, which was the Protective Housing Unit (PHU) at Corcoran State Prison. The PHU unit houses inmates who would be in jeopardy if held in the general population. PHU inmates had the following benefits:

- Educational and support programs
- Law library privileges
- Dayroom available in the morning and afternoon
- PHU inmates could freely interact with other PHU prisoners
- Yard access in the evenings
- Collect telephone calls were permitted
- Contact visits twice a week
- Televisions allowed in their cells

On November 19, 2017, Charles Manson died.

Manson's parole hearing lies and rationalizations:

Manson made silly, mindless faces, and was disingenuous and devious in relating to authorities and others. He manipulated those who showed any weakness.

If you listen and watch various parole hearings for Charles Manson, such as on YouTube, you will hear Manson lie and rationalize his crimes of murder. Manson usually ordered his followers to do the dirty work of killing, which he commanded. When confronted, here are samples of his statements concerning the Tate/LaBianca mass murders, the Gary Hinman murder, and the Donald "Shorty" Shea murder:

At parole hearings Manson asserted:

"I didn't have nothing to do with killing those people!"

"I wasn't around when they were killed!"

"I didn't tell nobody to go in and do nothing to anybody that I wouldn't want done to me!"

"Everyone says I was the leader of those people, but I was actually the follower!"

Manson aspired to be a rock star. Manson's guitar playing and singing his crazy lyrics attracted some mixed-up, alienated young girls to his Manson Family.

"Helter Skelter was an after-hours club at Spahn's Ranch, which had no license to operate."

"When I got out of prison, I said I'm not breakin' no laws. I'll eat out of garbage cans. I ain't breakin' no law!"

After the parole authority read Charles Manson's crimes he was convicted for, they asked him for any corrections or additions he might have. He said:

"How could anybody know what was said twenty-five years ago? I wouldn't lie. I know I never said nothin' to nobody I wouldn't want done to me. Listen, if I spit on you, that gives you the God-given right to spit on me back. Anything I do to you, you can do back to me. I been in jail long enough to know that if you beat somebody, sooner or later somebody's going to beat you up..."

Left: Barbara Hoyt, Manson Family member, who testified against the Manson Family murderers after some Manson Family members attempted to murder her. Right: Charles Manson, circa 1970.

When Manson was read his history of crime starting back in the 1940s, he interrupted and demanded they listen to him. He then launched into ranting and raving about the prison system and state using his reputation as a monster to spend hundreds of millions on prisons. Charlie complained people were making money from books about him and his songs.

The speaker for the parole board then continued revealing Manson's criminal history and crimes. He mentioned nine adult convictions from 1955 to 1969. He used various drugs, including LSD, marijuana, and alcohol, which he admitted. Manson then made excuses about his teenage years in jails, that he didn't have parents and people lied to him. He got married and stole a car, etc. He then ended up in Terminal Island prison. He said he had no parents, no education, and no money. He said he learned from older criminals.

Left: Charles Manson, circa 1970. Right: Manson, 2009.

When confronted with threatening prison staff, Manson asserted, "You back up to your women. I don't back up to my women. I don't take no lip from my women. I don't give 'em none. But I don't take none. If they disrespect me, I'll disrespect them back. If they hit me, I'll hit them back…"

The parole board official told him of another incident where Manson threatened prison staff. When Manson was interrogated, he tended to ramble on with irrelevant statements. Charlie said he was a dumb hillbilly and was like a third-grade kid. He didn't know what was right or wrong because older criminals in jail told him what was what.

Everybody was pushing him. He used to be five foot seven; now he's five foot two. In a few years, he'll be four feet tall because everybody is pushing on him. He said he was stupid because he had no parents, no education, and no money. You have to have parents and be educated to be smart, he said.

INTERVIEW COMMENTS – CHARLES MANSON:

Tom Snyder interviewed Charles Manson in 1981:

Snyder: Were you happy when you found out you weren't going to the gas chamber, Charles?

Manson: I knew I wasn't going to the gas chamber because I hadn't done anything wrong.

Snyder: Are you scared to die?

Manson: Sometimes, I feel scared to live. Living is what scares me. Dying is easy. How long have I been in jail? 34 years?

Snyder: Out of 47 years, you've been in jail 34 years?

Manson: I've been in every reform school, jail, and prison since I was 10. I've had pain. I've had my ass whipped. You learn from pain.

Snyder: Do remember telling the authorities, "Don't let me out. I can't cope with the outside world?"

Manson: Yeah, I can't cope with the maniacs on the outside.

Snyder: How are you different from the maniacs on the outside? Because you know, people think you're a maniac.

Manson: I'm a reflection of your negative. I been handling that. I been in and out of these nut wards for the last 10 years. I'm playin' for my life. You are workin' for money.

Snyder: What would you do if you got out of prison?

Manson: I'd probably go out in front on the grass and sit down.

Snyder: If you got out of here, there are a lot of people who say you'd start killing again.

Manson: Again? I have not killed anyone. You've been misinformed. I didn't break the law. Judge knew that. But people wanted me in prison. Just because you're convicted in a courtroom doesn't mean your guilty of something.

Snyder: Did you kill Donald "Shorty" Shea?

Manson: Hell, no.

Snyder: Did you cut Gary Hinman's ear off?

Manson: Hell, yes. I told Hinman to do exactly what I told him. He said no. All this hocus pocus, Helter Skelter, is a fairy tale. You put me on *Life* magazine and had me convicted before I went to court.

Diane Sawyer interviewed Charles Manson as part of a documentary:

Manson: When I stand on the mountain and say, "Do it!", it gets done. If it don't get done, then I'll move on it. And that's the last thing in the world you want me to do.

Leslie Van Houten: I knew that people would die. I knew that there would be killing.

Manson: Every one of you out there has tried to kill me for the last 25 years, and I'm still here. Hahaha. Now what?

Geraldo Rivera interviewed Charles Manson:

Manson: Crime factories are buyin' and sellin' crime. This fuckin' crime factory is for jobs and money.

Rivera: Why are there 20,000 murders a year?

Manson: Because you're buyin' it and sellin' it. ...This San Quentin prison is where you keep all your children you don't want. ...I killed nobody. I broke no law.

Rivera: You broke no law? But Charlie, you were in prison half your life.

Manson: So what? ...I didn't have no parents. They gotta take you off the street and throw you somewhere. I been in here since I was 9-years old.

Left to right: Ozzie Osbourne, Axl Rose, Charles Manson, Paul McCartney, and Neil Young. Manson had an impact on the music scene.

Manson, like a typical antisocial or psychopath with no conscience or moral structure, convicted of nine murders, yet denies his guilt.

If you want to hear more from Manson in interviews you can find many of them on YouTube.

Potential and impact of Charles Manson's music on the rock scene:

Charles Manson had some raw talent for songwriting, even if he was not a great singer. Manson had crossed paths with Dennis Wilson of the Beach Boys, Neil Young, and some other players in the rocker music industry while he was in Los Angeles in the late 1960s. Bobby Beausoleil murdered Gary Hinman. However, Beausoleil was a musician.

Manson's songwriting and dark image influenced The Beach Boys, Nine Inch Nails, Guns N' Roses, Marilyn Manson, and other rock music acts.

Dennis Wilson, Neil Young, and Bobby Beausoleil all recognized Manson's primitive-songwriting talent. Did Charlie's songs have some commercial potential? Charles Manson was an unstable psychopath, hardcore criminal, and lacked discipline. These negatives interfered with his development as a musician.

Beausoleil remarked that Manson did not have the patience, endurance, and self-control to develop his rough-draft songs into a commercial-rock album. Manson, when he was in a recording studio, wanted to knock out his songs once. But a rock-music record required more time. He did not understand the creative process and developing songs with an experienced producer. Manson could not take constructive criticism. To be successful in music or any entertainment area, one had to master a process of development.

Of course, while Manson had some talent in songwriting perhaps as a sort of badass Bob Dylan, he did not have the personality to make connections and keep them. Manson did not have the discipline or work habits to stick to the creative process needed in developing songs and producing a rock-music album. For example, Manson connected with Dennis Wilson but burned his bridge to the Beach Boys and their music producer contacts.

Left: Marilyn Manson. Right: Ozzy Osbourne. Marilyn Manson and Ozzy Osbourne were two artists influenced by Charles Manson's songs and reputation as a mass murderer.

The Manson Family moved into Dennis Wilson's Pacific Palisades mansion and proceeded to trash his place, exploit Wilson for money, food, cars, and medical treatment. Eventually, Wilson's manager kicked Manson and his cult out of the house. Manson then made death threats against Dennis Wilson and Terry Melcher, Wilson's music producer. I think Manson had the songwriting talent to be successful as a rocker at some level in the music industry.

But Charles Manson did not have the self-restraint, the moral character, self-control, and personality to build on his talent and become successful. If Manson had taken an honest job as a waiter or whatever and patiently accepted the slow-development process to record a rock album, he would have had a chance for some musical success. But he continued his petty criminal and later serial murders to ruin his opportunities.

Left: Neil Young, ca 1960s. Center: Mo Ostin. Right: Charles Manson. Neil Young recommended Charles Manson to Mo Ostin, a music producer, as a possible artist for a record deal.

Charlie's weird ranting and raving about the Beatles' Helter Skelter, like some paranoid, grandiose maniac, eliminated his potential success. And the Manson Family revenge murders topped-off Charlie's demise. Manson was able to influence successful rocker acts such as Ozzie Osbourne, who was inspired by Manson's dark messages.

Guns N' Roses covered one of Charles Manson's songs. The Beach Boys revised one of Manson's songs and recorded it. The Beach Boys took Charlie's diamond-in-the-rough song Cease to Exist and retitled it Never Learn Not to Love after a rewrite. Dennis Wilson and the Beach Boys gave Manson a motorcycle and some money for the song. But naturally, paranoid-killer Charles Manson claimed they stole it from him and threatened to murder them.

Both Dennis Wilson and Neil Young tried to help Manson get a recording contract. Young viewed Manson's songwriting as kind of an eccentric, twisted Bob Dylan style. Young spoke about Manson's songs: "His songs were off-the-cuff things he made up as he went along, and they were never the same twice in a row."

Left: Ain't It? Babe, a folk-pop single, Catherine "Gypsy" Share (center) cut in 1965 under her stage name, Charity Shayne. Right: Bobby Beausoleil, ca 1965. Beausoleil's contacts helped Share get the Ain't It?, Babe record deal.

Neil Young later wrote in his autobiography: "Kind of like Bob Dylan, but different because it was hard to glimpse a true message in them, but the songs were fascinating. He was quite good. I asked him if he had a recording contract. He told me he didn't yet, but he wanted to make records. I told Mo Ostin at Reprise about him, and recommended that Reprise check him out." Young said, "Reprise rejected Manson's songs. Manson did not take rejection well. It really pissed him off. He wasn't a songwriter, he was a song spewer. Manson was a little out of control." Young implied Manson sort of vomited songs instead of writing them.

But to send Charles Manson to successful-music producers like Mo Ostin and Terry Melcher, was like throwing a wild mountain lion into an upper-class, Malibu cocktail party. For example, after a few meetings with Terry Melcher, Manson managed to turn-off Melcher. When Melcher went to Spahn's Movie Ranch to listen to Manson and his girls sing and play his songs, he gave Manson $50 because the Manson Family looked like they were starving. Melcher passed on a recording-contract deal.

Left: Never Learn Not to Love, from The Beach Boys, was initially written by Charles Manson (right) as Ceased to Exist. Dennis Wilson (center) revised it and got the songwriter credit. Capitol Records released it.

Bobby Beausoleil, a Manson Family associate, and Catherine "Gypsy" Share, a Manson Family member, both had legit music industry track records. Beausoleil tried to help Manson record and develop his songwriting. But Manson refused to accept any advice, supervision, or professional music producer structure. Charlie had zero discipline. Beausoleil was in the band Love and did a music soundtrack on Kenneth Anger's film *Lucifer Rising*.

Beausoleil introduced Catherine "Gypsy" Share to the right people at the Autumn label, and she cut a folk-pop single in 1965 called Ain't It? Babe under her stage name, Charity Shayne. Sly Stone and the Beau Brummels were recorded on the Autumn label. Share's record was way before she joined the Manson Family. Both Beausoleil and Share could have helped Manson. But psychopath Manson was an out-of-control egomaniac with a sense of entitlement.

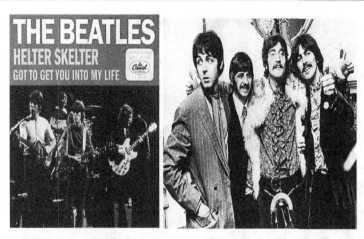

Left: Helter Skelter, The Beatles (1976). Right: The Beatles at the time of the re-release of the White Album including Helter Skelter, ca 1968.

Manson's songs were recorded and later influenced various rockers. Carl and Brian Wilson co-produced about ten unreleased Manson songs at Brian's home studio. Terry Melcher, who produced the Byrds, was approached by Manson via his connection to Dennis Wilson. Manson wanted his songs published, a rock record deal to make him a star, and demanded too much. He visited Melcher's home at 10050 Cielo Drive in the Benedict Canyon section of Los Angeles. Terry was living with Candice Bergen, his girlfriend.

Roman Polanski and Sharon Tate leased the house Terry Melcher and Candice Bergen had rented. I think to get revenge against the establishment and for not getting a record deal, Manson sent his Manson Family killers to kill everybody at the Tate residence. In Manson's Helter Skelter paranoia, he had his crew write messages like PIG, RISE, and HELTER SKELTER in the victims' blood at the Tate and LaBlanca homes. Manson got the words from the Beatles' songs and twisted the meaning.

Left: Rob Zombie. Right: The Lemonheads. Zombie and the Lemonheads covered Charles Manson's Ceased to Exist.

Ironically, after Manson was in jail, his friend Phil Kaufman issued Manson's album: Lie: The Love and Terror Cult. It had thirteen tracks including the original Cease to Exist, Sick City, People Say I'm No Good, Ego, and Don't Do Anything Illegal. Manson's other recordings were made in prison and surfaced, at times, over the decades. Kaufman's album of Manson's songs only sold 300 copies.

Black Sabbath's 1970s creepy doom rock was in reaction to the Manson Family murders and Manson's oddball songs. Ozzie Osbourne said in his autobiography: "The Manson murders were all over the telly, so anything with a dark edge was in big demand. Before he turned psycho, Manson had been a big part of the L.A. music scene. If he hadn't gone to jail, we probably would have ended up hanging out with him."

In court, Manson blamed the Beatles White Album for his twisted version of Helter Skelter. Manson testified: "Helter Skelter is confusion. Confusion is coming down fast. If you can't see the confusion coming down around you fast – you can call it what you wish. It is not my conspiracy. It is not my music. I hear what it relates. It says Rise. It says Kill. Why blame it on me? I didn't write the music."

Left: Charles Manson. Center/right: Alvin "Creepy" Karpis taught Manson to play guitar in the early 1960s while they were in prison.

Neil Young, inspired by Manson's crimes, wrote a dark song, Revolution Blues, which was in 1974's *On the Beach* from a psychopathic killer's viewpoint. Lyrics included: *"I see bloody fountains and 10 million dune buggies comin' down the mountains. Well, I hear that Laurel Canyon is full of famous stars, but I hate them worse than lepers."*

Dennis Wilson introduced Manson to Neil Young. Young concluded that Manson was some weirdly-talented poet: "He had this kind of music that nobody else was doing. He would sit down with a guitar and start playing and making up stuff, different every time. It just kept comin' out, comin' out. Then he would stop and you would never hear that one again. Musically, I thought he was very unique. I thought he had something crazy, something great. He was like a living poet."

As darker punk and the metal music scenes emerged, more of Manson's songs were recorded or inspired darker tunes. GG Allin released a new version of Garbage Dump in 1987. Rob Zombie and the Lemonheads covered Cease to Exist, and Home Is Where You're Happy on 1988's Creator. In the 1990's Lovey, Evan Dando referred to Big Iron Door. Redd Kross, on their 1982 debut, also covered Ceased to Exist.

Look at Your Game, Girl, a bonus track from
Guns N' Roses' 1993 album, "The Spaghetti Incident?",
was written by Charles Manson.

The song was in Manson's album Lie: The Love and Terror Cult.
It was released in 1970 to help pay for his legal counsel.

23 years after its initial release, AXL Rose insisted that GN'R do a
cover version of that song and include it in their album.

Manson lost a lawsuit filed against him by one of his victim's family in 1971.
The court ordered him to pay $500,000 to Voytek Frykowski's family.

Manson's royalty payment from GN'R's album was given to Voytek
Frykowski's son. For every 1,000,000 album copies the band sells,
Geffen label will pay him $62,000.   CRACKED.com

Other bands either influenced by Manson or who covered his songs
included Psychic TV, Cabaret Voltaire, Nine Inch Nails, and Marilyn
Manson.

Manson asked Alvin "Creepy" Karpis to teach him to play the
guitar in the early 1960s while both were in prison. Karpis told
Manson he'd be more significant than the Beatles. Well, at least
Manson had a dark influence over the music culture. When Manson
was able to use his Manson Family girls to get a relationship going
with Dennis Wilson, Manson was excited to meet record producer
Terry Melcher, son of Doris Day. But the violent vibe at Spahn's
Movie Ranch scared off Melcher.

Left: Trent Reznor, Nine Inch Nails. Right: Guns N' Roses.

Manson became increasingly paranoid and violent and used a twisted, misinterpretation of the Beatles' Helter Skelter as a basis for his crazy apocalyptic theory of a black-white race war. Helter Skelter, to Manson, meant a worldwide revolution based on a black-white conflict, which would result in Manson ruling the world with his Manson Family. Manson wanted to kill some successful examples of the bourgeois classes like Sharon Tate, her friends, and the LaBiancas.

Did Manson turn the 1960s countercultural dream into a nightmare because of the summer of 1969 mass murders? As I've written in the first part of the Manson Family psychology, the Summer of Love in 1967 had turned dark and hostile by the fall of 1967. Psychopaths like Charles Manson and hardcore drug dealers had infiltrated the peach-and-love-flower children or hippie culture.

After the Tate/LaBianca murders, Ringo Star commented: "It was upsetting. I mean, I knew Roman Polanski and Sharon Tate and - God! It was a rough time. It stopped everyone in their tracks because suddenly, all this violence came out amid all this love and peace and psychedelia. It was pretty miserable, actually, and everyone got really insecure - not just us, not just the rockers, but everyone in LA felt: 'Oh, God, it can happen to anybody.'"

Left: Steve Railsback. Right: Railsback portraying Charles Manson. Released just five years after Manson was convicted of murder, *Helter Skelter* featured actor Steve Railsback portraying the violent criminal. The television miniseries was based on a 1974 book of the same name, written by attorney Vincent Bugliosi, who prosecuted Manson's case. The series depicts the capture and subsequent trial of Manson, who would eventually be sentenced to life in prison for his involvement in the 1969 Tate murders, among other crimes.

Manson did damage the image of the peace-loving hippies who were no longer assumed to be harmless-counterculture freaks. As George Harrison said: "Another thing I found offensive was that Manson suddenly portrayed the long hair beard and mustache kind of image, as well as that of a murderer. Up until then, the long hair and the beard were more to do with not having your hair cut and not having a shave - a case of just being a scruff or something."

Manson's paranoia, his Helter Skelter vision included hiding his Manson Family in some underground hideout in Death Valley. Sonic Youth's Death Valley '69 is about Manson. Sonic Youth wrote a song with murderous, dark lyrics combined with a violent video. Who would have guessed that Manson's batshit-crazy ranting and raving would form the basis of rock songs?

Left: Australian actor Damon Herriman. Right: Herriman portraying Charles Manson in *Once Upon a Time in Hollywood*, a 2019 movie. Herriman played Charles Manson in two projects. He also portrayed Manson in David Fincher's Netflix show *Mindhunter*.

There was controversy over the Guns N' Roses cover of Look at Your Game, Girl. Axl Rose and Dizzy Reed performed on the track with the acoustic guitar played by session musician Carlos Booy. It was from the Lie: The Love and Terror Cult album released in 1970. The royalties due Manson went to the family of Manson murder victim Wojciech Frykowski.

The Ramones album Leave Home included Glad to See You Go which was from a killer's point of view who fantasizes about getting famous through *violence such as mass murder like Manson did. Lyrics include: "Gonna smile, I'm gonna laugh they're gonna want my autograph/And in a moment of passion get the glory like Charles Manson."*

The band Kasabian was named after Linda Kasabian, the prosecution's star witness against the Manson Family killers. Trent Reznor of Nine Inch Nails moved into 10050 Cielo Drive, the scene of the Tate murders. He built a music studio there and recorded The Downward Spiral at the former Tate residence. Reznor recalled: "Sometimes I'd come home and find bouquets of dead roses and lit candles in the front gate. It was really eerie. Who were they leaving the shrines for — Tate or Manson?" Later, the frontman took the front door as a memento of his time there.

Actor Jeremy Davies played Manson in this 2004 TV movie, *Helter Skelter*, which was a remake of the 1976 original. *But I'm a Cheerleader* star Clea Duvall, and Eric Dane of *Euphoria* and *Grey's Anatomy* also appeared in the film. Much like the first film, 2004's version of *Helter Skelter* focused primarily on Manson himself and was based on Bugliosi's book.

Manson's ecology or environmental beliefs were capsulized in the term ATWA by Manson. System of a Down wrote ATWA in Toxicity as a reference to Manson's acronym for Air, Trees, Water, and Animals. Guitarist Daron Malakian said: "It's something that he tends to really be focused on. The Charles Manson everybody sees on television – everything is always one-sided on television..."

"I don't agree with killing anybody. I don't agree with going in and slashing anybody's throats or anything, writing shit on the walls. That's not what I'm into. That's not the side of the Charles Manson that I'm into. It's more of his ideas and his thoughts on society." Lynette "Squeaky" Fromme is also very big on ATWA.

Bob Odenkirk is the star of the *Breaking Bad* spinoff series *Better Call Saul*. While there are numerous portrayals of Manson, Odenkirk's is one of the few that treats Manson as the butt of a joke — in addition to portraying him as a deranged criminal. Odenkirk played the convicted killer in sketches for *The Ben Stiller Show*, a sketch comedy program that aired on Fox from 1992 to 1993. Manson featured heavily during the show's single season, with Odenkirk appearing as the character in a variety of sketches. In one of the more memorable segments from the show, the writers reimagined the classic show, *Lassie,* with Odenkirk's Manson as the obedient, if incoherent, companion.

Other plays on the Manson connection included Siouxsie and the Banshees and their nightmarish cover of Helter Skelter in 1978. But ten years later, U2's cover of the song opened Rattle and Hum, the album, with Bono singing, "Charles Manson stole this song from The Beatles. We're stealing it back."

Left: *Helter Skelter* movie poster. Right: *Manson Family Vacation* movie poster.

Film and TV portrayals of Charles Manson:

- Charles Manson, the infamous criminal and leader of the Manson Family, has been portrayed numerous times on TV and in movies since he became notorious for the murders of movie star Sharon Tate and others in the late 1960s.
- Stars like Bob Odenkirk, Evan Peters, *Game of Thrones* star Gethin Anthony have all played the crazed cult leader onscreen.
- Damon Herriman, who played Manson on the Netflix show *Mindhunter*, played the convicted murderer again in Quentin Tarantino's film *Once Upon a Time in Hollywood.*

Documentaries on Charles Manson and the Manson Family:

- 1973: *Manson,* directed by Robert Hendrickson and Laurence Merrick
- 1989: *Charles Manson Superstar,* directed by Nikolas Schreck
- 2014: *Life After Manson,* directed by Olivia Klaus

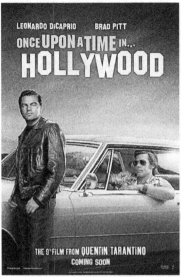

Once Upon a Time in Hollywood movie posters.

- 2017: *Manson: Inside the Mind of a Mad Man*, a television documentary about Reet Jurvetson.
- 2017: *Murder Made Me Famous, Charles Manson: What Happened?.*
- 2017: *Inside the Manson Cult: The Lost Tapes*
- 2017: *Charles Manson: The Final Words*, narrated by Rob Zombie, focuses on the Manson Family murders told from Manson's perspective, directed by James Buddy Day.
- 2018: *Inside the Manson Cult: The Lost Tapes*, narrated by Liev Schreiber, looks inside the darkest Manson Family.
- 2019: *I Lived with a Killer: The Manson Family*. Dianne Lake discusses what she witnessed of Manson's "peace-and-love hippie philosophy" as it became "dark, dangerous and evil."
- 2019: *Charles Manson: The Funeral*, directed by James Buddy Day.
- 2019: *Manson: The Women*, featuring Lynette "Squeaky" Fromme, Sandra "Blue" Good, Catherine "Gypsy" Share, and Diane "Snake" Lake, documentary special on Oxygen Channel, directed by James Buddy Day.

Movie posters: *Manson: My Name is Evil* and *Charlie Says*.

Pop cultural fictional novels, films, and TV inspired by Charles Manson and the Manson Family:

- 1976: *Helter Skelter*, television drama
- 1984: Manson Family Movies, film drama
- 1990: *The Manson Family*, musical opera by John Moran
- 1990: Assassins, Broadway musical with references to Manson.
- 1992: *The Ben Stiller Show*, skit show with Manson as a recurring character portrayed by Bob Odenkirk.
- 1998: "Merry Christmas, Charles Manson!", an episode of *South Park* centered around Manson.
- 2003: *The Dead Circus*, a novel that includes the activities of the Manson Family as a major plot point.
- 2003: *The Manson Family*, a crime drama horror film centered around the Manson Family.
- 2004: *Helter Skelter*, a crime film about the Manson Family and Linda Kasabian

Movie posters: *The Manson Family Massacre* and *The Manson Family*.

- 2006: *Live Freaky! Die Freaky!*, a stop-motion animated film based on the murders.
- 2014: *House of Manson*, a biographical feature film focusing on the life of Charles Manson from his childhood to arrest.
- 2014: *Honky Holocaust*, an alternate reality film where the Manson family successfully ignites the race war prophesized by Helter Skelter and emerge from their underground refuge to confront the blacks now in power.
- 2015: *Manson Family Vacation*, an indie comedy inspired by Manson
- 2015–16: *Aquarius*, television crime drama that includes storylines inspired by actual events that involved Manson.
- 2016: *The Girls*, a novel by Emma Cline, loosely inspired by the Manson Family.
- 2017: *Mindhunter*, the first episode of season 1, used Charles Manson as a case study. Manson is featured in the second season.
- 2017: *American Horror Story: Cult*, the seventh season of the horror anthology series *American Horror Story*.
- 2018: Charlie Says, a film centered around Manson and three of his followers.

- 2019: *The Haunting of Sharon Tate*, directed by Daniel Farrands, the film revolves around Tate during the last evening of her life.
- 2019: *Once Upon a Time in Hollywood*, directed by Quentin Tarantino, the film has a plot revolving around Manson and the Manson Family.

Charles Manson's summary: Manson, until he died in 2017, showed no remorse or regret for the murders he was convicted of committing or his other crimes. If you listen to his comments at parole hearings and interviews, he tends to ramble on with either irrelevant nonsense or claim that he is a victim of society and the prison system.

Manson said that he was a victim because he had no parents, no education, and no money. He even claimed that he was not the leader of the Manson Family; he was a follower. And further, that since he was not at the murder scenes while his cult killers were committing murders Manson ordered, that he was not responsible.

As I've discussed in this chapter, Manson did have some raw talent and potential to be successful in the music business. However, his psychopathic and hardcore criminal lifestyle interfered with his rock-star aspirations.

How could the Manson cult's Tate/LaBianca mass murders, other murders, and crimes happen?

How did the Manson mass murders happen? How could sex, drugs, and rock and roll be a bad thing? Manson was a delusional cult leader, coupled with psychedelic drugs, and an alienated, brainwashed population of young people, in a countercultural, pseudo-hippie environment that reinforced it.

A gradual desensitization and conditioning process changed Charlie's cult members. Manson had committed many crimes as a career criminal and he got his cult doing crimes like he was.

Charlie probably was genetically predisposed to psychopathy, and his dysfunctional family life and Manson's time in jail helped trigger his criminal behavior. However, Charlie and his Manson criminal cult still had a choice to go straight or commit crimes including murder.

Made in the USA
Las Vegas, NV
23 June 2024

91394162R00302